LOVE ME TENDER

STORY AND ART BY
TERRY MOORE

"You know what I like about cars, Andy? You can depend on them. You turn the wheel left, they go left. You always know which way they're going to turn."

-Pontiac Moon

Contents

Acknowledgements

I am very grateful to Jim Lee for his involvement and support of Strangers In Paradise during the making of these issues. His rendition of the opening five page dream sequence (with Josh Wiesenfeld's inks) was a wonderful gift, and added a definitive touch of "realism" to the super-hero fantasy.

Grateful acknowledgement also to Jonathan Peterson, Jeff Mariotte, Nick Bell, Joe Cotrupe, Sarah Ditzer, Chris Provinzano, John Nee, James Rochelle, Steve Oliff, Claudia Chong and Bob Matson for lending their time and talents to this work.

Strangers In Paradise: Love Me Tender is published by Abstract Studio, Inc. P.O. Box 271487, Houston, Texas, U.S.A. All Contents except where otherwise noted TM©1997 Terry Moore. The title, Strangers In Paradise and the likeness of its characters are TM ©1997 Terry Moore, and any unauthorized use other than brief passages used for the purpose of review or promotion without the express consent of Terry Moore is pro-hibited by law. Any inquiries or requests should be addressed Email: Sipnet@StrangersInParadise.com or visit our website at www.StrangersInParadise.com
Fourth printing   Printed in Canada.
ISBN: 1-892597-03-9

Strangers No More

Dear Terry,

Thank you so much for producing such a beautiful book. In addition to a personal bimonthly joy, Strangers In Paradise, like so much of the material emerging these days, makes our jobs as retailers so much easier. Without creators like yourself, brave and talented enough to produce a book which appeals to so many different people, we'd never be able to begin marketing comics to the general public. Believe me, there are retailers out there who leap with joy every time a new quality title emerges which we can not only enjoy ourselves, but promote and sell to the rest of the world who've yet to find a comic they might enjoy. . .

Stephen L. Holland
Page 45, March 7th, 1995

So began a very lucrative, mutually-beneficial partnership and a wonderful friendship now almost three years old between ourselves at **Page 45** (Mark, Dominique and myself), and Terry and Robyn Moore, which I could characterise, succinctly, as a transatlantic, telephonic tennis-rally, consisting from both sides almost exclusively of the phrase "thank you".

Well, that's not strictly true.

The lucrative, mutually-beneficial partnership began the day we received our first issue of Terry's life-breathing comic, and it was cemented but moments later when we sold our first of what have since turned into thousands of copies, to an audience at least 50% female and almost wholly new to comics.

Once we knew what we had in our hands it was relatively easy for us. We didn't have to create the fiction, we just bought it in, promoted it, took the money, said "thank you very much", and watched the broad, broad smiles of those returning for the very next issue, the next collection, or a further suggestion to add to their comic book reading list.

It will come as no surprise to you, therefore, that this fine work of fiction, about two highly individual girls from Houston, has, for some time now, been our biggest single selling title. Particularly in this format, the collections.

Early in 1997 **Page 45** had the pleasure of playing host to Terry and Robyn for a Strangers In Paradise signing, and Terry, four hours in (jet-lag no doubt playing havoc with his brain), had a hand so cramped from continuous sketching that. . . that he just continued to sign and sketch for another full hour. No moans, no protestations, just pure glee and excitement that he was here, with those who cared about his stories as much as he did. Robyn and I caught him shaking that wrist beneath the counter to liven it up, and on he went.

The very last couple in line were a mother and daughter, whose names, I regret, elude me during this, a very tight deadline. Neither had read a copy of Strangers previously, but had heard about Terry's presence and the book, and were intrigued. The mother bought a copy of Jon J. Muth's beautiful, watercolour reinterpretation of **Dracula**, the daughter, well under 16 and armed with some of her own spectacularly promising sketches, bought the first episode of the book you hold in your hands.

Do you know what they said, the very next week, was their favorite segment? The piece about the transsexual marriage. Oh Terry Moore, the love you spread. . .

In a society bombarded with messages of hate, from the tabloid newspapers and self-serving politicians to the more vocal members of organised religions, it is so heart-warming to come across a book whose priorities lie firmly in what was, to me, the key Christian doctrine: *Love Thy Neighbor*. I don't remember any post-script, qualification or specification exceptions being made; seems a fairly clear and concise commandment to me.

So, here we go again, Terry: "Thank you".

Thank you for Francine, for David and Katchoo. Thank you for Darcy Parker, Louis and Phoebe, Freddie, Chuck, Rachel, Tambi and all the others. Thank you for such beautiful brush strokes, such moving poetry, and the *joie de vivre* you pack into your work.

Stephen L. Holland
Page 45
Nottingham, England, 1997

Ahem.

This is where I put Terry's altruism to the test, for I would be a lamentable retailer if I didn't suggest that if you enjoyed this and other volumes of Strangers In Paradise, you will love Nabiel Kanan's **Exit**, Adrian Tomine's **Optic Nerve**, Dave Sim & Gerhard's **Jaka's Story**, Kyle Baker's **Why I Hate Saturn**, Bryan Talbot's **The Tale Of One Bad Rat**, Will Eisner's **To The Heart Of The Storm** or **Dropsie Avenue**, Donna Barr's **Desert Peach**, Seth's **It's A Good Life If You Don't Weaken**, and Jeremy Dennis' **3InABed**, all of which overflow with what I would call a tender narrative. Indeed, there are so many more that I could fill this entire book with suggestions, but I'm being presumptuous enough as it is. Talk to the comic book retailer from whom you bought this collection; she or he will have suggestions of their own, and point you in the right direction.

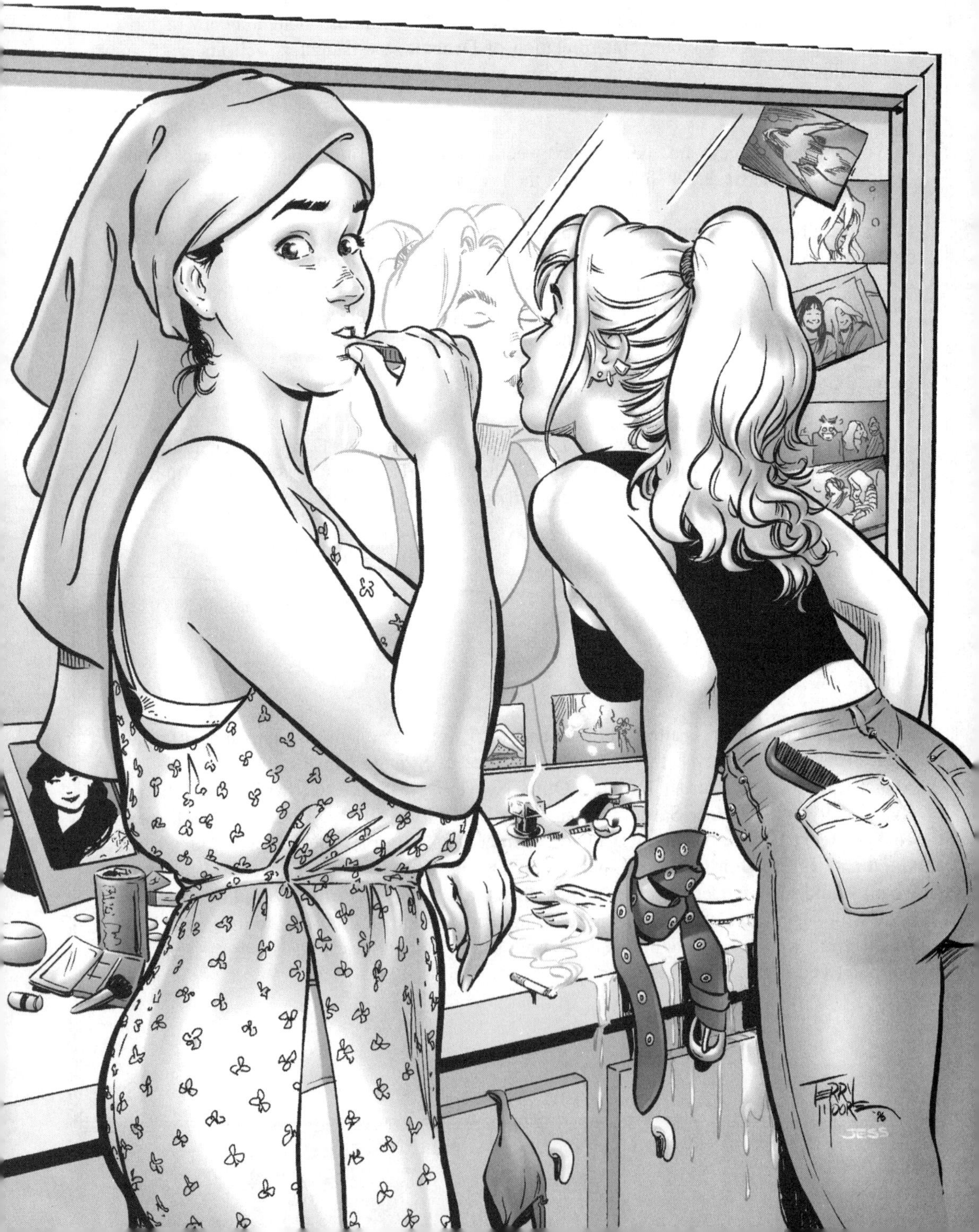

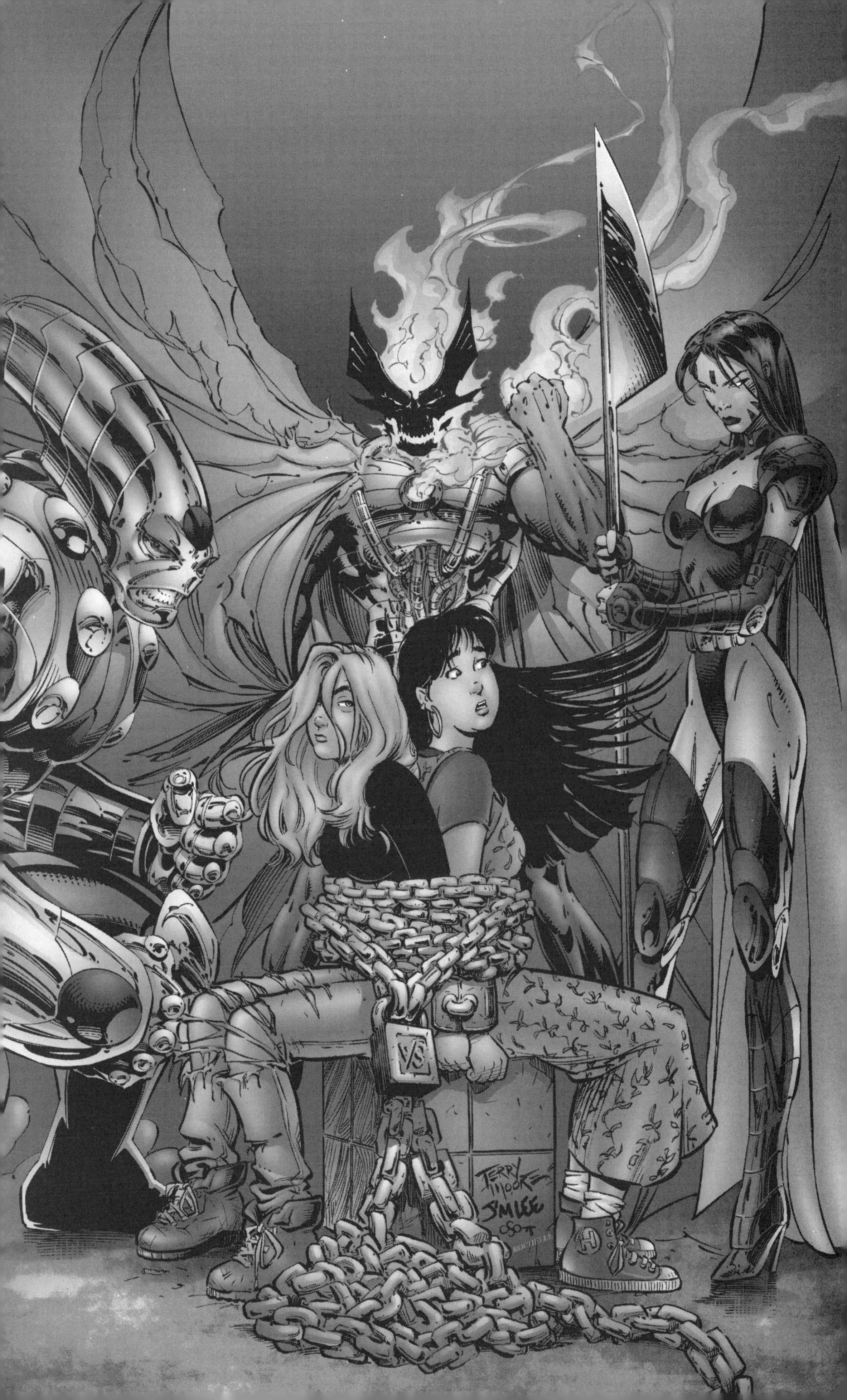
VS
TERRY MOORE
JIM LEE

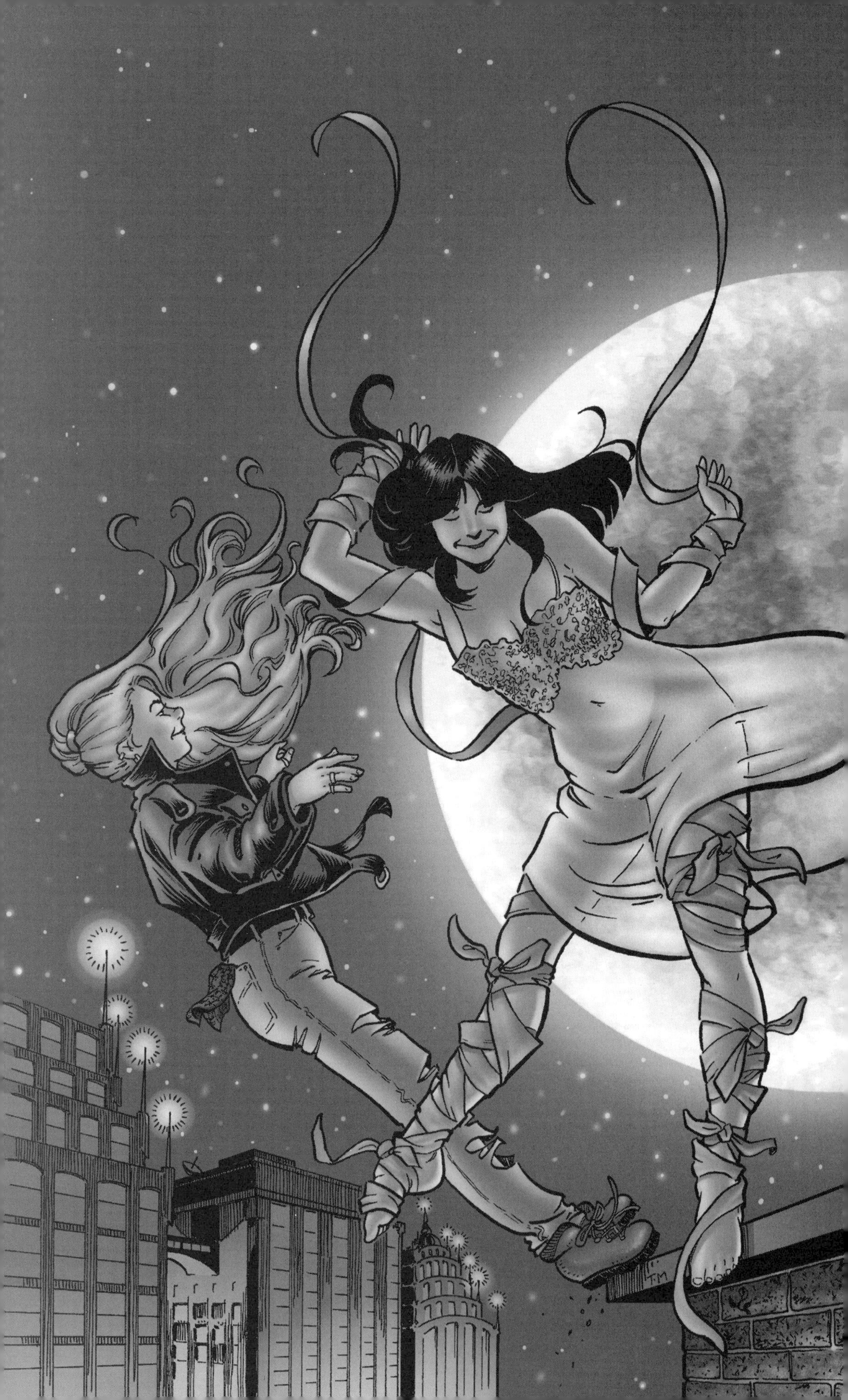

SO, WHAT DO WE FEEL LIKE DOING TONIGHT?

OH, I DON'T KNOW. MAYBE LITTLE *BRUCE* WOULD LIKE TO GO TO A *MOVIE?*

YEAH! COPS AND ROBBERS! RATATATA-RATATAT!

STAY BACK OR I'LL *BLAST YA!*

LOOK OUT!

OH DEAR!

STOP THAT MAN!

NEATO!

HELP! WE'VE BEEN *ROBBED!*

HO HUM. *ANOTHER* STATUE UNVEILING. HOW COME THE PAPER NEVER SENDS US WHERE THE *ACTION* IS, FRANCINE?

THIS IS DANGEROUS ENOUGH FOR *ME*, THANK YOU VERY MUCH. YOU KNOW HOW I HATE VIOLENCE, DAVID!

UH OH! MY *SUPER HEARING* TELLS ME *THERE'S TROUBLE* AT THE BANK ON 5TH AND ELM!

DARN! I'M OUT OF FILM. I HAVE TO GO BACK TO THE CAR AND RE-LOAD.

WHAT? THIS HAPPENS *EVERY TIME* WE GO SOME-WHERE! CAN'T YOU REMEMBER TO CARRY EXTRA FILM IN YOUR PURSE?

SORRY! I'LL JUST BE A MINUTE.

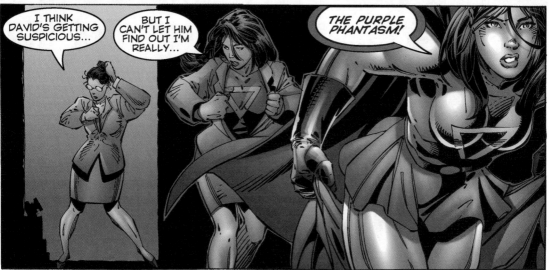

I THINK DAVID'S GETTING SUSPICIOUS...

BUT I CAN'T LET HIM FIND OUT I'M REALLY...

THE PURPLE PHANTASM!

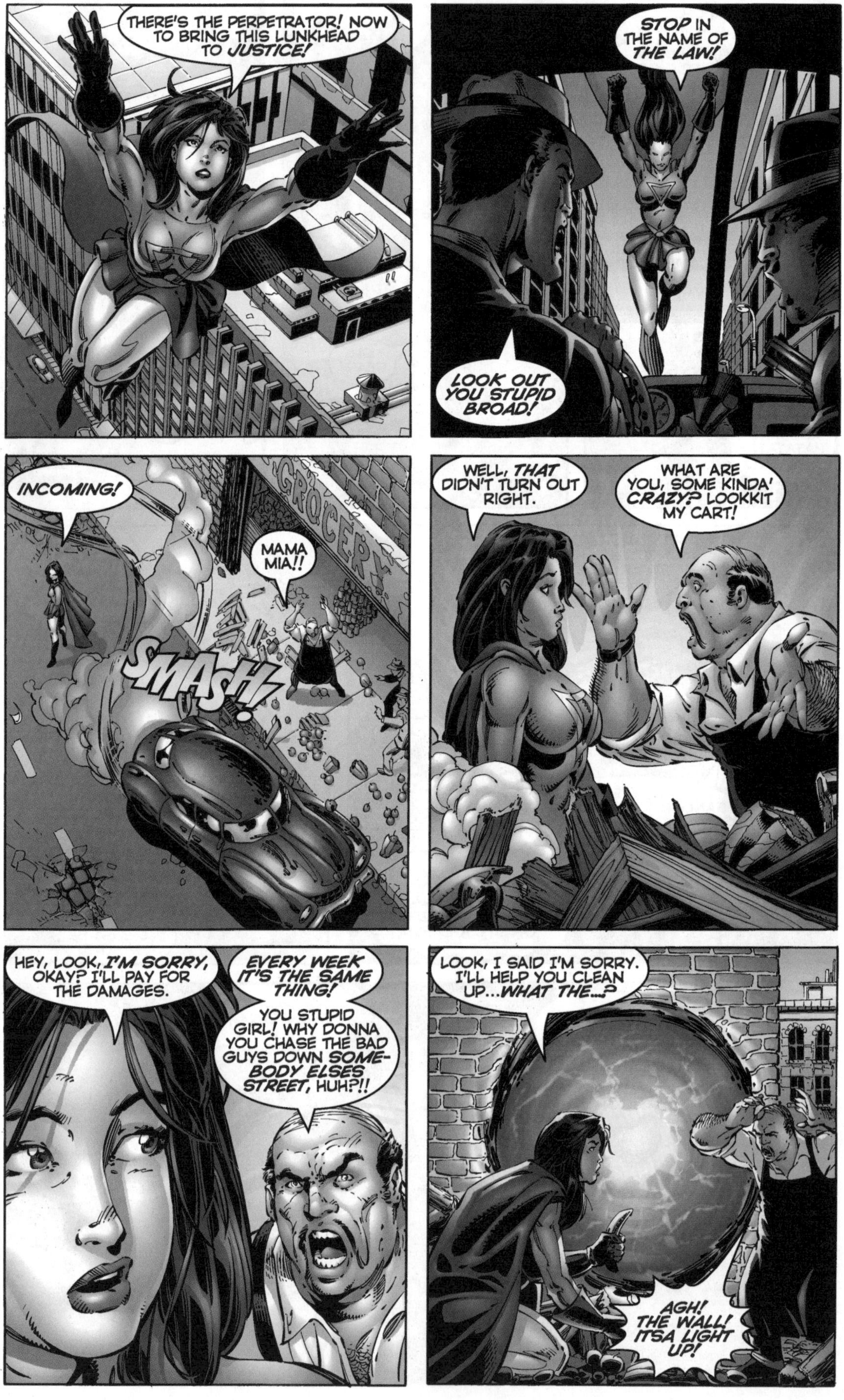
THERE'S THE PERPETRATOR! NOW TO BRING THIS LUNKHEAD TO JUSTICE!
STOP IN THE NAME OF THE LAW!
LOOK OUT YOU STUPID BROAD!
INCOMING!
MAMA MIA!!
SMASH!
WELL, THAT DIDN'T TURN OUT RIGHT.
WHAT ARE YOU, SOME KINDA' CRAZY? LOOKKIT MY CART!
HEY, LOOK, I'M SORRY, OKAY? I'LL PAY FOR THE DAMAGES.
EVERY WEEK IT'S THE SAME THING!
YOU STUPID GIRL! WHY DONNA YOU CHASE THE BAD GUYS DOWN SOMEBODY ELSES STREET, HUH?!!
LOOK, I SAID I'M SORRY. I'LL HELP YOU CLEAN UP...WHAT THE...?
AGH! THE WALL! ITSA LIGHT UP!

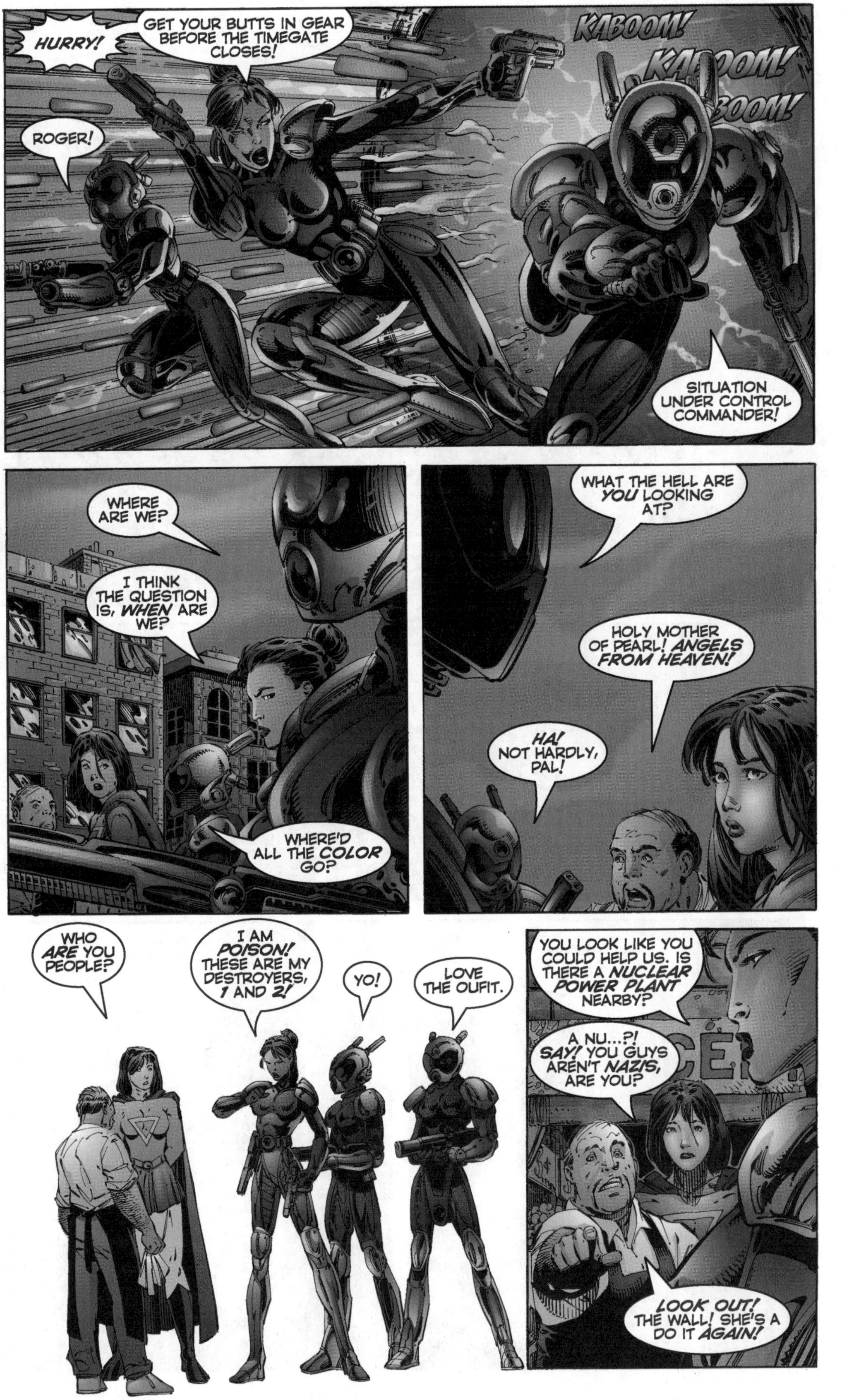
HURRY!
GET YOUR BUTTS IN GEAR BEFORE THE TIMEGATE CLOSES!
KABOOM!
KABOOM!
BOOM!
ROGER!
SITUATION UNDER CONTROL COMMANDER!
WHERE ARE WE?
I THINK THE QUESTION IS, WHEN ARE WE?
WHERE'D ALL THE COLOR GO?
WHAT THE HELL ARE YOU LOOKING AT?
HOLY MOTHER OF PEARL! ANGELS FROM HEAVEN!
HA! NOT HARDLY, PAL!
WHO ARE YOU PEOPLE?
I AM POISON! THESE ARE MY DESTROYERS, 1 AND 2!
YO!
LOVE THE OUFIT.
YOU LOOK LIKE YOU COULD HELP US. IS THERE A NUCLEAR POWER PLANT NEARBY?
A NU...?! SAY! YOU GUYS AREN'T NAZIS, ARE YOU?
LOOK OUT! THE WALL! SHE'S A DO IT AGAIN!

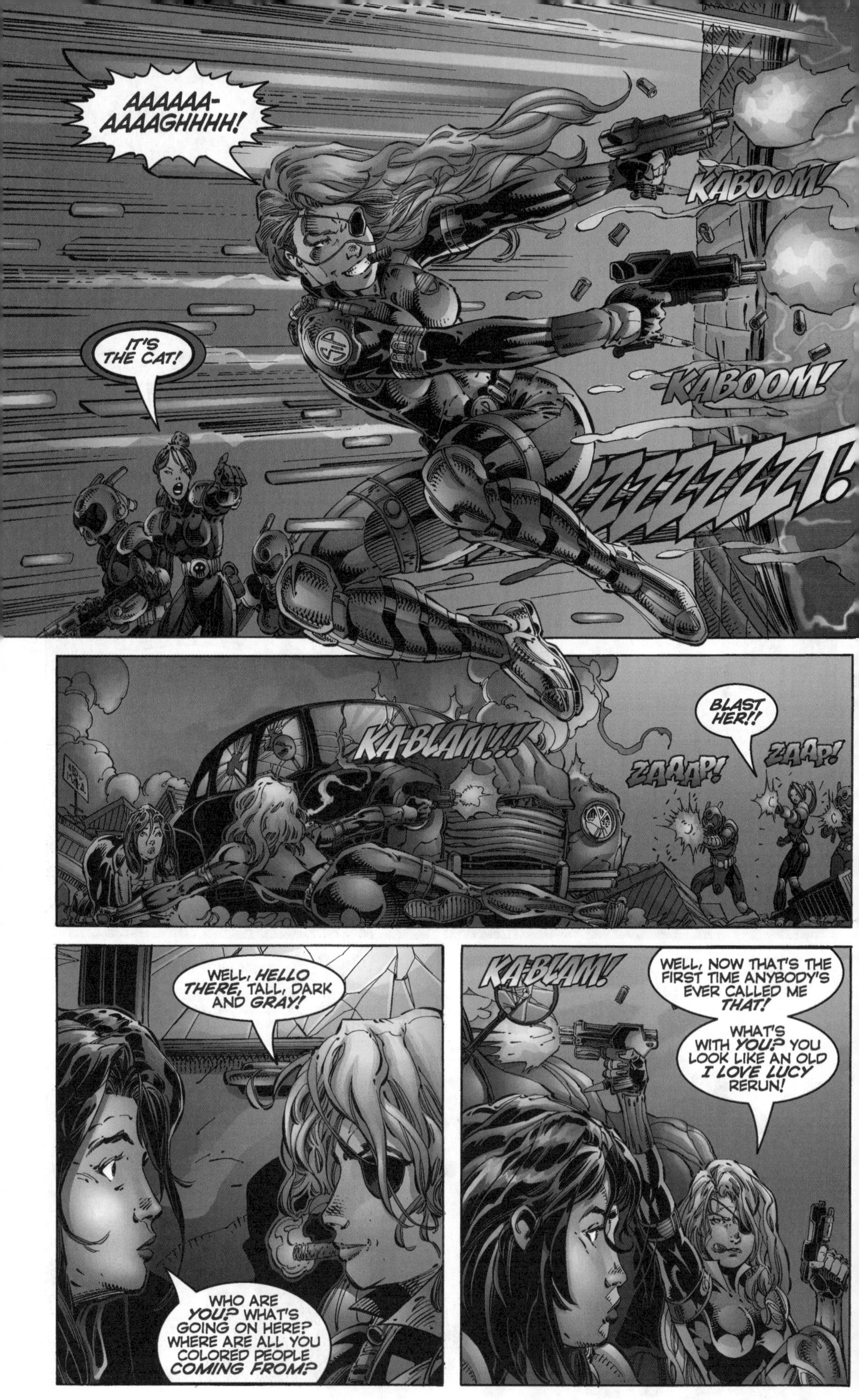
AAAAAA-AAAAGHHHH!
IT'S THE CAT!
KABOOM!
KABOOM!
ZZZZZZZZT!
KA-BLAM!!!
BLAST HER!!
ZAAAP!
ZAAP!
WELL, HELLO THERE, TALL, DARK AND GRAY!
WHO ARE YOU? WHAT'S GOING ON HERE? WHERE ARE ALL YOU COLORED PEOPLE COMING FROM?
KA-BLAM!
WELL, NOW THAT'S THE FIRST TIME ANYBODY'S EVER CALLED ME THAT!
WHAT'S WITH YOU? YOU LOOK LIKE AN OLD I LOVE LUCY RERUN!

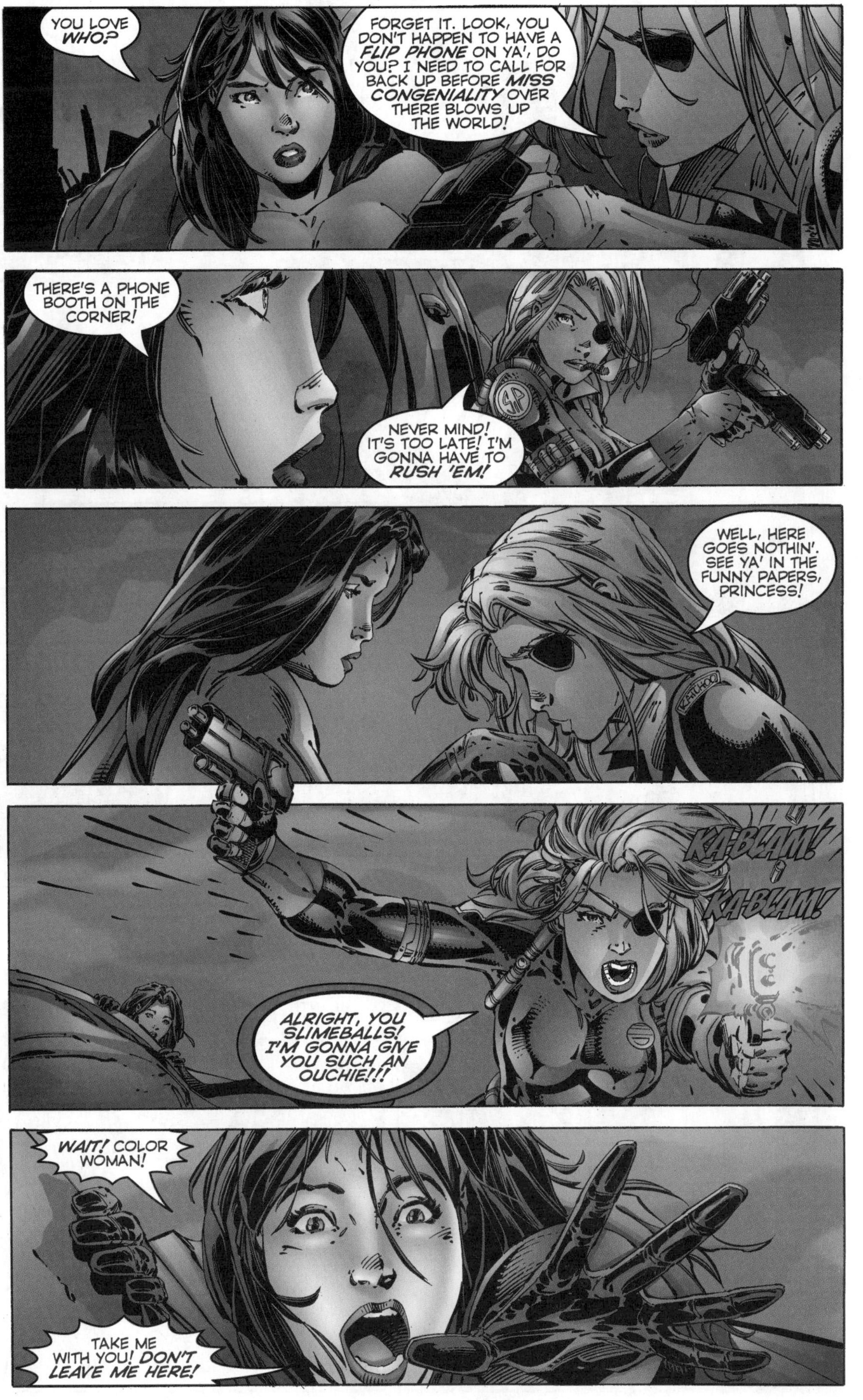
YOU LOVE WHO?
FORGET IT. LOOK, YOU DON'T HAPPEN TO HAVE A FLIP PHONE ON YA', DO YOU? I NEED TO CALL FOR BACK UP BEFORE MISS CONGENIALITY OVER THERE BLOWS UP THE WORLD!
THERE'S A PHONE BOOTH ON THE CORNER!
NEVER MIND! IT'S TOO LATE! I'M GONNA HAVE TO RUSH 'EM!
WELL, HERE GOES NOTHIN'. SEE YA' IN THE FUNNY PAPERS, PRINCESS!
KA-BLAM!
KA-BLAM!
ALRIGHT, YOU SLIMEBALLS! I'M GONNA GIVE YOU SUCH AN OUCHIE!!!
WAIT! COLOR WOMAN!
TAKE ME WITH YOU! DON'T LEAVE ME HERE!

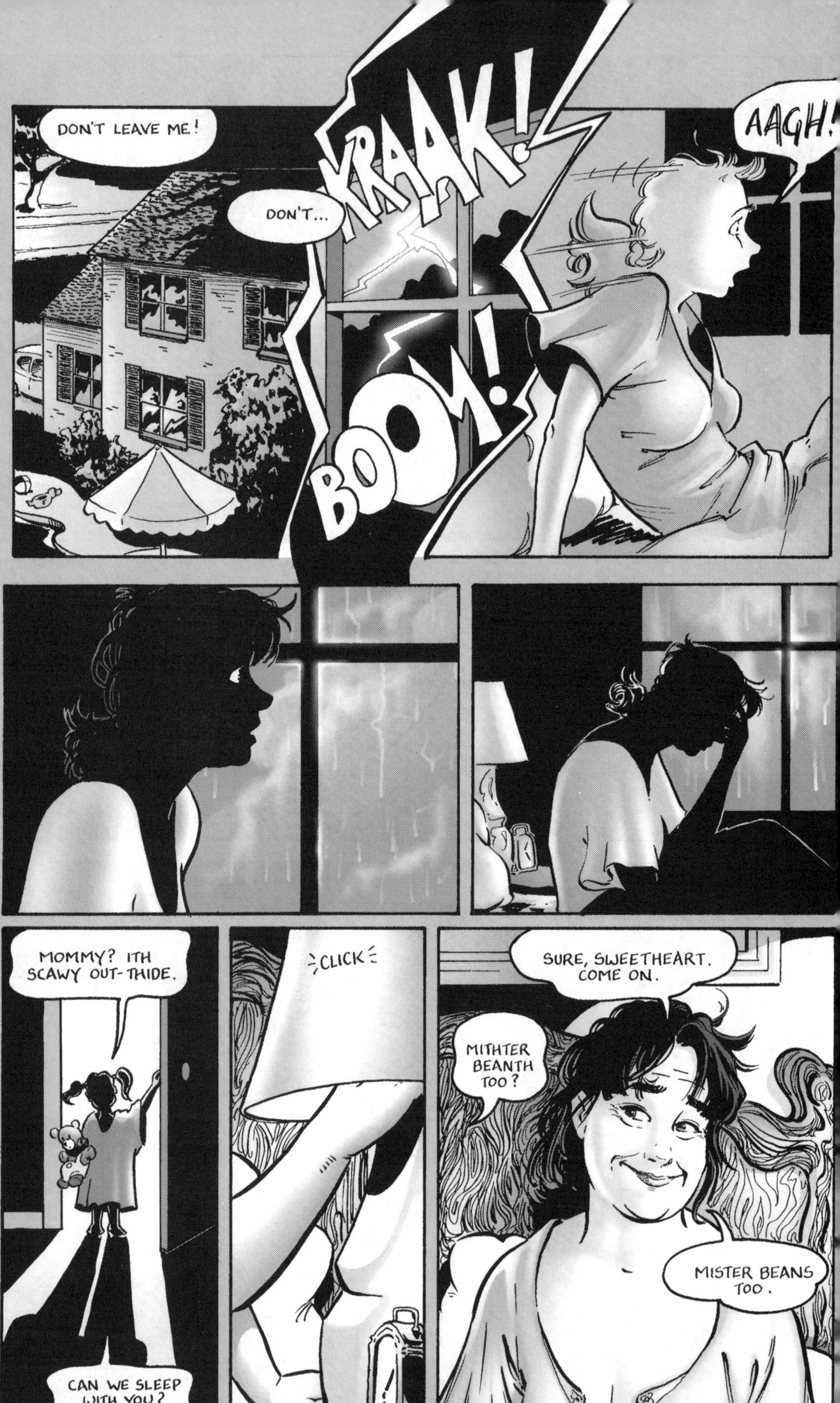
DON'T LEAVE ME!
DON'T...
KRAAK!
AAGH!
BOOM!
MOMMY? ITH SCAWY OUT-THIDE.
CAN WE SLEEP WITH YOU?
CLICK
SURE, SWEETHEART. COME ON.
MITHTER BEANTH TOO?
MISTER BEANS TOO.

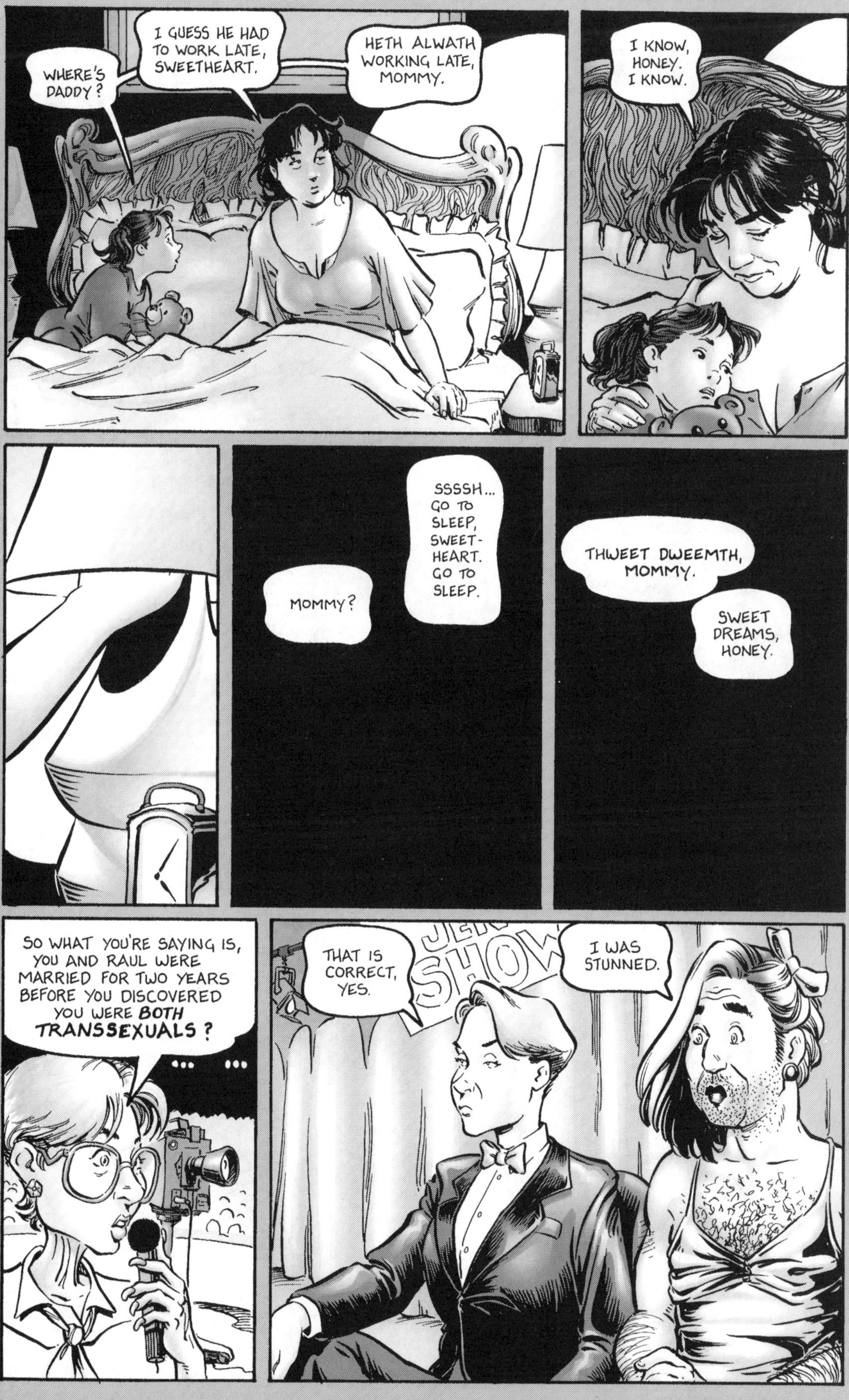
WHERE'S DADDY?
I GUESS HE HAD TO WORK LATE, SWEETHEART.
HETH ALWATH WORKING LATE, MOMMY.
I KNOW, HONEY. I KNOW.
MOMMY?
SSSSH... GO TO SLEEP, SWEET-HEART. GO TO SLEEP.
THWEET DWEEMTH, MOMMY.
SWEET DREAMS, HONEY.
SO WHAT YOU'RE SAYING IS, YOU AND RAUL WERE MARRIED FOR TWO YEARS BEFORE YOU DISCOVERED YOU WERE **BOTH TRANSSEXUALS**?
THAT IS CORRECT, YES.
I WAS STUNNED.

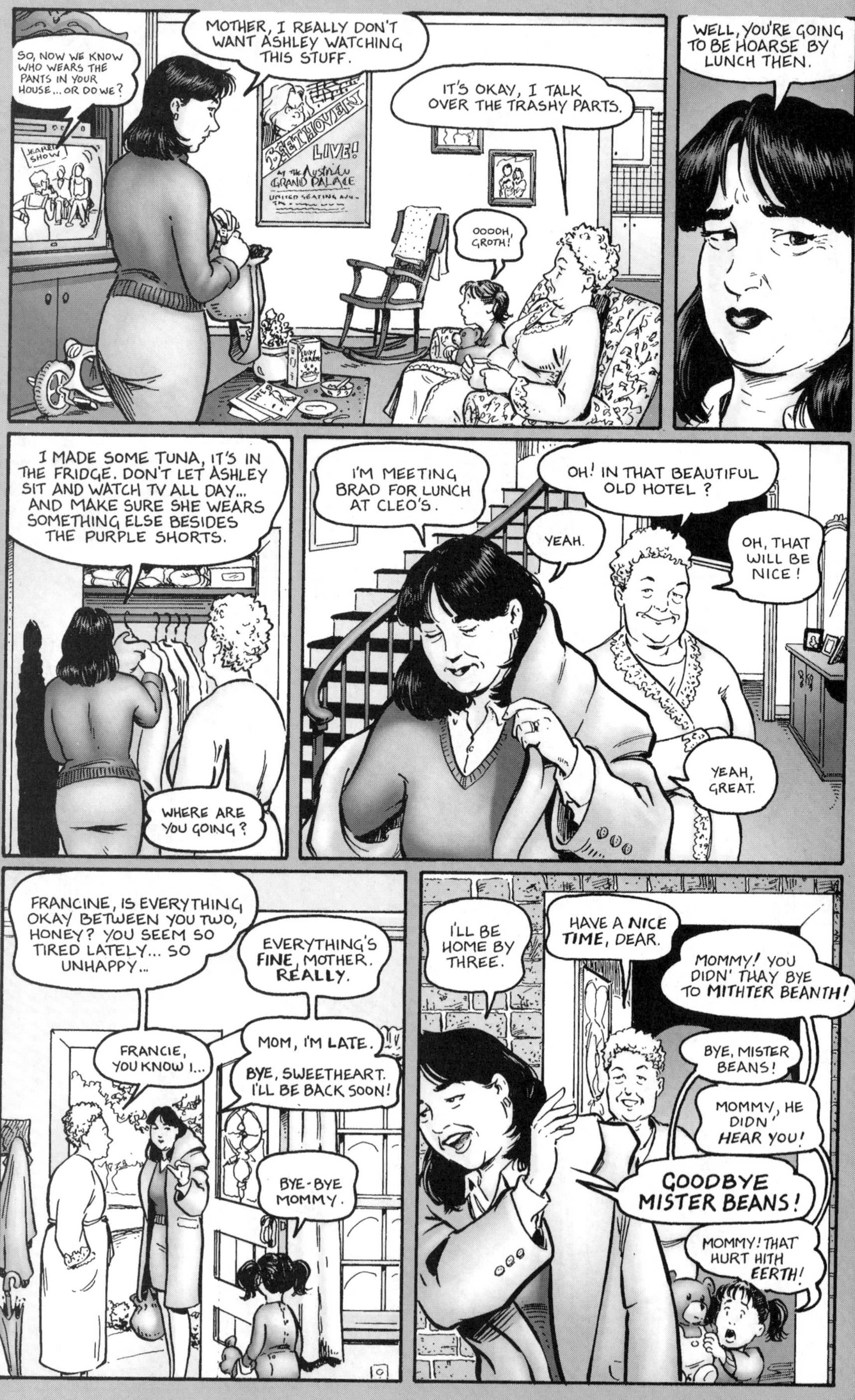

SO, NOW WE KNOW WHO WEARS THE PANTS IN YOUR HOUSE... OR DO WE?
MOTHER, I REALLY DON'T WANT ASHLEY WATCHING THIS STUFF.
BEETHOVEN LIVE!
IT'S OKAY, I TALK OVER THE TRASHY PARTS.
OOOOH, GROTH!
WELL, YOU'RE GOING TO BE HOARSE BY LUNCH THEN.
I MADE SOME TUNA, IT'S IN THE FRIDGE. DON'T LET ASHLEY SIT AND WATCH TV ALL DAY... AND MAKE SURE SHE WEARS SOMETHING ELSE BESIDES THE PURPLE SHORTS.
WHERE ARE YOU GOING?
I'M MEETING BRAD FOR LUNCH AT CLEO'S.
OH! IN THAT BEAUTIFUL OLD HOTEL?
YEAH.
OH, THAT WILL BE NICE!
YEAH, GREAT.
FRANCINE, IS EVERYTHING OKAY BETWEEN YOU TWO, HONEY? YOU SEEM SO TIRED LATELY... SO UNHAPPY...
EVERYTHING'S FINE, MOTHER. REALLY.
FRANCIE, YOU KNOW I...
MOM, I'M LATE.
BYE, SWEETHEART. I'LL BE BACK SOON!
BYE-BYE MOMMY.
I'LL BE HOME BY THREE.
HAVE A NICE TIME, DEAR.
MOMMY! YOU DIDN' THAY BYE TO MITHTER BEANTH!
BYE, MISTER BEANS!
MOMMY, HE DIDN' HEAR YOU!
GOODBYE MISTER BEANS!
MOMMY! THAT HURT HITH EERTH!

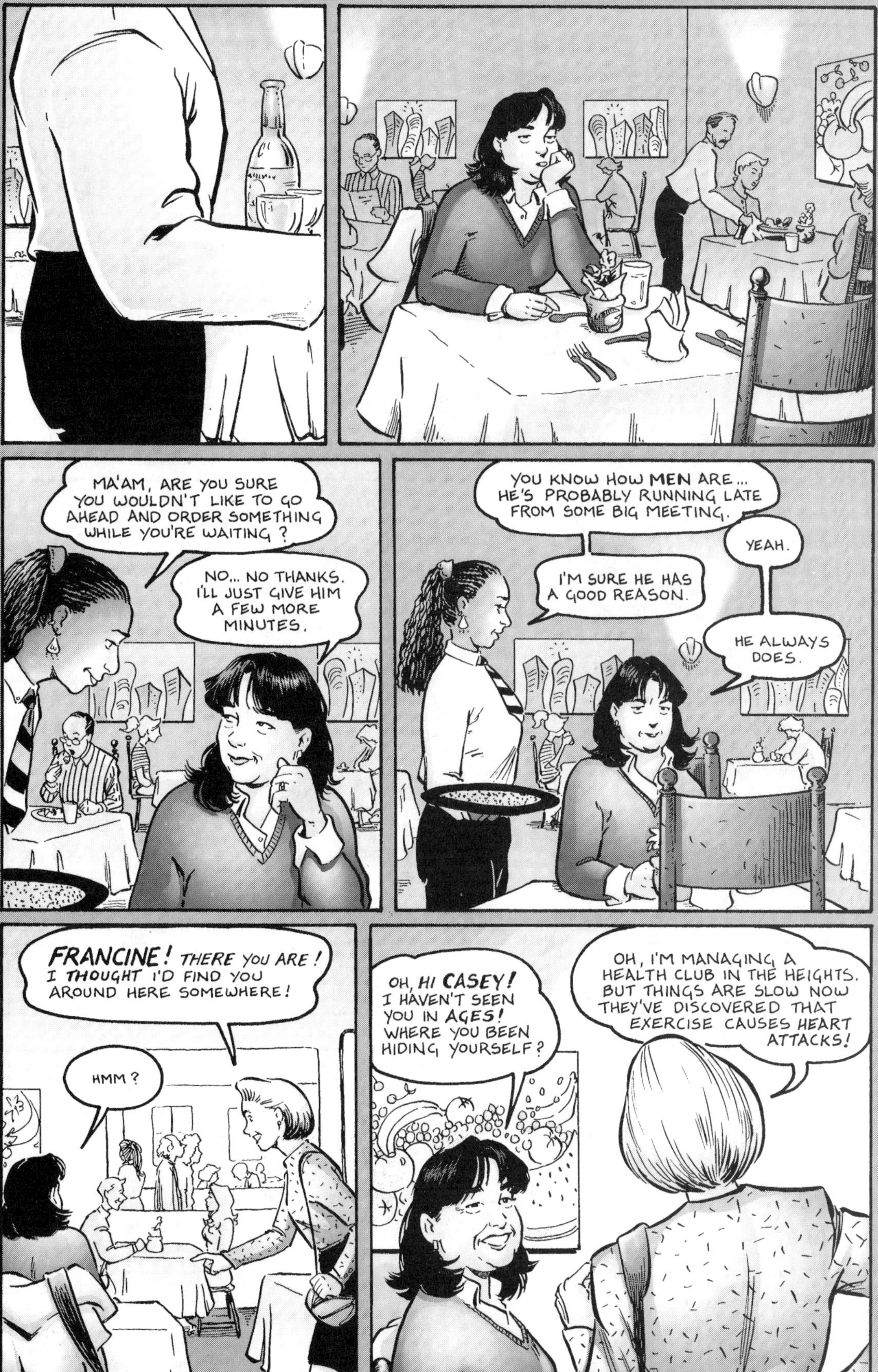
MA'AM, ARE YOU SURE YOU WOULDN'T LIKE TO GO AHEAD AND ORDER SOMETHING WHILE YOU'RE WAITING ?
NO... NO THANKS. I'LL JUST GIVE HIM A FEW MORE MINUTES.
YOU KNOW HOW MEN ARE... HE'S PROBABLY RUNNING LATE FROM SOME BIG MEETING.
I'M SURE HE HAS A GOOD REASON.
YEAH.
HE ALWAYS DOES.
FRANCINE! THERE YOU ARE! I THOUGHT I'D FIND YOU AROUND HERE SOMEWHERE!
HMM ?
OH, HI CASEY! I HAVEN'T SEEN YOU IN AGES! WHERE YOU BEEN HIDING YOURSELF ?
OH, I'M MANAGING A HEALTH CLUB IN THE HEIGHTS. BUT THINGS ARE SLOW NOW THEY'VE DISCOVERED THAT EXERCISE CAUSES HEART ATTACKS!

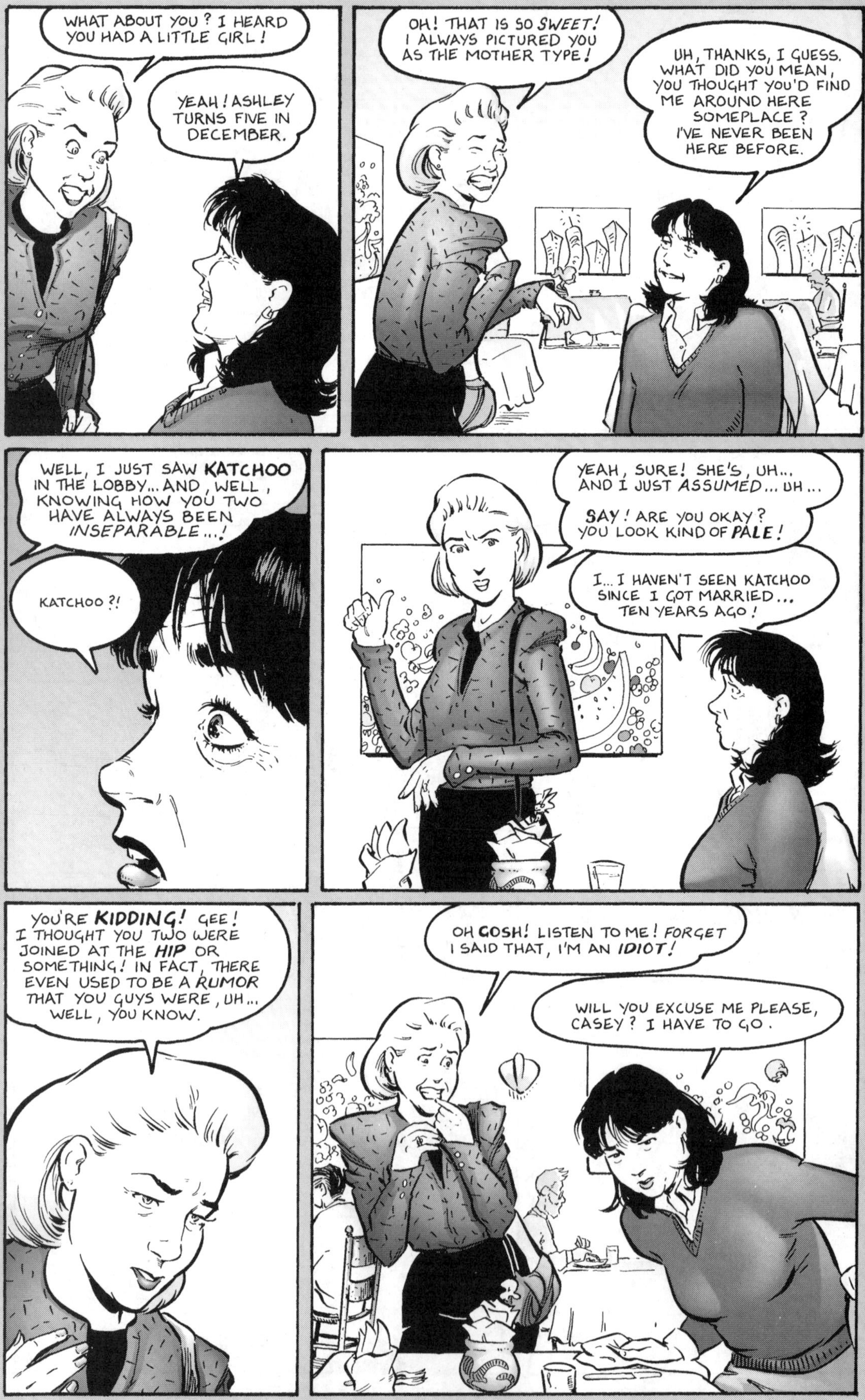
WHAT ABOUT YOU? I HEARD YOU HAD A LITTLE GIRL!
YEAH! ASHLEY TURNS FIVE IN DECEMBER.
OH! THAT IS SO *SWEET*! I ALWAYS PICTURED YOU AS THE MOTHER TYPE!
UH, THANKS, I GUESS. WHAT DID YOU MEAN, YOU THOUGHT YOU'D FIND ME AROUND HERE SOMEPLACE? I'VE NEVER BEEN HERE BEFORE.
WELL, I JUST SAW **KATCHOO** IN THE LOBBY... AND, WELL, KNOWING HOW YOU TWO HAVE ALWAYS BEEN *INSEPARABLE*...!
KATCHOO?!
YEAH, SURE! SHE'S, UH... AND I JUST *ASSUMED*... UH...
SAY! ARE YOU OKAY? YOU LOOK KIND OF **PALE**!
I... I HAVEN'T SEEN KATCHOO SINCE I GOT MARRIED... TEN YEARS AGO!
YOU'RE **KIDDING**! GEE! I THOUGHT YOU TWO WERE JOINED AT THE **HIP** OR SOMETHING! IN FACT, THERE EVEN USED TO BE A *RUMOR* THAT YOU GUYS WERE, UH... WELL, YOU KNOW.
OH **GOSH**! LISTEN TO ME! *FORGET* I SAID THAT, I'M AN **IDIOT**!
WILL YOU EXCUSE ME PLEASE, CASEY? I HAVE TO GO.

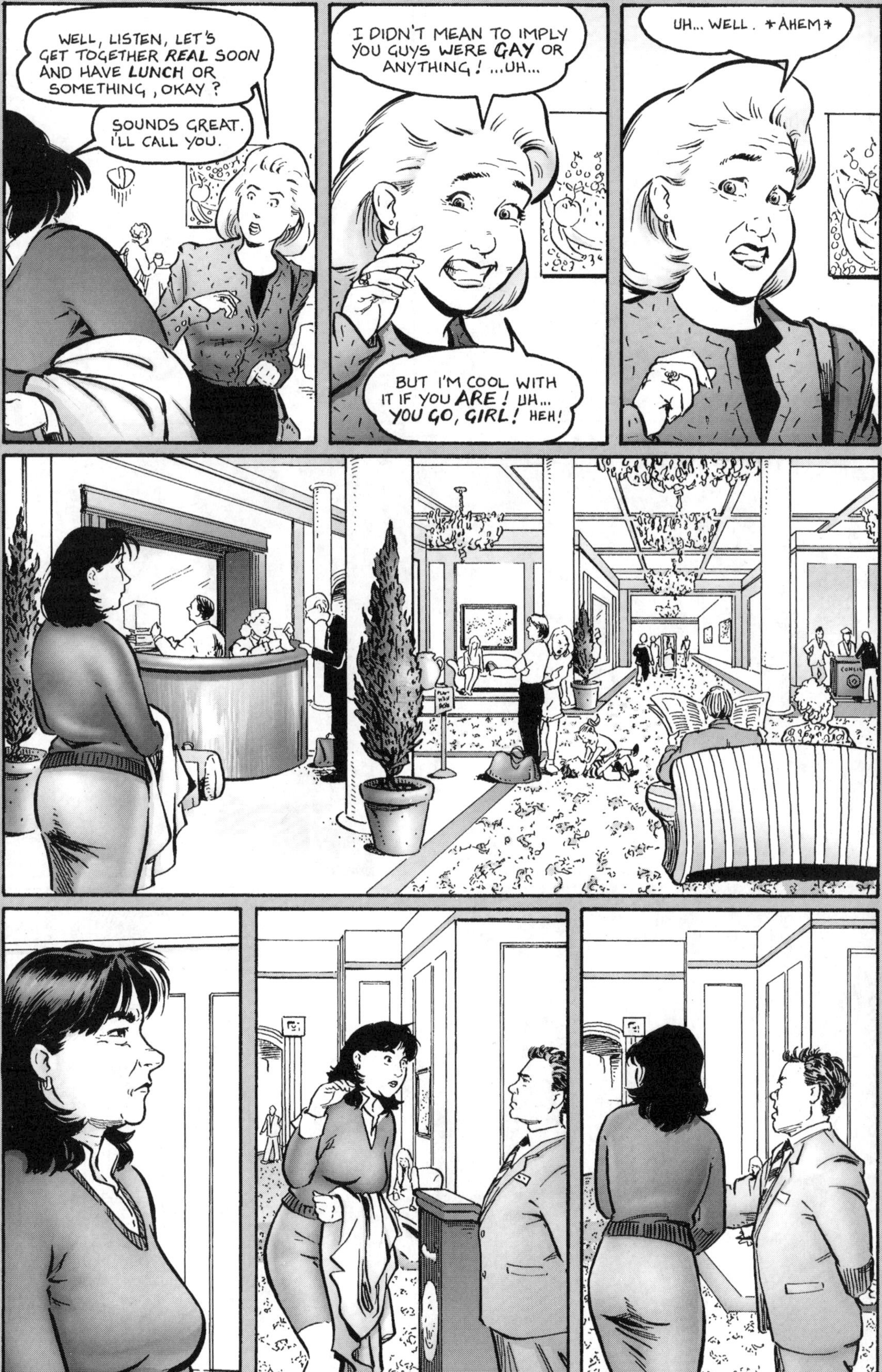

WELL, LISTEN, LET'S GET TOGETHER REAL SOON AND HAVE LUNCH OR SOMETHING, OKAY?
SOUNDS GREAT. I'LL CALL YOU.
I DIDN'T MEAN TO IMPLY YOU GUYS WERE GAY OR ANYTHING! ...UH...
BUT I'M COOL WITH IT IF YOU ARE! UH... YOU GO, GIRL! HEH!
UH... WELL. *AHEM*

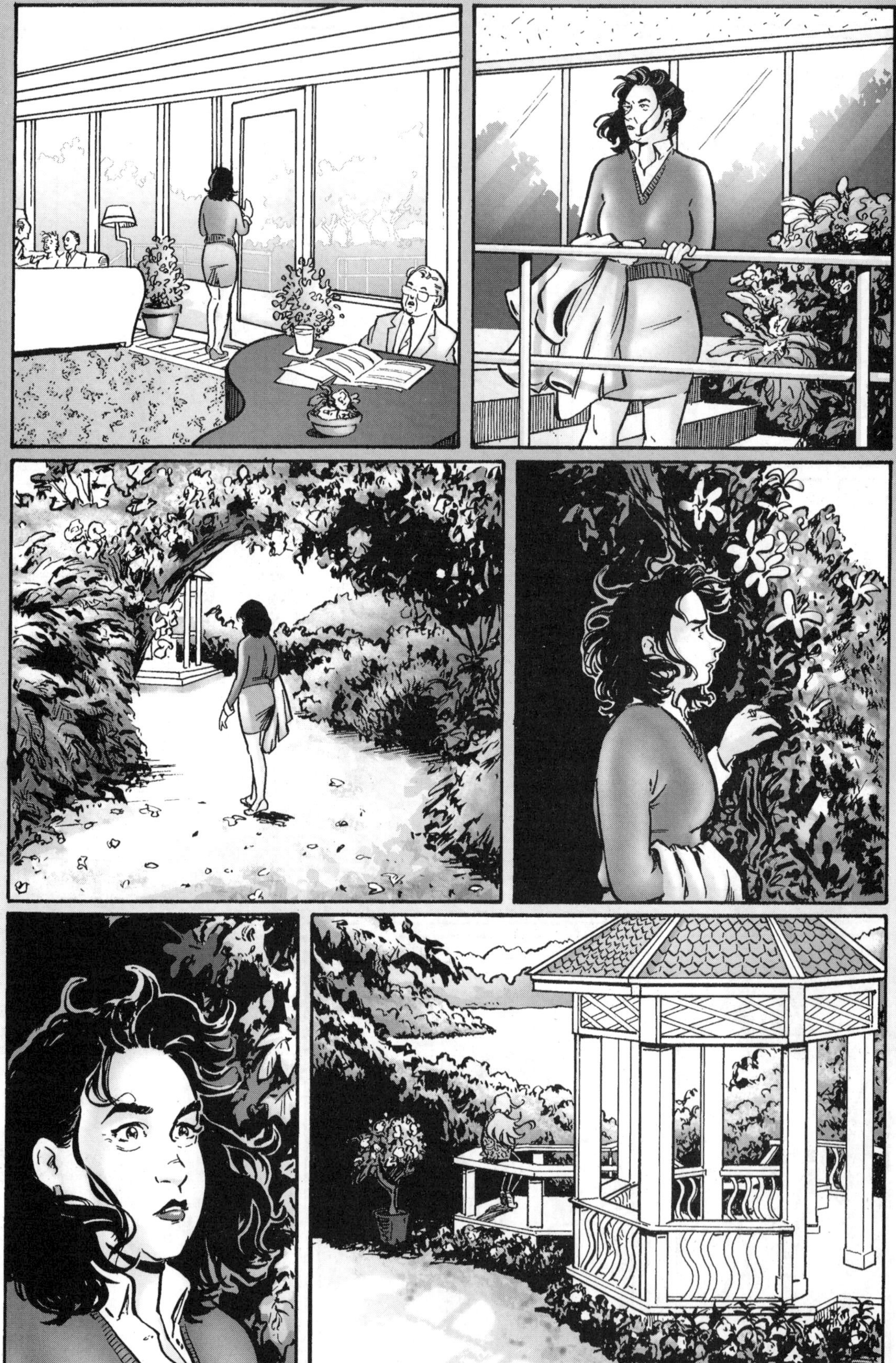

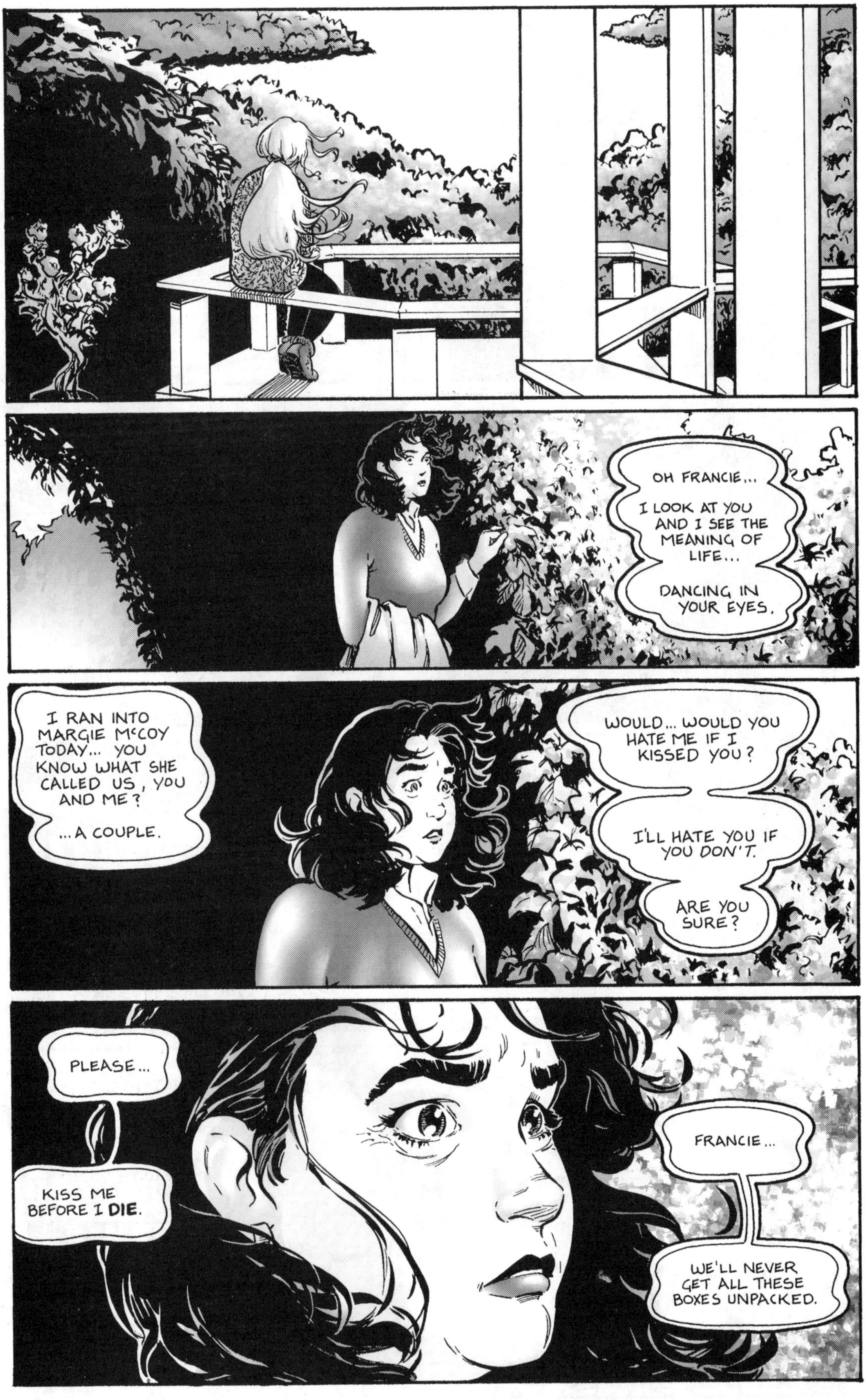
OH FRANCIE... I LOOK AT YOU AND I SEE THE MEANING OF LIFE... DANCING IN YOUR EYES.
I RAN INTO MARGIE McCOY TODAY... YOU KNOW WHAT SHE CALLED US, YOU AND ME? ...A COUPLE.
WOULD... WOULD YOU HATE ME IF I KISSED YOU?
I'LL HATE YOU IF YOU DON'T.
ARE YOU SURE?
PLEASE...
KISS ME BEFORE I DIE.
FRANCIE...
WE'LL NEVER GET ALL THESE BOXES UNPACKED.

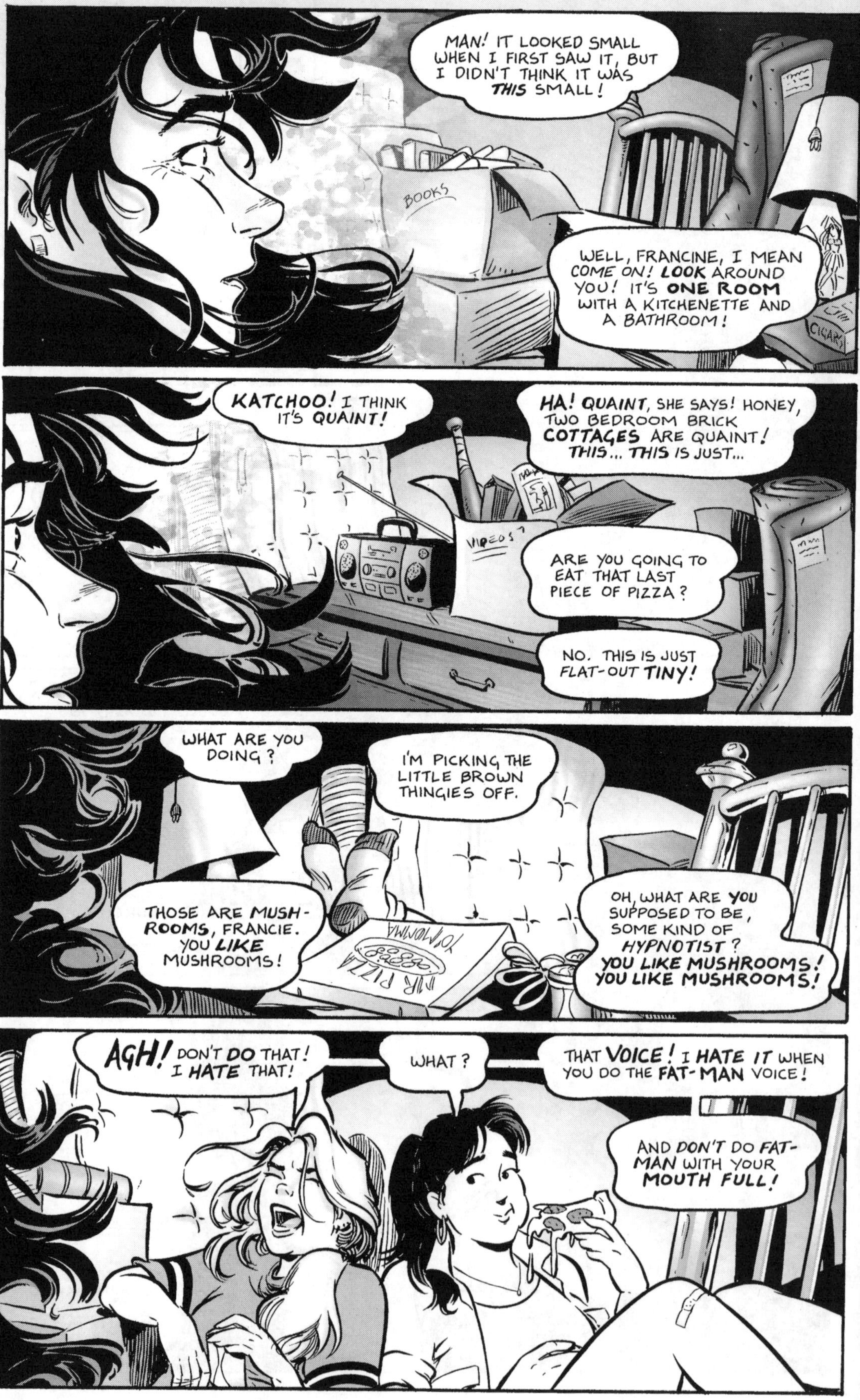
MAN! IT LOOKED SMALL WHEN I FIRST SAW IT, BUT I DIDN'T THINK IT WAS **THIS** SMALL!
BOOKS
WELL, FRANCINE, I MEAN COME ON! **LOOK** AROUND YOU! IT'S **ONE ROOM** WITH A KITCHENETTE AND A BATHROOM!
CIGARS
KATCHOO! I THINK IT'S **QUAINT!**
HA! **QUAINT**, SHE SAYS! HONEY, TWO BEDROOM BRICK **COTTAGES** ARE QUAINT! **THIS... THIS** IS JUST...
VIDEOS
ARE YOU GOING TO EAT THAT LAST PIECE OF PIZZA?
NO. THIS IS JUST FLAT-OUT **TINY!**
WHAT ARE YOU DOING?
I'M PICKING THE LITTLE BROWN THINGIES OFF.
THOSE ARE **MUSH-ROOMS**, FRANCIE. YOU **LIKE** MUSHROOMS!
OH, WHAT ARE **YOU** SUPPOSED TO BE, SOME KIND OF **HYPNOTIST**? **YOU LIKE MUSHROOMS! YOU LIKE MUSHROOMS!**
AGH! DON'T **DO** THAT! I **HATE** THAT!
WHAT?
THAT **VOICE!** I **HATE IT** WHEN YOU DO THE **FAT-MAN** VOICE!
AND **DON'T** DO **FAT-MAN** WITH YOUR **MOUTH FULL!**

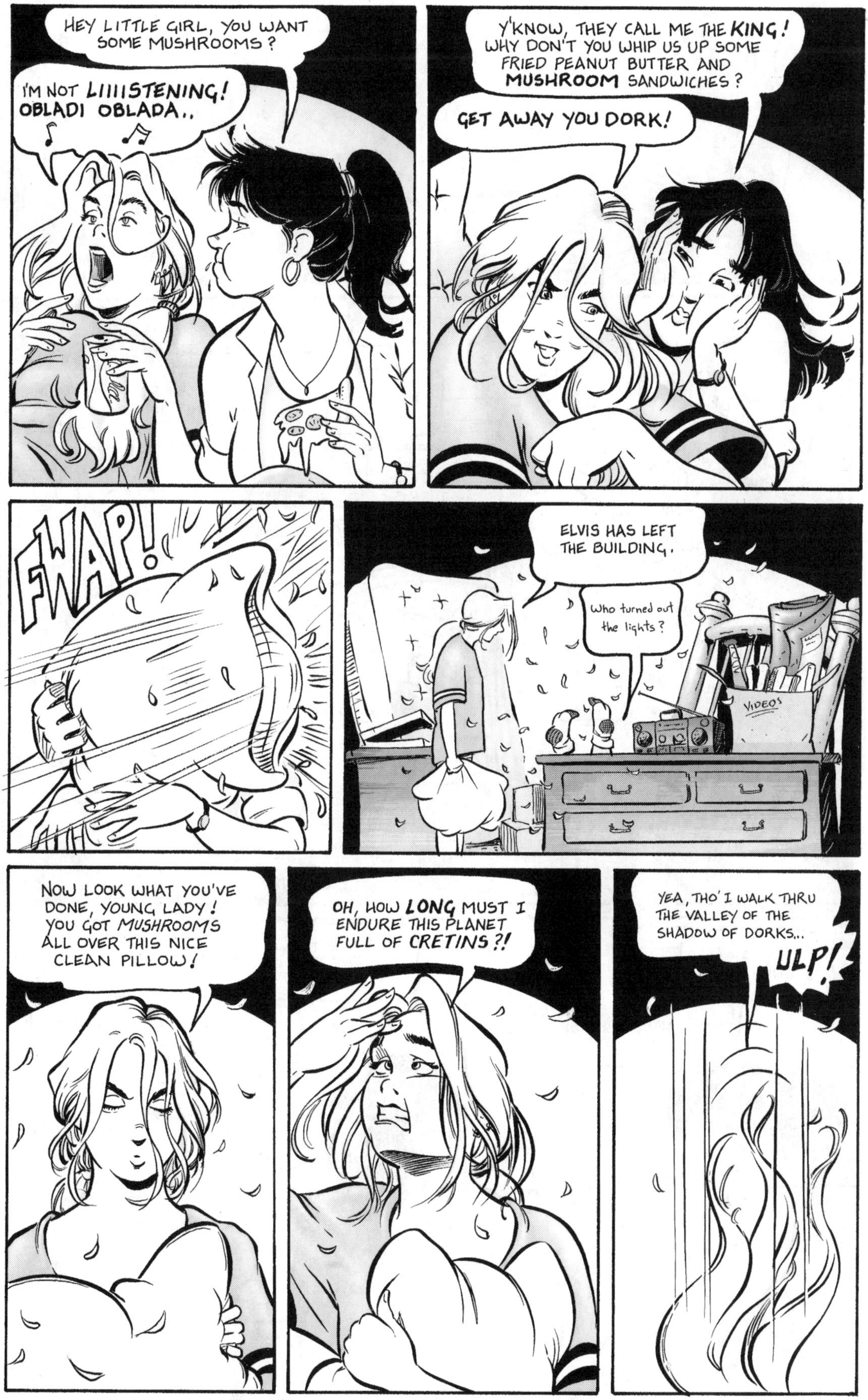
HEY LITTLE GIRL, YOU WANT SOME MUSHROOMS?
I'M NOT LIIIISTENING! OBLADI OBLADA..
Y'KNOW, THEY CALL ME THE KING! WHY DON'T YOU WHIP US UP SOME FRIED PEANUT BUTTER AND MUSHROOM SANDWICHES?
GET AWAY YOU DORK!
FWAP!
ELVIS HAS LEFT THE BUILDING.
Who turned out the lights?
VIDEOS
NOW LOOK WHAT YOU'VE DONE, YOUNG LADY! YOU GOT MUSHROOMS ALL OVER THIS NICE CLEAN PILLOW!
OH, HOW LONG MUST I ENDURE THIS PLANET FULL OF CRETINS?!
YEA, THO' I WALK THRU THE VALLEY OF THE SHADOW OF DORKS..
ULP!

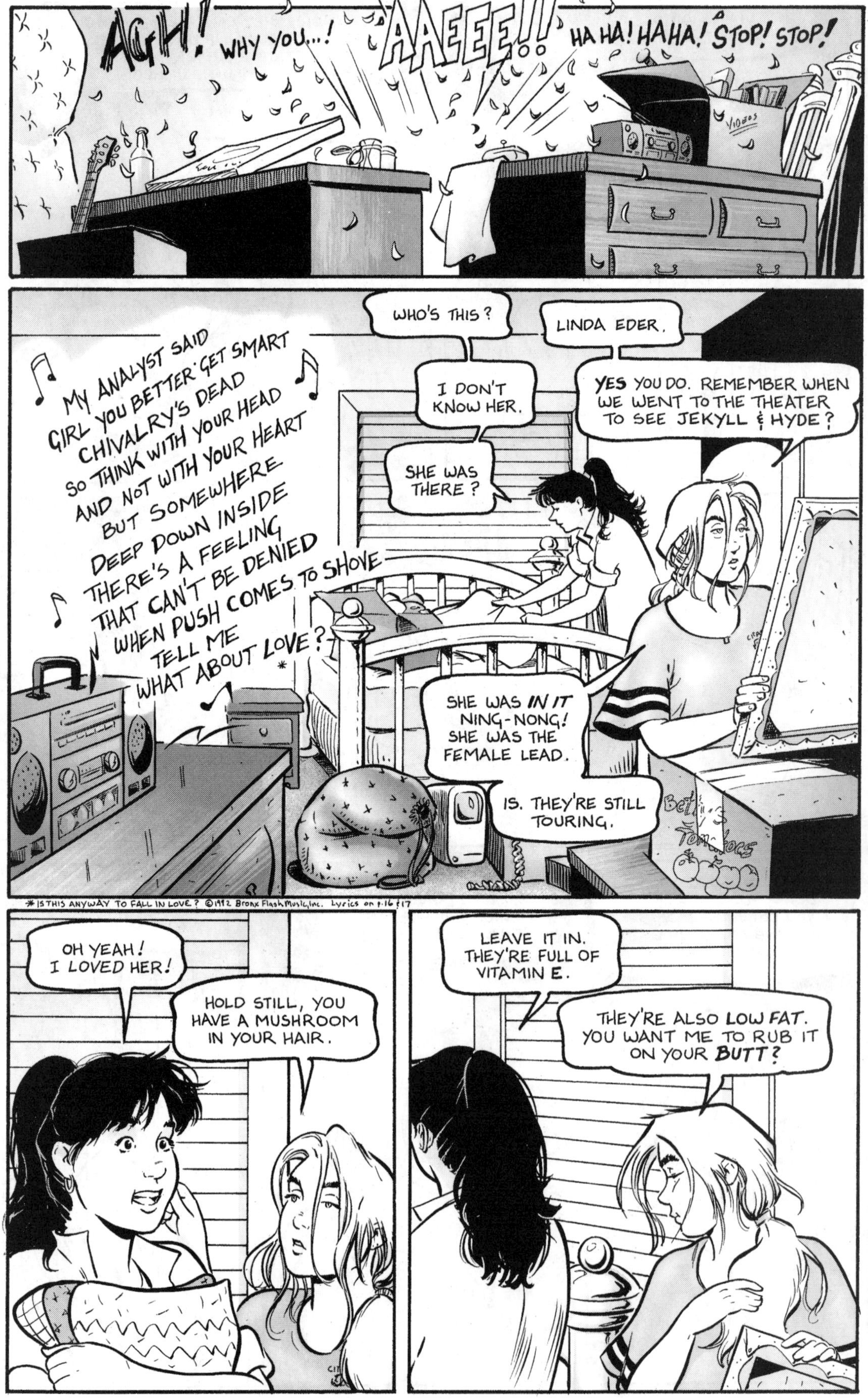
AGH!
WHY YOU...!
AAEEE!!
HA HA! HAHA! STOP! STOP!
VIDEOS
WHO'S THIS?
I DON'T KNOW HER.
LINDA EDER.
MY ANALYST SAID GIRL YOU BETTER GET SMART CHIVALRY'S DEAD SO THINK WITH YOUR HEAD AND NOT WITH YOUR HEART BUT SOMEWHERE DEEP DOWN INSIDE THERE'S A FEELING THAT CAN'T BE DENIED WHEN PUSH COMES TO SHOVE TELL ME WHAT ABOUT LOVE?*
YES YOU DO. REMEMBER WHEN WE WENT TO THE THEATER TO SEE JEKYLL & HYDE?
SHE WAS THERE?
SHE WAS IN IT NING-NONG! SHE WAS THE FEMALE LEAD.
IS. THEY'RE STILL TOURING.
* IS THIS ANYWAY TO FALL IN LOVE? ©1992 Bronx Flash Music, Inc. Lyrics on p.16 & 17
OH YEAH! I LOVED HER!
HOLD STILL, YOU HAVE A MUSHROOM IN YOUR HAIR.
LEAVE IT IN. THEY'RE FULL OF VITAMIN E.
THEY'RE ALSO LOW FAT. YOU WANT ME TO RUB IT ON YOUR BUTT?

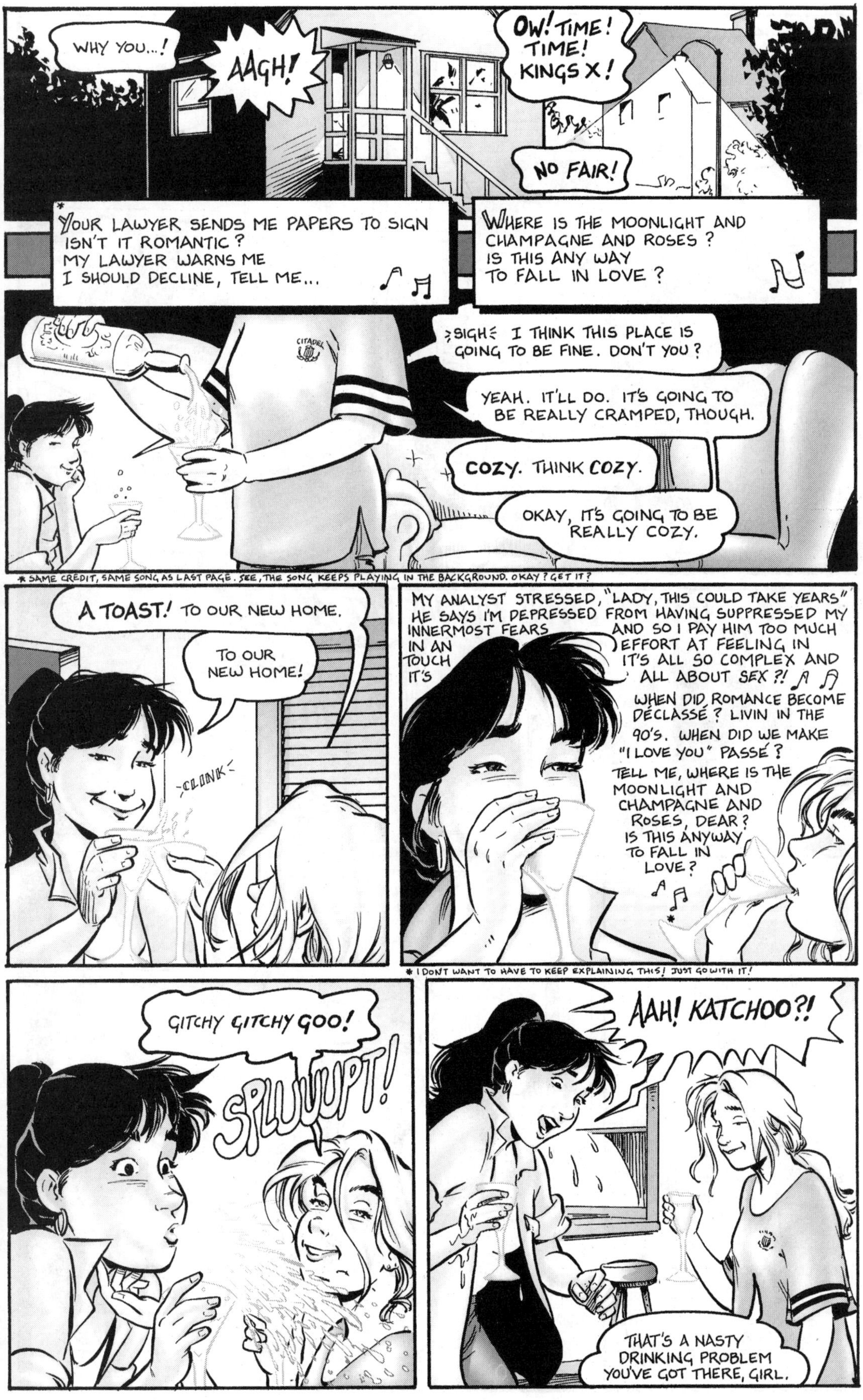

WHY YOU...!
AAGH!
OW! TIME! TIME! KINGS X!
NO FAIR!
*YOUR LAWYER SENDS ME PAPERS TO SIGN ISN'T IT ROMANTIC? MY LAWYER WARNS ME I SHOULD DECLINE, TELL ME...
WHERE IS THE MOONLIGHT AND CHAMPAGNE AND ROSES? IS THIS ANY WAY TO FALL IN LOVE?
CITADEL
≥SIGH≤ I THINK THIS PLACE IS GOING TO BE FINE. DON'T YOU?
YEAH. IT'LL DO. IT'S GOING TO BE REALLY CRAMPED, THOUGH.
COZY. THINK COZY.
OKAY, IT'S GOING TO BE REALLY COZY.
* SAME CREDIT, SAME SONG AS LAST PAGE. SEE, THE SONG KEEPS PLAYING IN THE BACKGROUND. OKAY? GET IT?
A TOAST! TO OUR NEW HOME.
TO OUR NEW HOME!
CLINK
MY ANALYST STRESSED, "LADY, THIS COULD TAKE YEARS" HE SAYS I'M DEPRESSED FROM HAVING SUPPRESSED MY INNERMOST FEARS
AND SO I PAY HIM TOO MUCH
IN AN EFFORT AT FEELING IN TOUCH
IT'S ALL SO COMPLEX AND IT'S ALL ABOUT SEX?!
WHEN DID ROMANCE BECOME DÉCLASSÉ? LIVIN IN THE 90'S. WHEN DID WE MAKE "I LOVE YOU" PASSÉ?
TELL ME, WHERE IS THE MOONLIGHT AND CHAMPAGNE AND ROSES, DEAR? IS THIS ANYWAY TO FALL IN LOVE?
* I DONT WANT TO HAVE TO KEEP EXPLAINING THIS! JUST GO WITH IT!
GITCHY GITCHY GOO!
SPLUUUPT!
AAH! KATCHOO?!
THAT'S A NASTY DRINKING PROBLEM YOU'VE GOT THERE, GIRL.

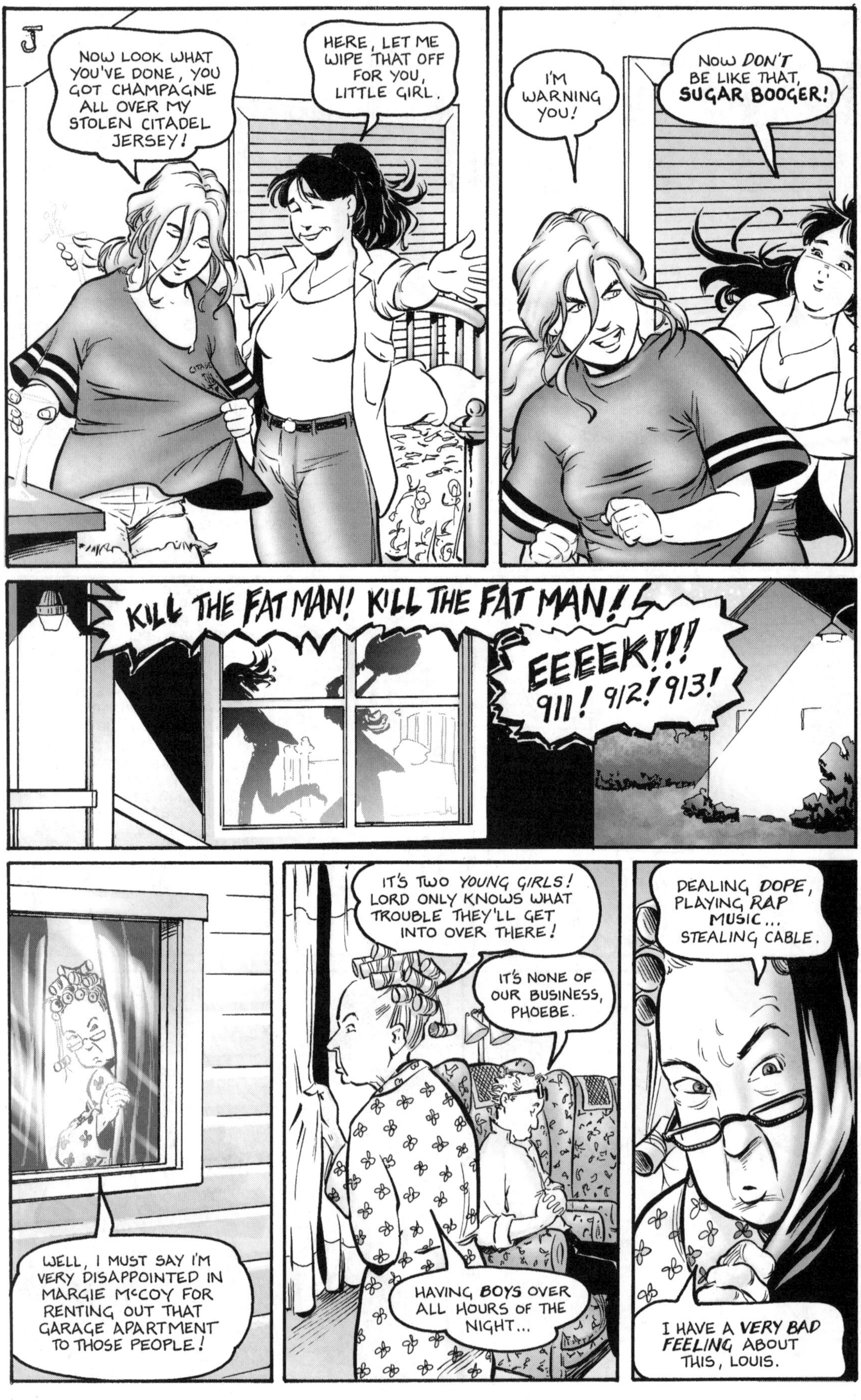

NOW LOOK WHAT YOU'VE DONE, YOU GOT CHAMPAGNE ALL OVER MY STOLEN CITADEL JERSEY!
HERE, LET ME WIPE THAT OFF FOR YOU, LITTLE GIRL.
I'M WARNING YOU!
NOW DON'T BE LIKE THAT, SUGAR BOOGER!
KILL THE FAT MAN! KILL THE FAT MAN!
EEEEK!!! 911! 912! 913!
WELL, I MUST SAY I'M VERY DISAPPOINTED IN MARGIE McCOY FOR RENTING OUT THAT GARAGE APARTMENT TO THOSE PEOPLE!
IT'S TWO YOUNG GIRLS! LORD ONLY KNOWS WHAT TROUBLE THEY'LL GET INTO OVER THERE!
IT'S NONE OF OUR BUSINESS, PHOEBE.
HAVING BOYS OVER ALL HOURS OF THE NIGHT...
DEALING DOPE, PLAYING RAP MUSIC... STEALING CABLE.
I HAVE A VERY BAD FEELING ABOUT THIS, LOUIS.

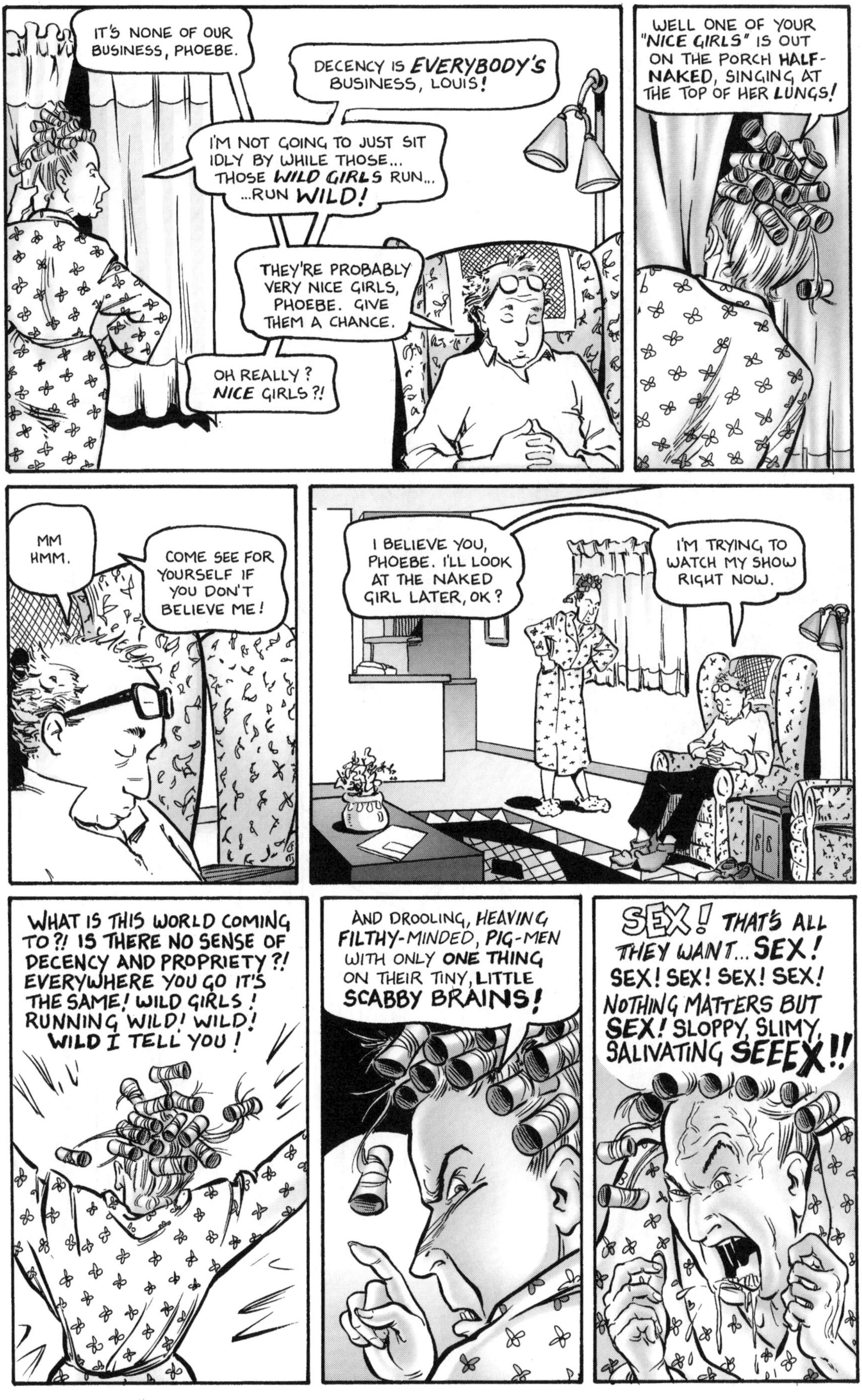

IT'S NONE OF OUR BUSINESS, PHOEBE.
DECENCY IS EVERYBODY'S BUSINESS, LOUIS!
I'M NOT GOING TO JUST SIT IDLY BY WHILE THOSE... THOSE WILD GIRLS RUN... ...RUN WILD!
THEY'RE PROBABLY VERY NICE GIRLS, PHOEBE. GIVE THEM A CHANCE.
OH REALLY? NICE GIRLS?!
WELL ONE OF YOUR "NICE GIRLS" IS OUT ON THE PORCH HALF-NAKED, SINGING AT THE TOP OF HER LUNGS!
MM HMM.
COME SEE FOR YOURSELF IF YOU DON'T BELIEVE ME!
I BELIEVE YOU, PHOEBE. I'LL LOOK AT THE NAKED GIRL LATER, OK?
I'M TRYING TO WATCH MY SHOW RIGHT NOW.
WHAT IS THIS WORLD COMING TO?! IS THERE NO SENSE OF DECENCY AND PROPRIETY?! EVERYWHERE YOU GO IT'S THE SAME! WILD GIRLS! RUNNING WILD! WILD! WILD I TELL YOU!
AND DROOLING, HEAVING FILTHY-MINDED, PIG-MEN WITH ONLY ONE THING ON THEIR TINY, LITTLE SCABBY BRAINS!
SEX! THAT'S ALL THEY WANT... SEX! SEX! SEX! SEX! SEX! NOTHING MATTERS BUT SEX! SLOPPY, SLIMY, SALIVATING SEEEX!!

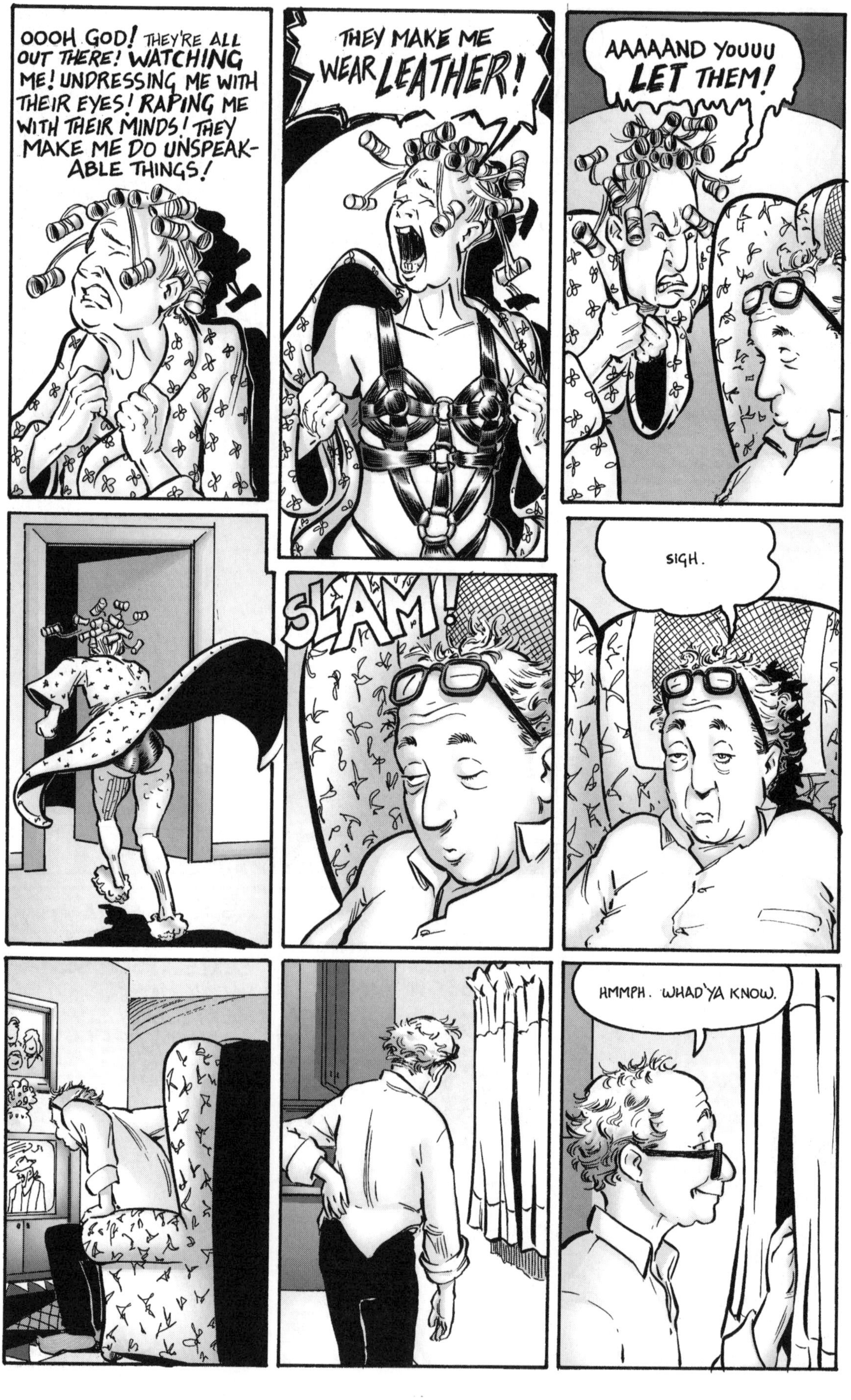
OOOH GOD! THEY'RE ALL OUT THERE! WATCHING ME! UNDRESSING ME WITH THEIR EYES! RAPING ME WITH THEIR MINDS! THEY MAKE ME DO UNSPEAKABLE THINGS!
THEY MAKE ME WEAR LEATHER!
AAAAAND YOUUU LET THEM!
SLAM!
SIGH.
HMMPH. WHAD'YA KNOW.

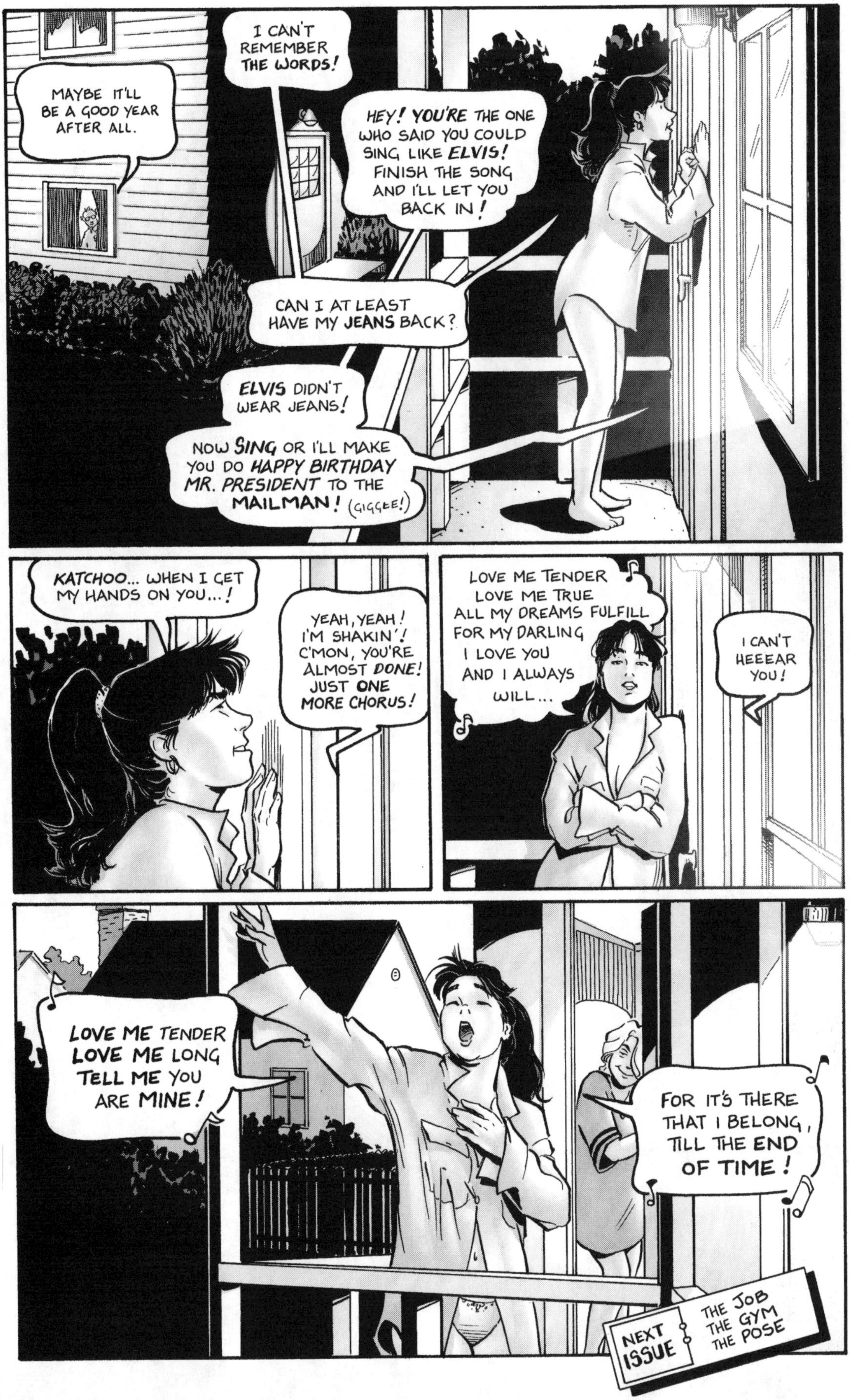
MAYBE IT'LL BE A GOOD YEAR AFTER ALL.
I CAN'T REMEMBER THE WORDS!
HEY! YOU'RE THE ONE WHO SAID YOU COULD SING LIKE ELVIS! FINISH THE SONG AND I'LL LET YOU BACK IN!
CAN I AT LEAST HAVE MY JEANS BACK?
ELVIS DIDN'T WEAR JEANS!
NOW SING OR I'LL MAKE YOU DO HAPPY BIRTHDAY MR. PRESIDENT TO THE MAILMAN! (GIGGLE!)
KATCHOO... WHEN I GET MY HANDS ON YOU...!
YEAH, YEAH! I'M SHAKIN'! C'MON, YOU'RE ALMOST DONE! JUST ONE MORE CHORUS!
LOVE ME TENDER LOVE ME TRUE ALL MY DREAMS FULFILL FOR MY DARLING I LOVE YOU AND I ALWAYS WILL...
I CAN'T HEEEAR YOU!
LOVE ME TENDER LOVE ME LONG TELL ME YOU ARE MINE!
FOR IT'S THERE THAT I BELONG, TILL THE END OF TIME!
NEXT ISSUE
THE JOB THE GYM THE POSE

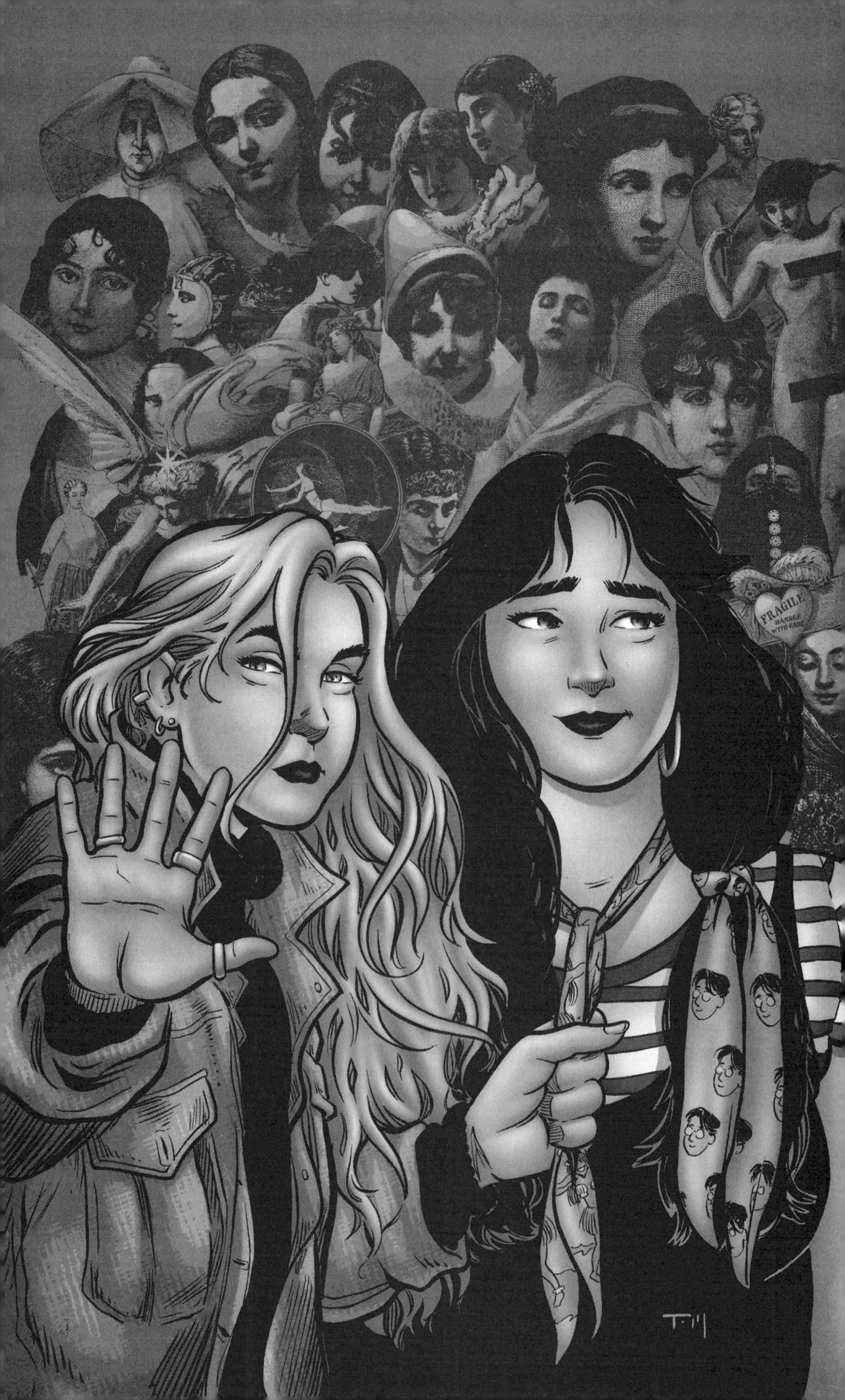
FRAGILE
HANDLE WITH CARE

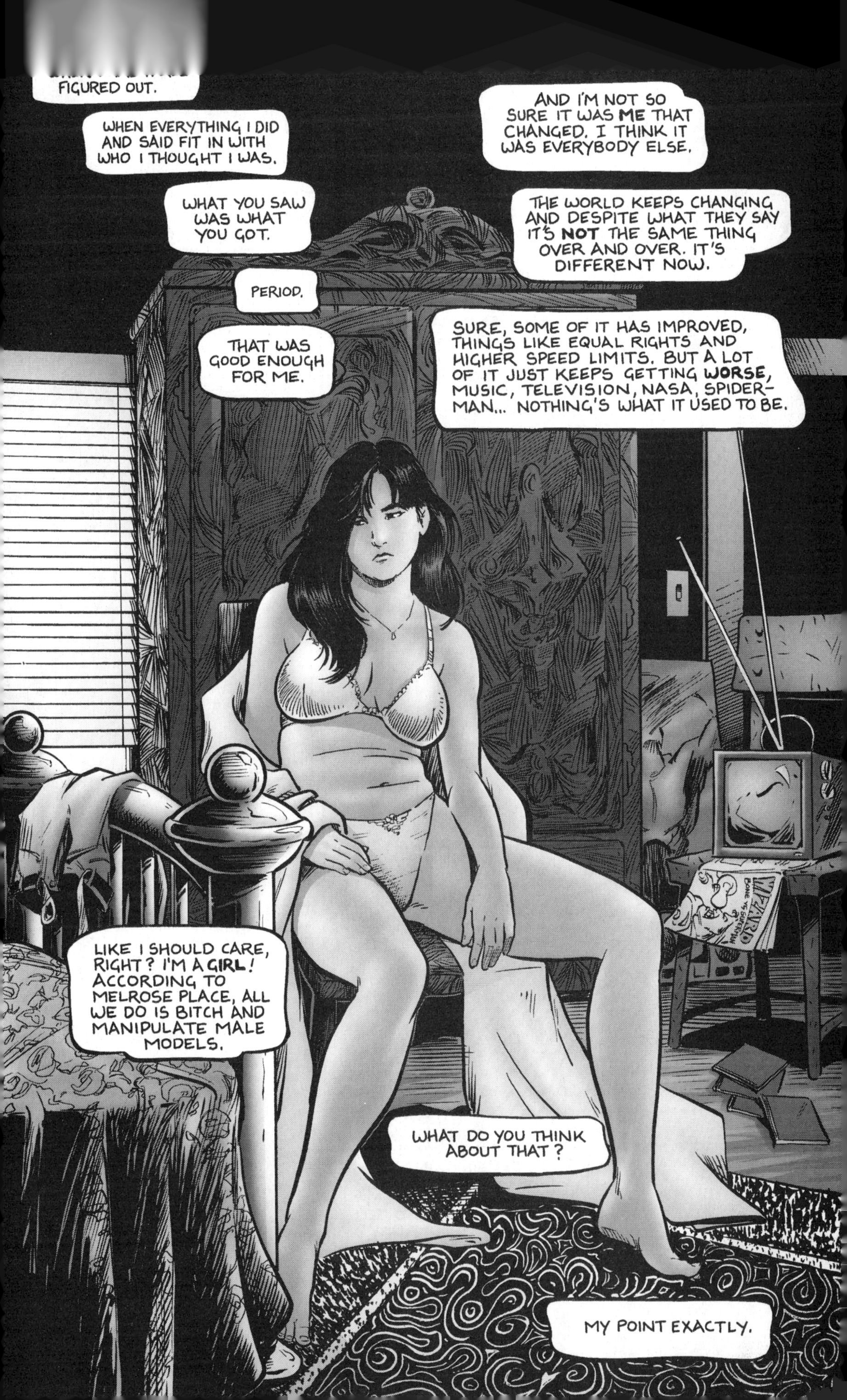
FIGURED OUT.
WHEN EVERYTHING I DID AND SAID FIT IN WITH WHO I THOUGHT I WAS.
WHAT YOU SAW WAS WHAT YOU GOT.
PERIOD.
THAT WAS GOOD ENOUGH FOR ME.
AND I'M NOT SO SURE IT WAS ME THAT CHANGED. I THINK IT WAS EVERYBODY ELSE.
THE WORLD KEEPS CHANGING AND DESPITE WHAT THEY SAY IT'S NOT THE SAME THING OVER AND OVER. IT'S DIFFERENT NOW.
SURE, SOME OF IT HAS IMPROVED, THINGS LIKE EQUAL RIGHTS AND HIGHER SPEED LIMITS. BUT A LOT OF IT JUST KEEPS GETTING WORSE, MUSIC, TELEVISION, NASA, SPIDER-MAN... NOTHING'S WHAT IT USED TO BE.
LIKE I SHOULD CARE, RIGHT? I'M A GIRL! ACCORDING TO MELROSE PLACE, ALL WE DO IS BITCH AND MANIPULATE MALE MODELS.
WHAT DO YOU THINK ABOUT THAT?
MY POINT EXACTLY.

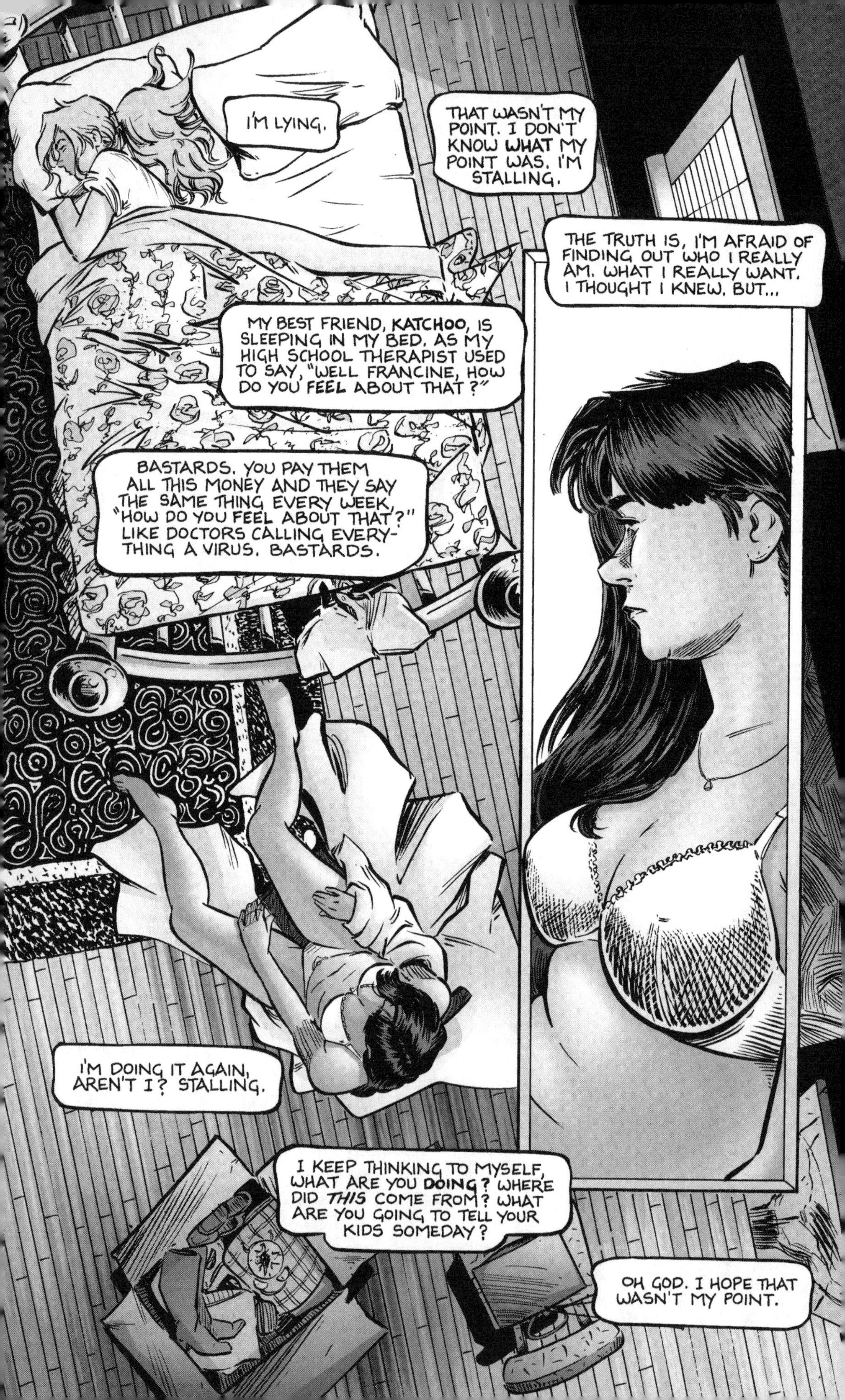
I'M LYING.
THAT WASN'T MY POINT. I DON'T KNOW WHAT MY POINT WAS. I'M STALLING.
THE TRUTH IS, I'M AFRAID OF FINDING OUT WHO I REALLY AM. WHAT I REALLY WANT. I THOUGHT I KNEW, BUT...
MY BEST FRIEND, KATCHOO, IS SLEEPING IN MY BED. AS MY HIGH SCHOOL THERAPIST USED TO SAY, "WELL FRANCINE, HOW DO YOU FEEL ABOUT THAT?"
BASTARDS. YOU PAY THEM ALL THIS MONEY AND THEY SAY THE SAME THING EVERY WEEK, "HOW DO YOU FEEL ABOUT THAT?" LIKE DOCTORS CALLING EVERYTHING A VIRUS. BASTARDS.
I'M DOING IT AGAIN, AREN'T I? STALLING.
I KEEP THINKING TO MYSELF, WHAT ARE YOU DOING? WHERE DID THIS COME FROM? WHAT ARE YOU GOING TO TELL YOUR KIDS SOMEDAY?
OH GOD. I HOPE THAT WASN'T MY POINT.

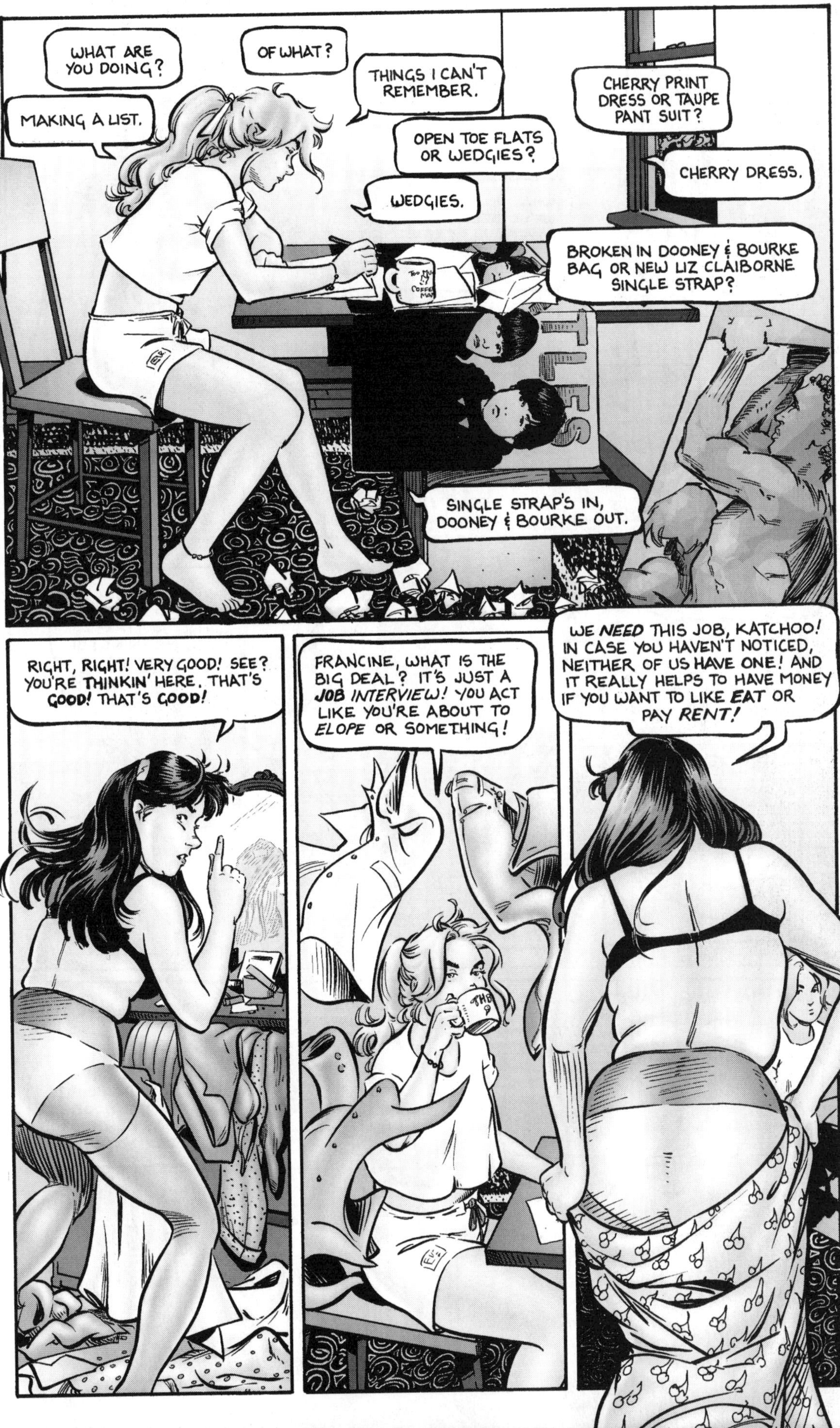
WHAT ARE YOU DOING?
MAKING A LIST.
OF WHAT?
THINGS I CAN'T REMEMBER.
OPEN TOE FLATS OR WEDGIES?
WEDGIES.
CHERRY PRINT DRESS OR TAUPE PANT SUIT?
CHERRY DRESS.
BROKEN IN DOONEY & BOURKE BAG OR NEW LIZ CLAIBORNE SINGLE STRAP?
SINGLE STRAP'S IN, DOONEY & BOURKE OUT.
RIGHT, RIGHT! VERY GOOD! SEE? YOU'RE THINKIN' HERE. THAT'S GOOD! THAT'S GOOD!
FRANCINE, WHAT IS THE BIG DEAL? IT'S JUST A JOB INTERVIEW! YOU ACT LIKE YOU'RE ABOUT TO ELOPE OR SOMETHING!
WE NEED THIS JOB, KATCHOO! IN CASE YOU HAVEN'T NOTICED, NEITHER OF US HAVE ONE! AND IT REALLY HELPS TO HAVE MONEY IF YOU WANT TO LIKE EAT OR PAY RENT!

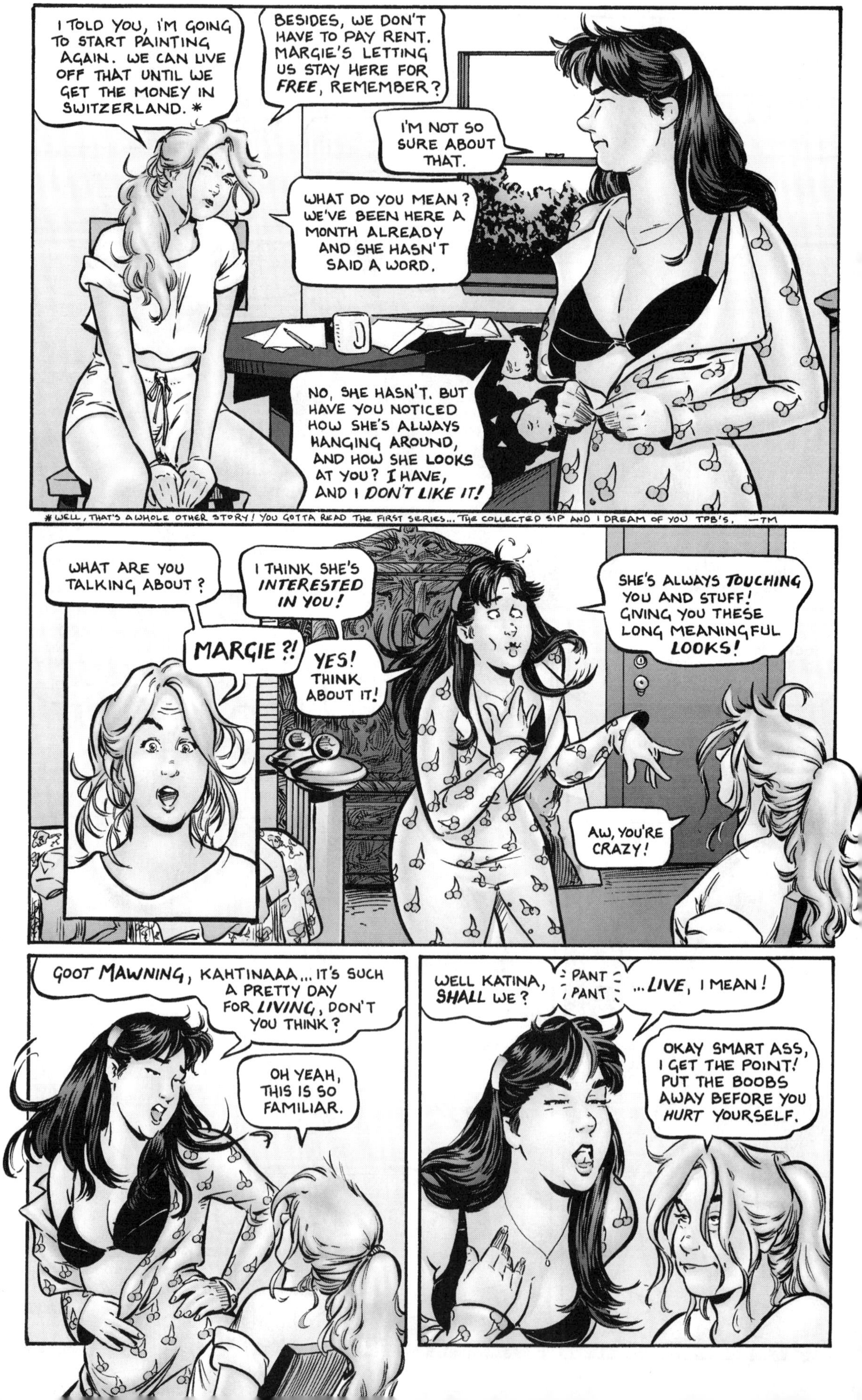
I TOLD YOU, I'M GOING TO START PAINTING AGAIN. WE CAN LIVE OFF THAT UNTIL WE GET THE MONEY IN SWITZERLAND. *
BESIDES, WE DON'T HAVE TO PAY RENT. MARGIE'S LETTING US STAY HERE FOR FREE, REMEMBER?
I'M NOT SO SURE ABOUT THAT.
WHAT DO YOU MEAN? WE'VE BEEN HERE A MONTH ALREADY AND SHE HASN'T SAID A WORD.
NO, SHE HASN'T. BUT HAVE YOU NOTICED HOW SHE'S ALWAYS HANGING AROUND, AND HOW SHE LOOKS AT YOU? I HAVE, AND I DON'T LIKE IT!
* WELL, THAT'S A WHOLE OTHER STORY! YOU GOTTA READ THE FIRST SERIES... THE COLLECTED SIP AND I DREAM OF YOU TPB'S. —TM
WHAT ARE YOU TALKING ABOUT?
I THINK SHE'S INTERESTED IN YOU!
MARGIE?!
YES! THINK ABOUT IT!
SHE'S ALWAYS TOUCHING YOU AND STUFF! GIVING YOU THESE LONG MEANINGFUL LOOKS!
AW, YOU'RE CRAZY!
GOOT MAWNING, KAHTINAAA... IT'S SUCH A PRETTY DAY FOR LIVING, DON'T YOU THINK?
OH YEAH, THIS IS SO FAMILIAR.
WELL KATINA, SHALL WE?
PANT PANT
...LIVE, I MEAN!
OKAY SMART ASS, I GET THE POINT! PUT THE BOOBS AWAY BEFORE YOU HURT YOURSELF.

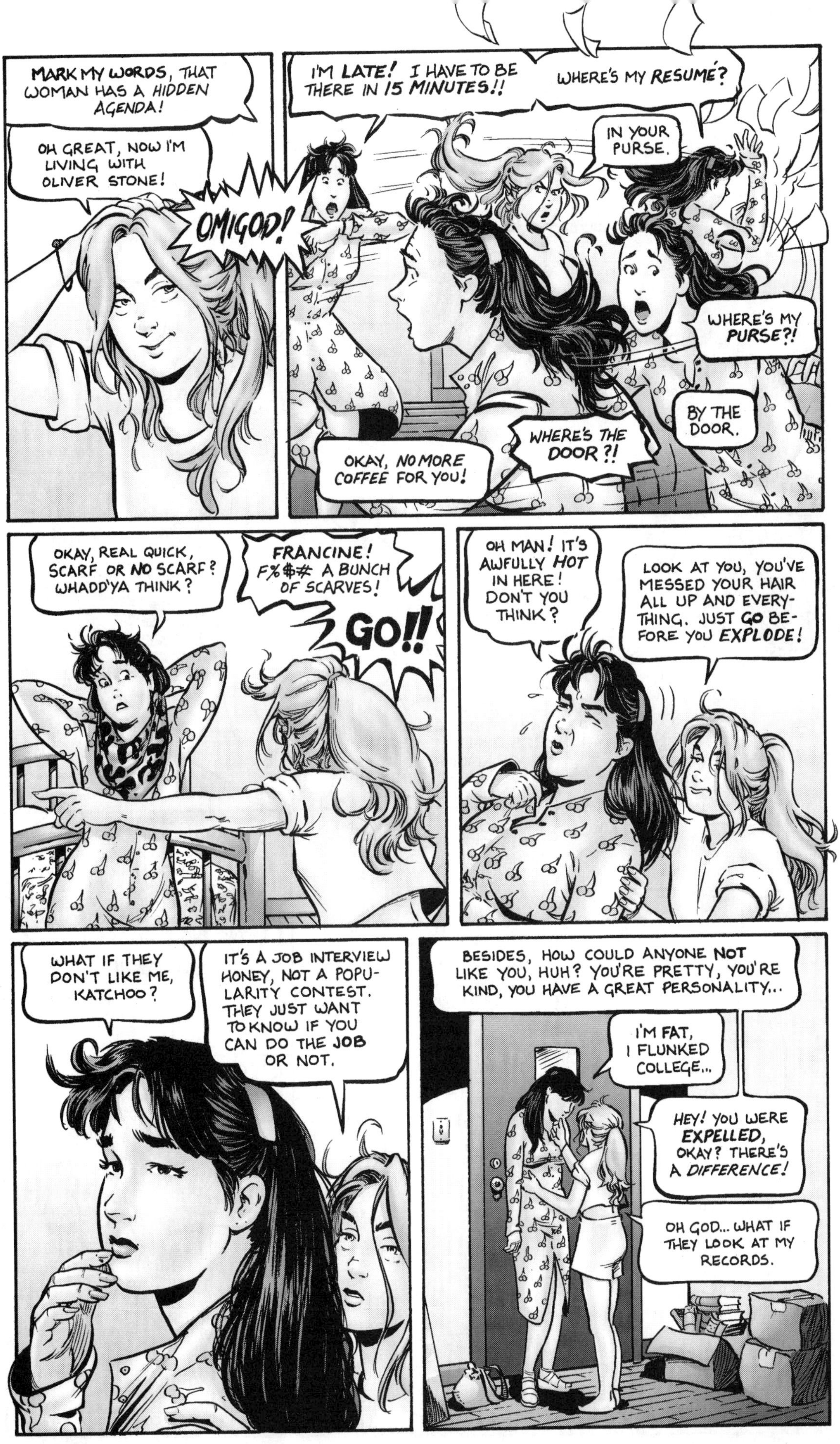

MARK MY WORDS, THAT WOMAN HAS A HIDDEN AGENDA!
OH GREAT, NOW I'M LIVING WITH OLIVER STONE!
OMIGOD!
I'M LATE! I HAVE TO BE THERE IN 15 MINUTES!!
WHERE'S MY RESUMÉ?
IN YOUR PURSE.
WHERE'S MY PURSE?!
BY THE DOOR.
WHERE'S THE DOOR?!
OKAY, NO MORE COFFEE FOR YOU!
OKAY, REAL QUICK, SCARF OR NO SCARF? WHADD'YA THINK?
FRANCINE! F%$# A BUNCH OF SCARVES!
GO!!
OH MAN! IT'S AWFULLY HOT IN HERE! DON'T YOU THINK?
LOOK AT YOU, YOU'VE MESSED YOUR HAIR ALL UP AND EVERY-THING. JUST GO BE-FORE YOU EXPLODE!
WHAT IF THEY DON'T LIKE ME, KATCHOO?
IT'S A JOB INTERVIEW HONEY, NOT A POPU-LARITY CONTEST. THEY JUST WANT TO KNOW IF YOU CAN DO THE JOB OR NOT.
BESIDES, HOW COULD ANYONE NOT LIKE YOU, HUH? YOU'RE PRETTY, YOU'RE KIND, YOU HAVE A GREAT PERSONALITY...
I'M FAT, I FLUNKED COLLEGE...
HEY! YOU WERE EXPELLED, OKAY? THERE'S A DIFFERENCE!
OH GOD... WHAT IF THEY LOOK AT MY RECORDS.

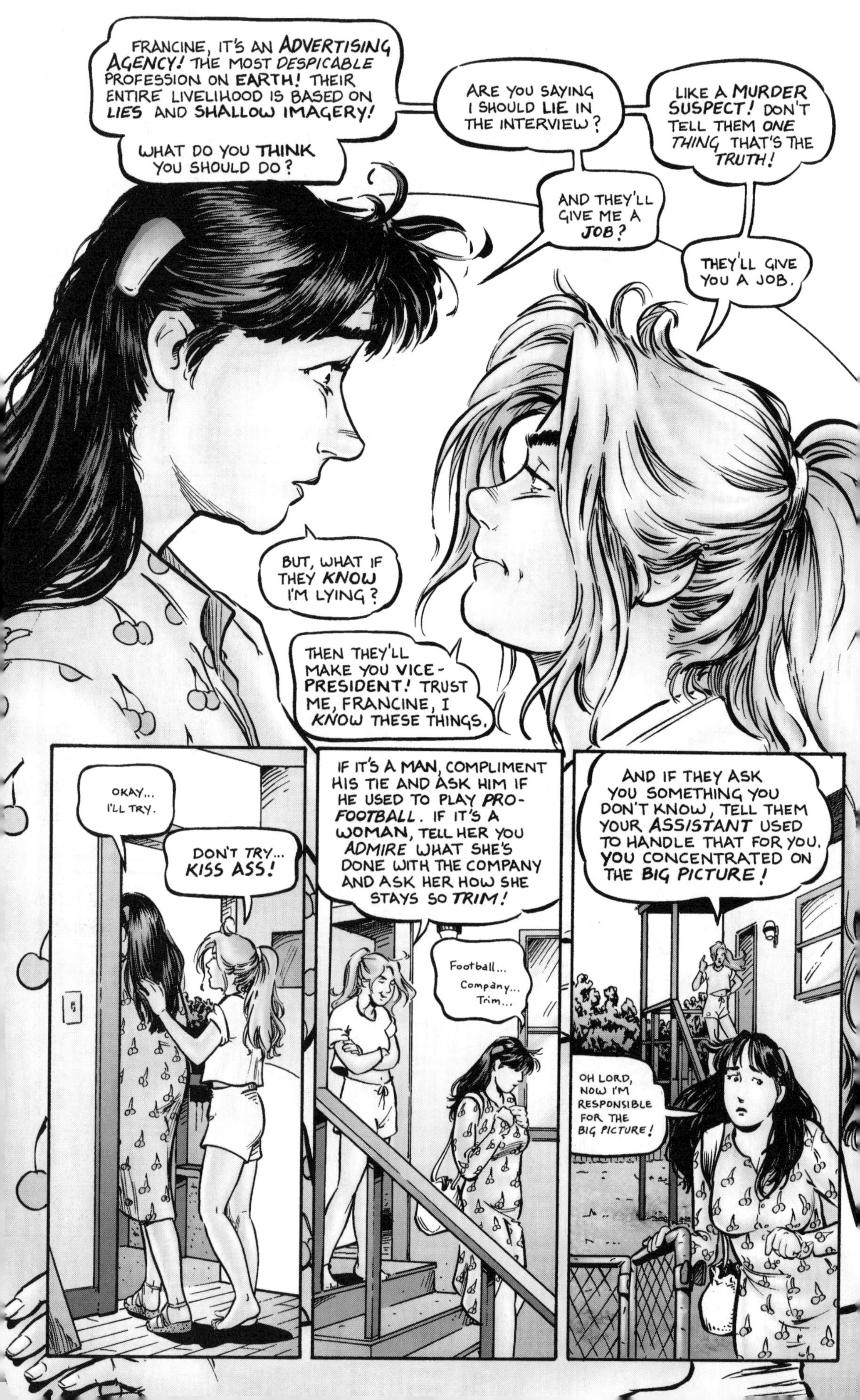

FRANCINE, IT'S AN ADVERTISING AGENCY! THE MOST DESPICABLE PROFESSION ON EARTH! THEIR ENTIRE LIVELIHOOD IS BASED ON LIES AND SHALLOW IMAGERY!
WHAT DO YOU THINK YOU SHOULD DO?
ARE YOU SAYING I SHOULD LIE IN THE INTERVIEW?
LIKE A MURDER SUSPECT! DON'T TELL THEM ONE THING THAT'S THE TRUTH!
AND THEY'LL GIVE ME A JOB?
THEY'LL GIVE YOU A JOB.
BUT, WHAT IF THEY KNOW I'M LYING?
THEN THEY'LL MAKE YOU VICE-PRESIDENT! TRUST ME, FRANCINE, I KNOW THESE THINGS.
OKAY... I'LL TRY.
DON'T TRY... KISS ASS!
IF IT'S A MAN, COMPLIMENT HIS TIE AND ASK HIM IF HE USED TO PLAY PRO-FOOTBALL. IF IT'S A WOMAN, TELL HER YOU ADMIRE WHAT SHE'S DONE WITH THE COMPANY AND ASK HER HOW SHE STAYS SO TRIM!
Football... Company... Trim...
AND IF THEY ASK YOU SOMETHING YOU DON'T KNOW, TELL THEM YOUR ASSISTANT USED TO HANDLE THAT FOR YOU. YOU CONCENTRATED ON THE BIG PICTURE!
OH LORD, NOW I'M RESPONSIBLE FOR THE BIG PICTURE!

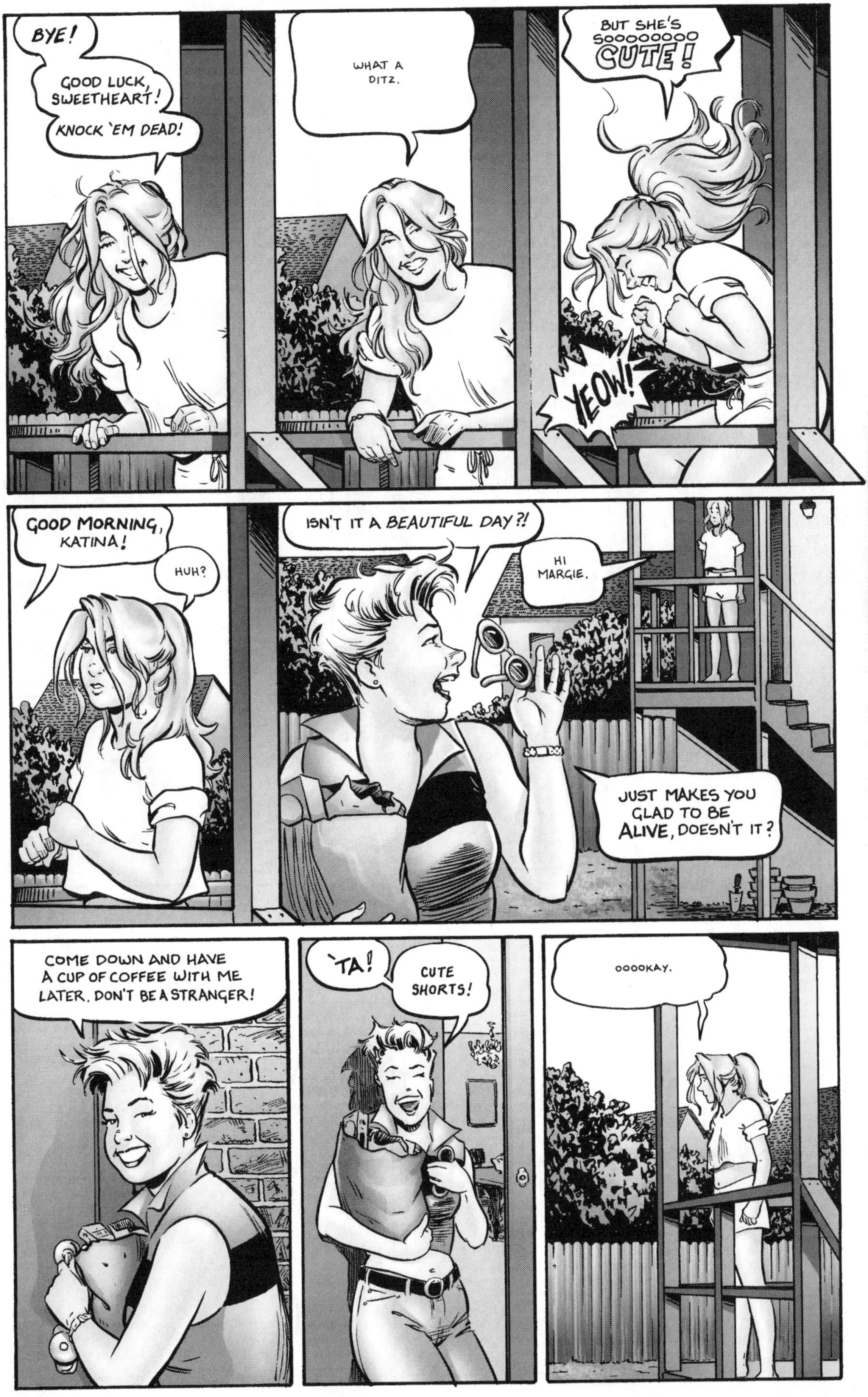
BYE!
GOOD LUCK, SWEETHEART!
KNOCK 'EM DEAD!
WHAT A DITZ.
BUT SHE'S SOOOOOOOO CUTE!
YEOW!
GOOD MORNING, KATINA!
HUH?
ISN'T IT A BEAUTIFUL DAY?!
HI MARGIE.
JUST MAKES YOU GLAD TO BE ALIVE, DOESN'T IT?
COME DOWN AND HAVE A CUP OF COFFEE WITH ME LATER. DON'T BE A STRANGER!
'TA!
CUTE SHORTS!
OOOOKAY.

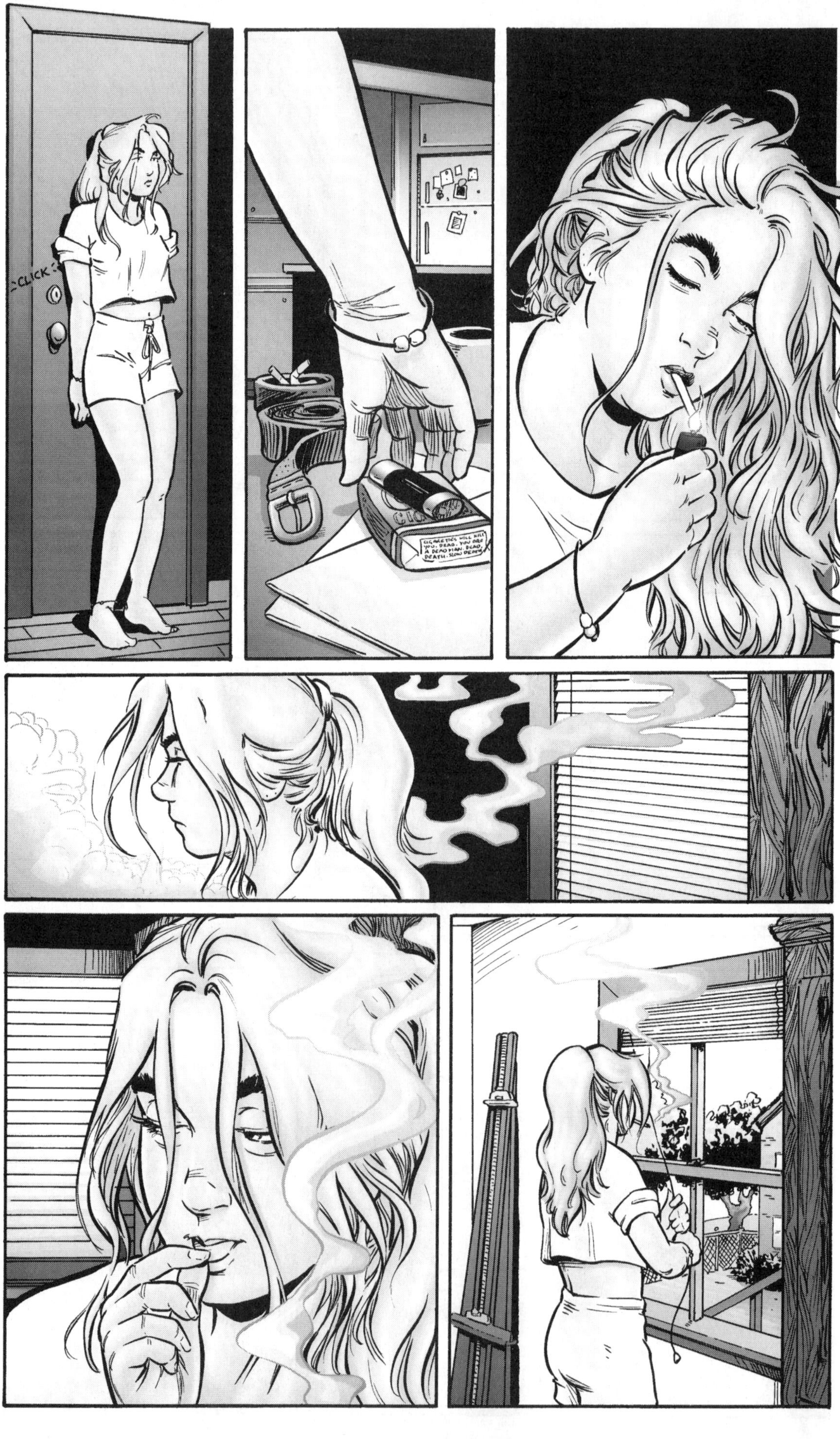
CLICK
CIGARETTES WILL KILL YOU. DEAD. YOU ARE A DEAD MAN. DEAD. DEATH. SLOW DEATH

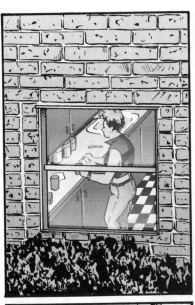

...SIGH...

HI! AGH!

KATCHOO? HEY! DID I STARTLE YOU?

KATCHOO?

YOU EVER HEARD OF KNOCKING DIPSHIT!

OH-HO MAN! I'M SORRY!

I GOTCHA', DIDN'T I?

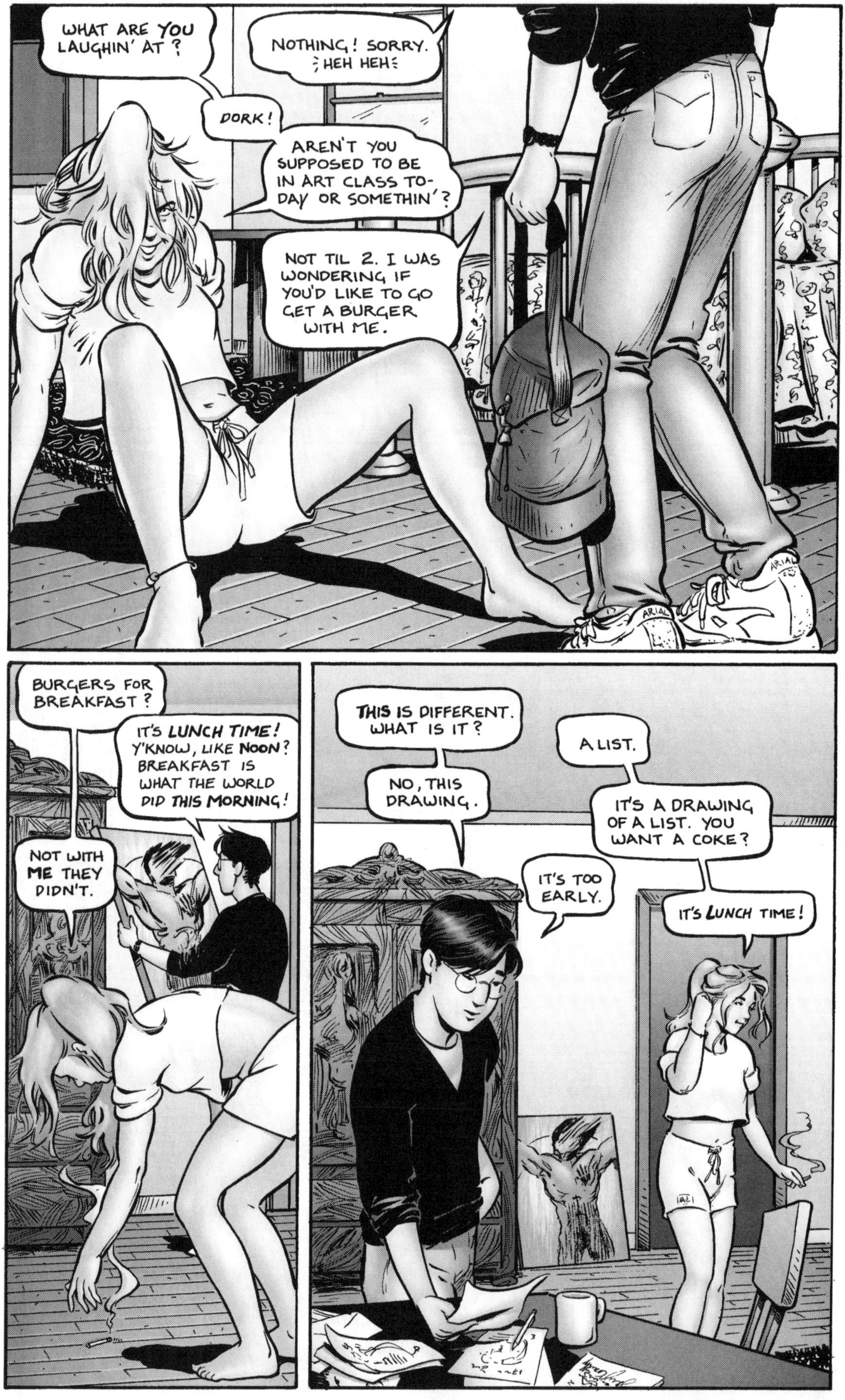

WHAT ARE YOU LAUGHIN' AT?
NOTHING! SORRY. HEH HEH
DORK!
AREN'T YOU SUPPOSED TO BE IN ART CLASS TO-DAY OR SOMETHIN'?
NOT TIL 2. I WAS WONDERING IF YOU'D LIKE TO GO GET A BURGER WITH ME.
BURGERS FOR BREAKFAST?
IT'S LUNCH TIME! Y'KNOW, LIKE NOON? BREAKFAST IS WHAT THE WORLD DID THIS MORNING!
NOT WITH ME THEY DIDN'T.
THIS IS DIFFERENT. WHAT IS IT?
A LIST.
NO, THIS DRAWING.
IT'S A DRAWING OF A LIST. YOU WANT A COKE?
IT'S TOO EARLY.
IT'S LUNCH TIME!

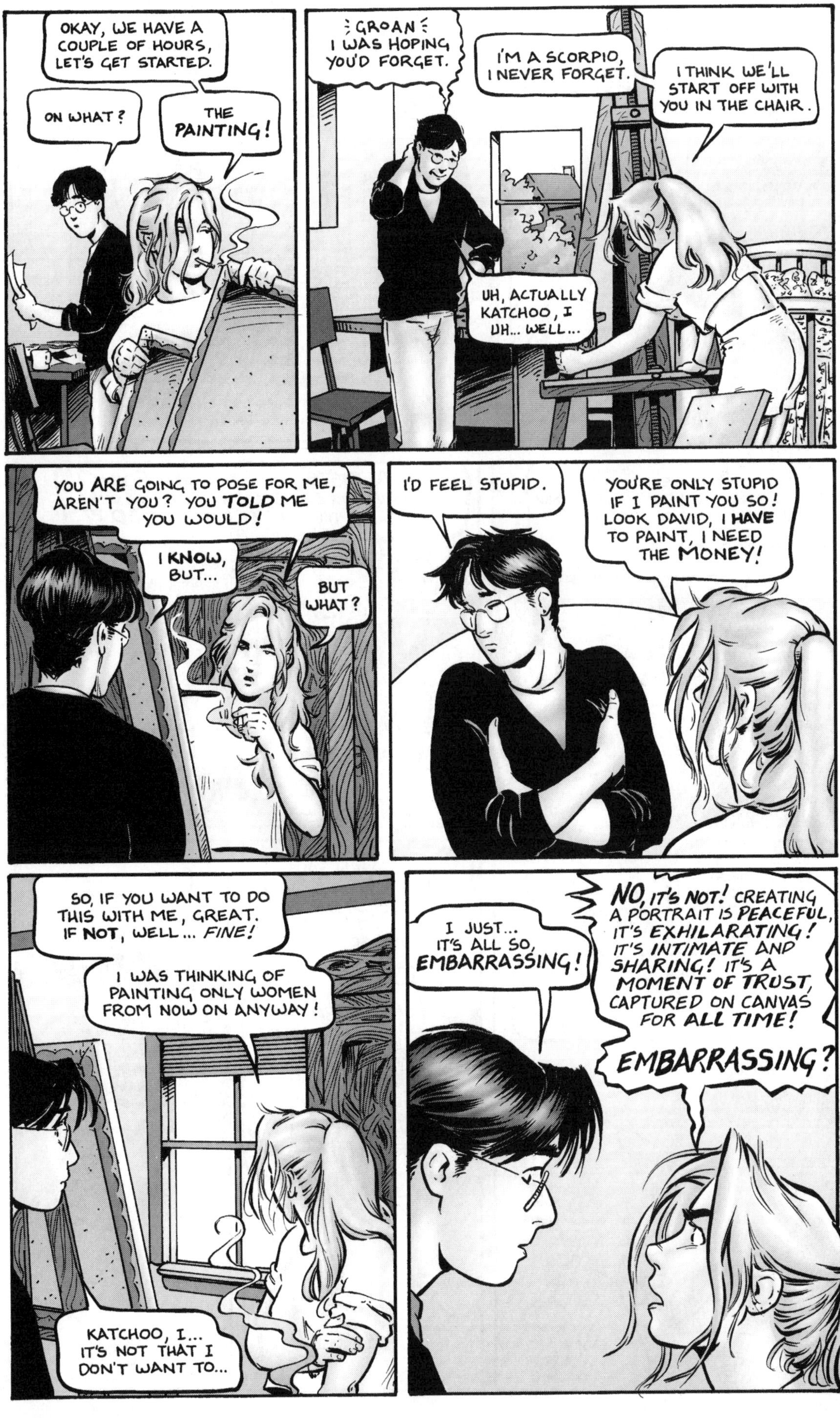
OKAY, WE HAVE A COUPLE OF HOURS, LET'S GET STARTED.
ON WHAT?
THE PAINTING!
GROAN I WAS HOPING YOU'D FORGET.
I'M A SCORPIO, I NEVER FORGET.
I THINK WE'LL START OFF WITH YOU IN THE CHAIR.
UH, ACTUALLY KATCHOO, I UH... WELL...
YOU ARE GOING TO POSE FOR ME, AREN'T YOU? YOU TOLD ME YOU WOULD!
I KNOW, BUT...
BUT WHAT?
I'D FEEL STUPID.
YOU'RE ONLY STUPID IF I PAINT YOU SO! LOOK DAVID, I HAVE TO PAINT, I NEED THE MONEY!
SO, IF YOU WANT TO DO THIS WITH ME, GREAT. IF NOT, WELL... FINE!
I WAS THINKING OF PAINTING ONLY WOMEN FROM NOW ON ANYWAY!
KATCHOO, I... IT'S NOT THAT I DON'T WANT TO...
I JUST... IT'S ALL SO, EMBARRASSING!
NO, IT'S NOT! CREATING A PORTRAIT IS PEACEFUL, IT'S EXHILARATING! IT'S INTIMATE AND SHARING! IT'S A MOMENT OF TRUST, CAPTURED ON CANVAS FOR ALL TIME!
EMBARRASSING?

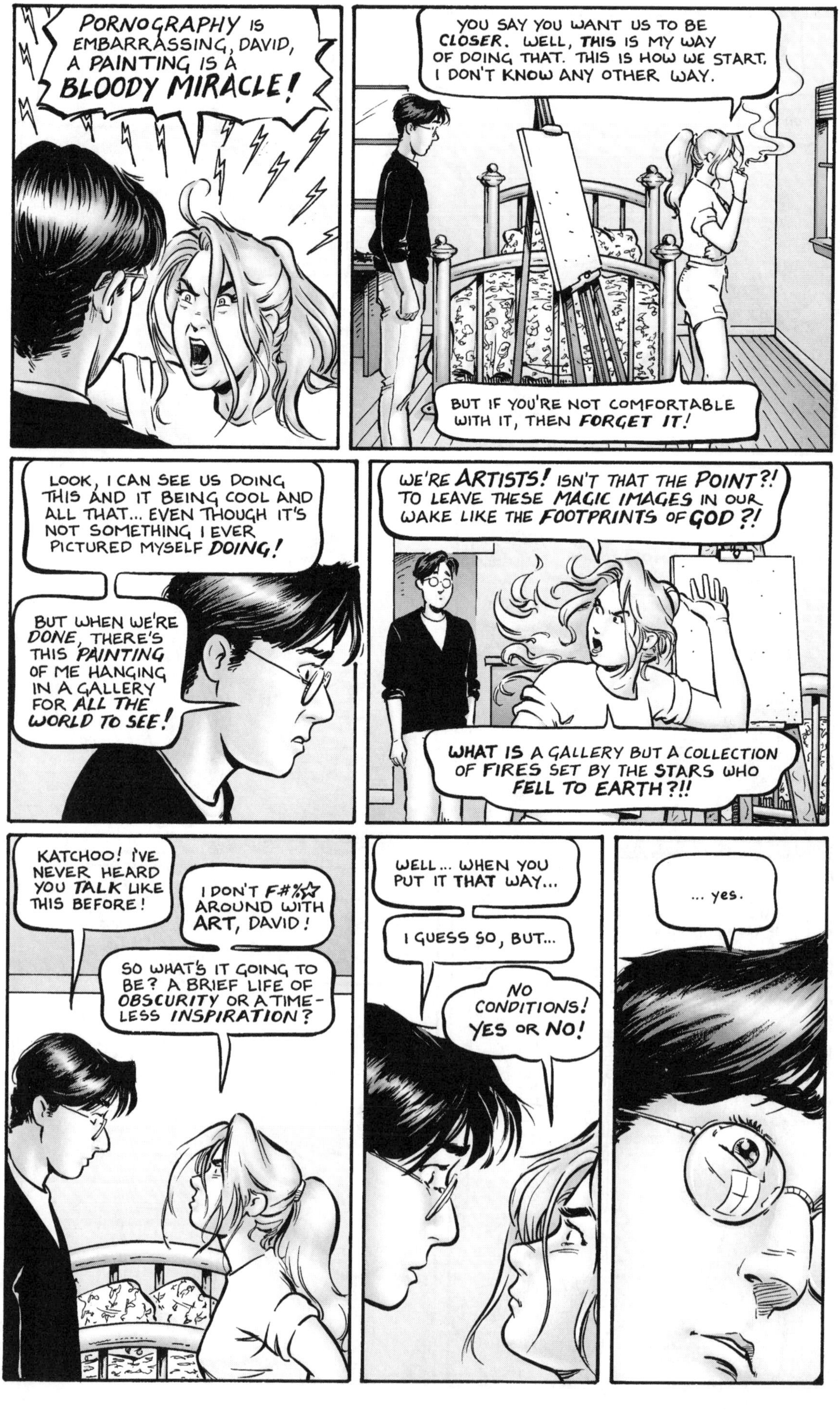
PORNOGRAPHY IS EMBARRASSING, DAVID, A PAINTING IS A BLOODY MIRACLE!
YOU SAY YOU WANT US TO BE CLOSER. WELL, THIS IS MY WAY OF DOING THAT. THIS IS HOW WE START. I DON'T KNOW ANY OTHER WAY.
BUT IF YOU'RE NOT COMFORTABLE WITH IT, THEN FORGET IT!
LOOK, I CAN SEE US DOING THIS AND IT BEING COOL AND ALL THAT... EVEN THOUGH IT'S NOT SOMETHING I EVER PICTURED MYSELF DOING!
BUT WHEN WE'RE DONE, THERE'S THIS PAINTING OF ME HANGING IN A GALLERY FOR ALL THE WORLD TO SEE!
WE'RE ARTISTS! ISN'T THAT THE POINT?! TO LEAVE THESE MAGIC IMAGES IN OUR WAKE LIKE THE FOOTPRINTS OF GOD?!
WHAT IS A GALLERY BUT A COLLECTION OF FIRES SET BY THE STARS WHO FELL TO EARTH?!!
KATCHOO! I'VE NEVER HEARD YOU TALK LIKE THIS BEFORE!
I DON'T F#%☆ AROUND WITH ART, DAVID!
SO WHAT'S IT GOING TO BE? A BRIEF LIFE OF OBSCURITY OR A TIME-LESS INSPIRATION?
WELL... WHEN YOU PUT IT THAT WAY...
I GUESS SO, BUT...
NO CONDITIONS! YES OR NO!
... yes.

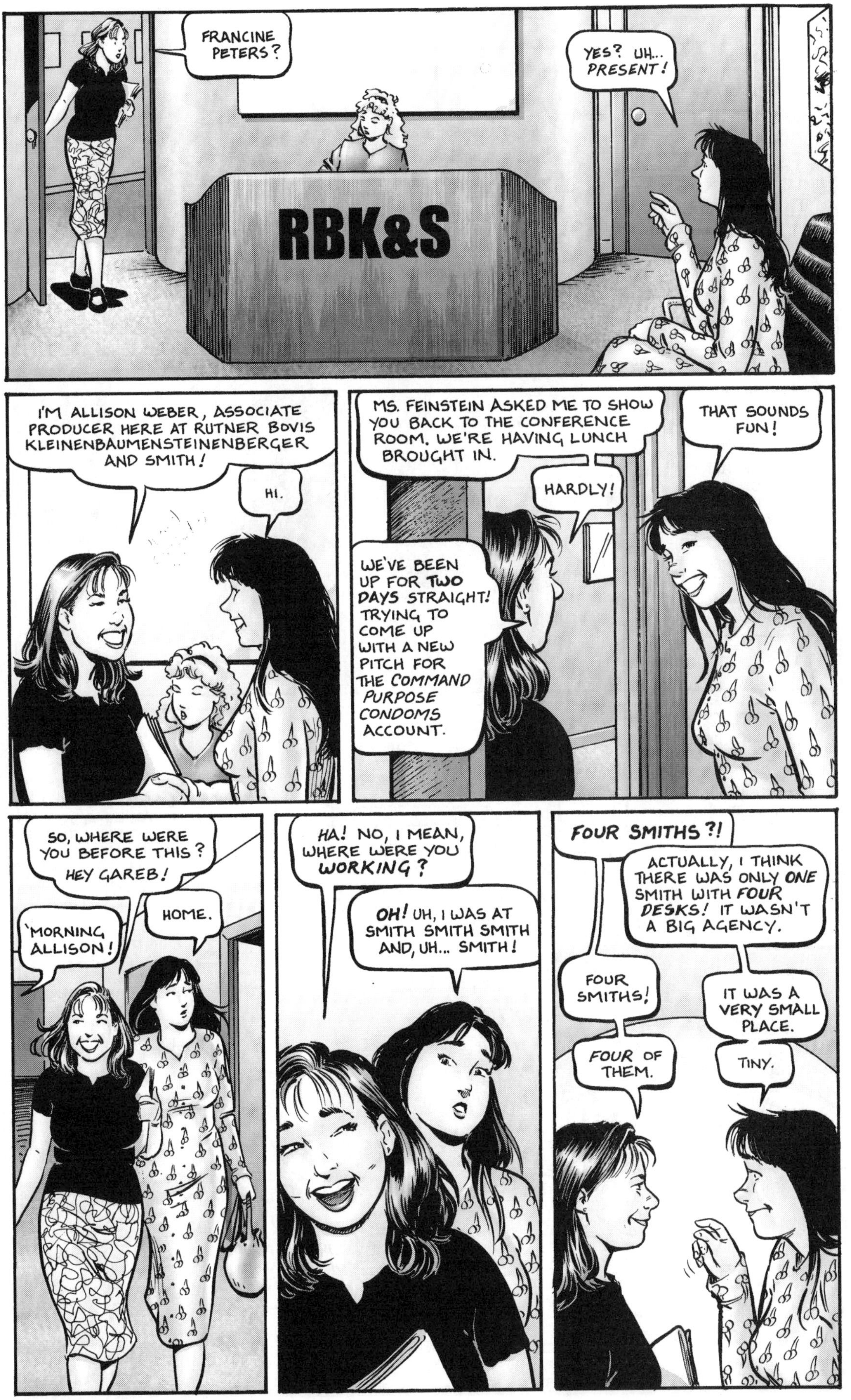
FRANCINE PETERS?
YES? UH... PRESENT!
RBK&S
I'M ALLISON WEBER, ASSOCIATE PRODUCER HERE AT RUTNER BOVIS KLEINENBAUMENSTEINENBERGER AND SMITH!
HI.
MS. FEINSTEIN ASKED ME TO SHOW YOU BACK TO THE CONFERENCE ROOM. WE'RE HAVING LUNCH BROUGHT IN.
THAT SOUNDS FUN!
HARDLY!
WE'VE BEEN UP FOR TWO DAYS STRAIGHT! TRYING TO COME UP WITH A NEW PITCH FOR THE COMMAND PURPOSE CONDOMS ACCOUNT.
SO, WHERE WERE YOU BEFORE THIS? HEY GAREB!
'MORNING ALLISON!
HOME.
HA! NO, I MEAN, WHERE WERE YOU WORKING?
OH! UH, I WAS AT SMITH SMITH SMITH AND, UH... SMITH!
FOUR SMITHS?!
ACTUALLY, I THINK THERE WAS ONLY ONE SMITH WITH FOUR DESKS! IT WASN'T A BIG AGENCY.
FOUR SMITHS!
IT WAS A VERY SMALL PLACE.
FOUR OF THEM.
TINY.

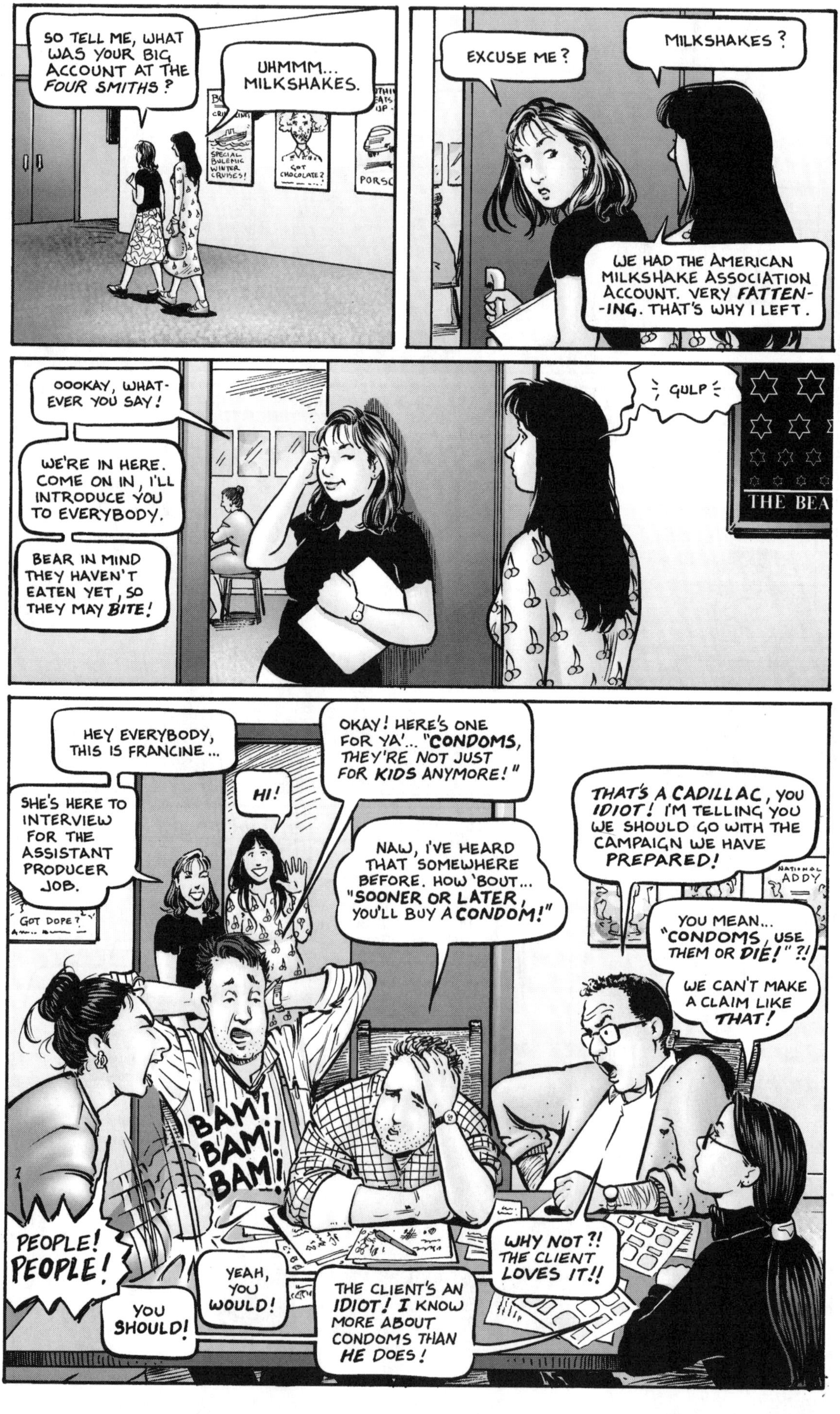
SO TELL ME, WHAT WAS YOUR BIG ACCOUNT AT THE *FOUR SMITHS* ?
UHMMM... MILKSHAKES.
SPECIAL BULEMIC WINTER CRUISES!
GOT CHOCOLATE?
EXCUSE ME?
MILKSHAKES?
WE HAD THE AMERICAN MILKSHAKE ASSOCIATION ACCOUNT. VERY ***FATTEN-ING***. THAT'S WHY I LEFT.
OOOKAY, WHAT-EVER YOU SAY!
WE'RE IN HERE. COME ON IN, I'LL INTRODUCE YOU TO EVERYBODY.
BEAR IN MIND THEY HAVEN'T EATEN YET, SO THEY MAY ***BITE***!
GULP
HEY EVERYBODY, THIS IS FRANCINE...
SHE'S HERE TO INTERVIEW FOR THE ASSISTANT PRODUCER JOB.
HI!
GOT DOPE?
OKAY! HERE'S ONE FOR YA'... "**CONDOMS**, THEY'RE NOT JUST FOR **KIDS** ANYMORE!"
NAW, I'VE HEARD THAT SOMEWHERE BEFORE. HOW 'BOUT... "**SOONER OR LATER**, YOU'LL BUY A **CONDOM!**"
*THAT'S A **CADILLAC**, YOU **IDIOT**!* I'M TELLING YOU WE SHOULD GO WITH THE CAMPAIGN WE HAVE **PREPARED!**
NATIONAL ADDY
YOU MEAN... "**CONDOMS**, USE THEM OR ***DIE!***" ?!
WE CAN'T MAKE A CLAIM LIKE ***THAT!***
BAM! BAM! BAM!
PEOPLE! PEOPLE!
YOU SHOULD!
YEAH, YOU **WOULD!**
THE CLIENT'S AN ***IDIOT! I*** KNOW MORE ABOUT CONDOMS THAN ***HE*** DOES!
WHY NOT?! THE CLIENT ***LOVES*** IT!!

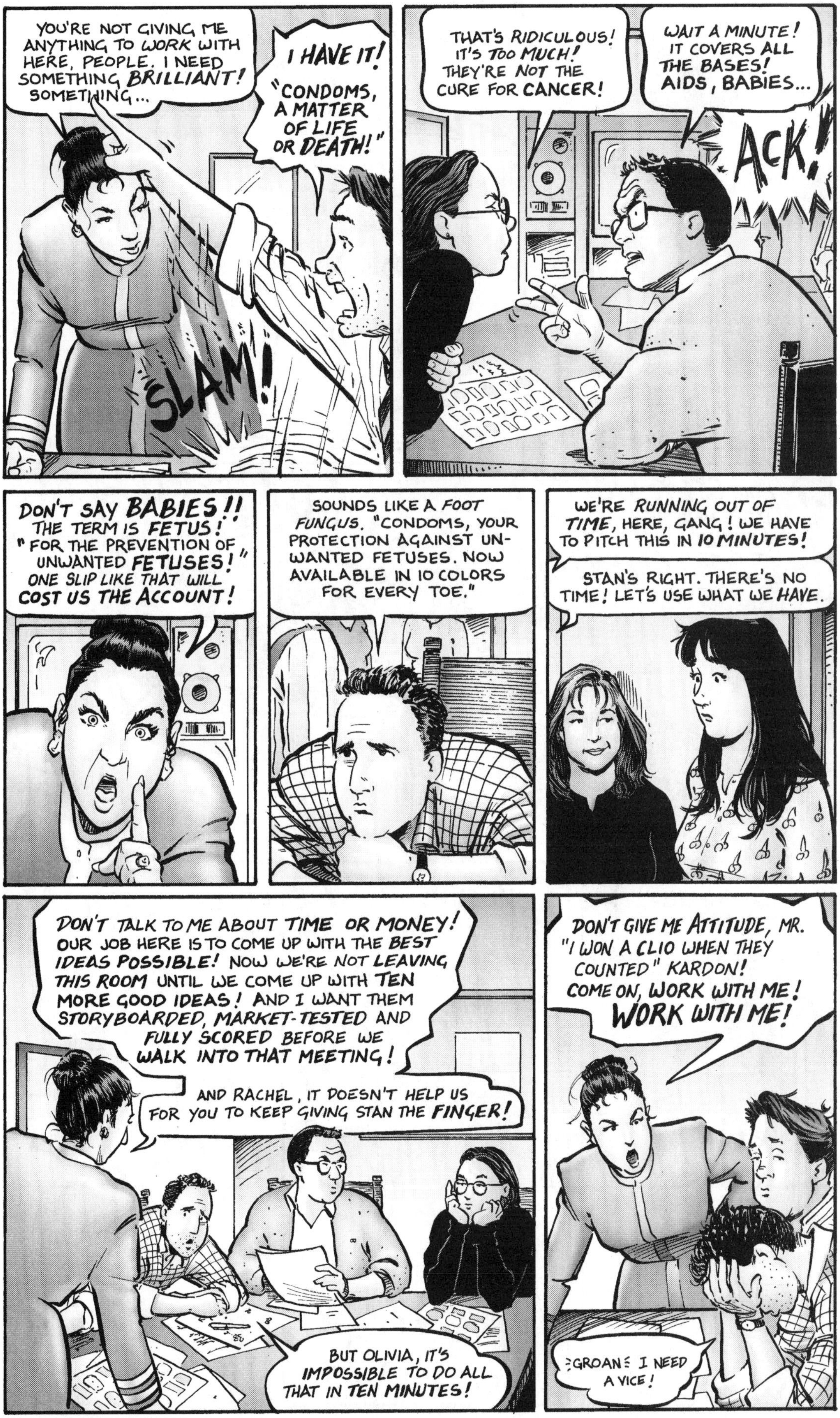
YOU'RE NOT GIVING ME ANYTHING TO WORK WITH HERE, PEOPLE. I NEED SOMETHING BRILLIANT! SOMETHING...
I HAVE IT! "CONDOMS, A MATTER OF LIFE OR DEATH!"
SLAM!
THAT'S RIDICULOUS! IT'S TOO MUCH! THEY'RE NOT THE CURE FOR CANCER!
WAIT A MINUTE! IT COVERS ALL THE BASES! AIDS, BABIES...
ACK!
DON'T SAY BABIES!! THE TERM IS FETUS! "FOR THE PREVENTION OF UNWANTED FETUSES!" ONE SLIP LIKE THAT WILL COST US THE ACCOUNT!
SOUNDS LIKE A FOOT FUNGUS. "CONDOMS, YOUR PROTECTION AGAINST UNWANTED FETUSES. NOW AVAILABLE IN 10 COLORS FOR EVERY TOE."
WE'RE RUNNING OUT OF TIME, HERE, GANG! WE HAVE TO PITCH THIS IN 10 MINUTES!
STAN'S RIGHT. THERE'S NO TIME! LET'S USE WHAT WE HAVE.
DON'T TALK TO ME ABOUT TIME OR MONEY! OUR JOB HERE IS TO COME UP WITH THE BEST IDEAS POSSIBLE! NOW WE'RE NOT LEAVING THIS ROOM UNTIL WE COME UP WITH TEN MORE GOOD IDEAS! AND I WANT THEM STORYBOARDED, MARKET-TESTED AND FULLY SCORED BEFORE WE WALK INTO THAT MEETING!
AND RACHEL, IT DOESN'T HELP US FOR YOU TO KEEP GIVING STAN THE FINGER!
BUT OLIVIA, IT'S IMPOSSIBLE TO DO ALL THAT IN TEN MINUTES!
DON'T GIVE ME ATTITUDE, MR. "I WON A CLIO WHEN THEY COUNTED" KARDON! COME ON, WORK WITH ME! WORK WITH ME!
GROAN I NEED A VICE!

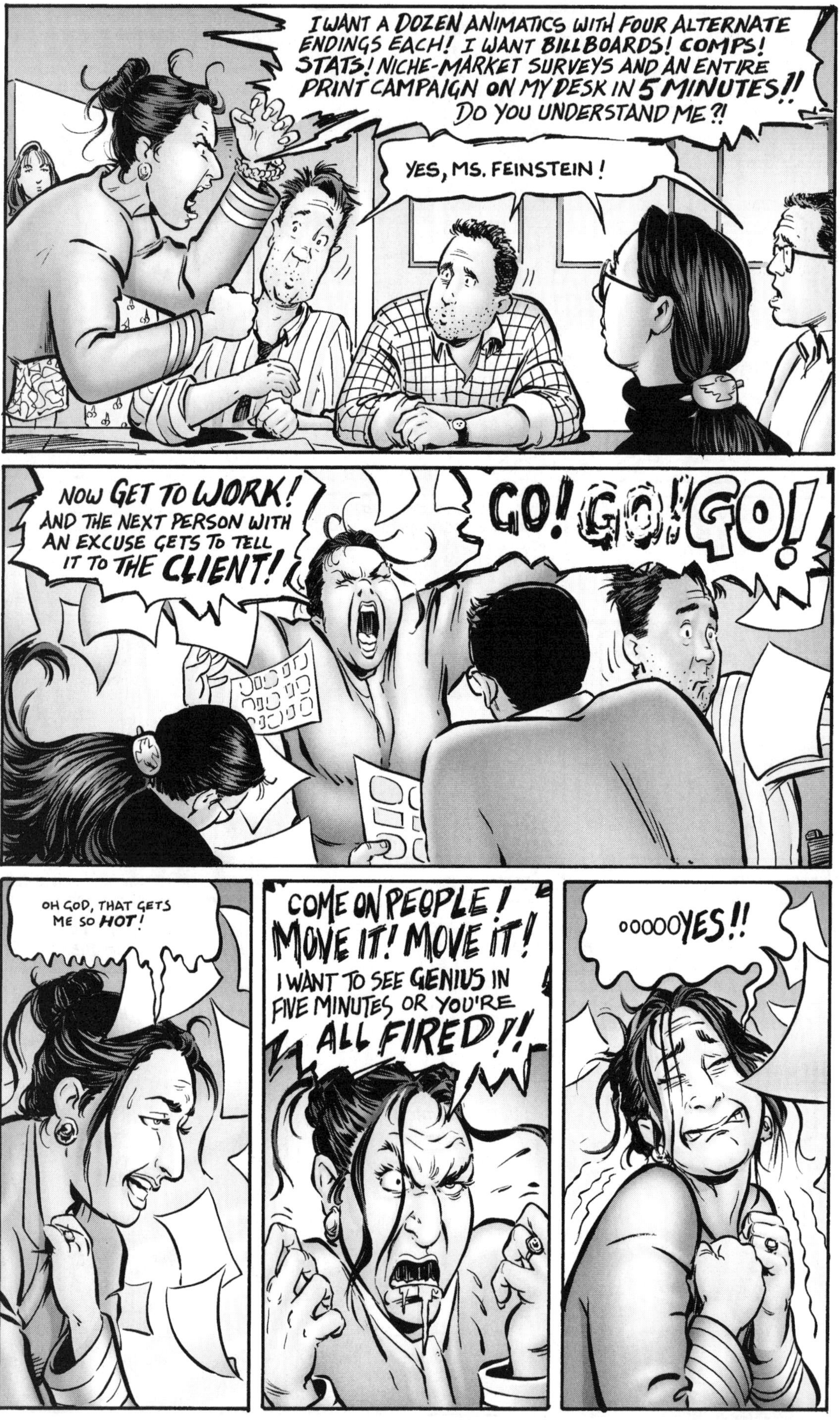

I WANT A DOZEN ANIMATICS WITH FOUR ALTERNATE ENDINGS EACH! I WANT BILLBOARDS! COMPS! STATS! NICHE-MARKET SURVEYS AND AN ENTIRE PRINT CAMPAIGN ON MY DESK IN 5 MINUTES!! DO YOU UNDERSTAND ME?!
YES, MS. FEINSTEIN!
NOW GET TO WORK! AND THE NEXT PERSON WITH AN EXCUSE GETS TO TELL IT TO THE CLIENT!
GO! GO! GO!
OH GOD, THAT GETS ME SO HOT!
COME ON PEOPLE! MOVE IT! MOVE IT! I WANT TO SEE GENIUS IN FIVE MINUTES OR YOU'RE ALL FIRED?!
oooooYES!!

...

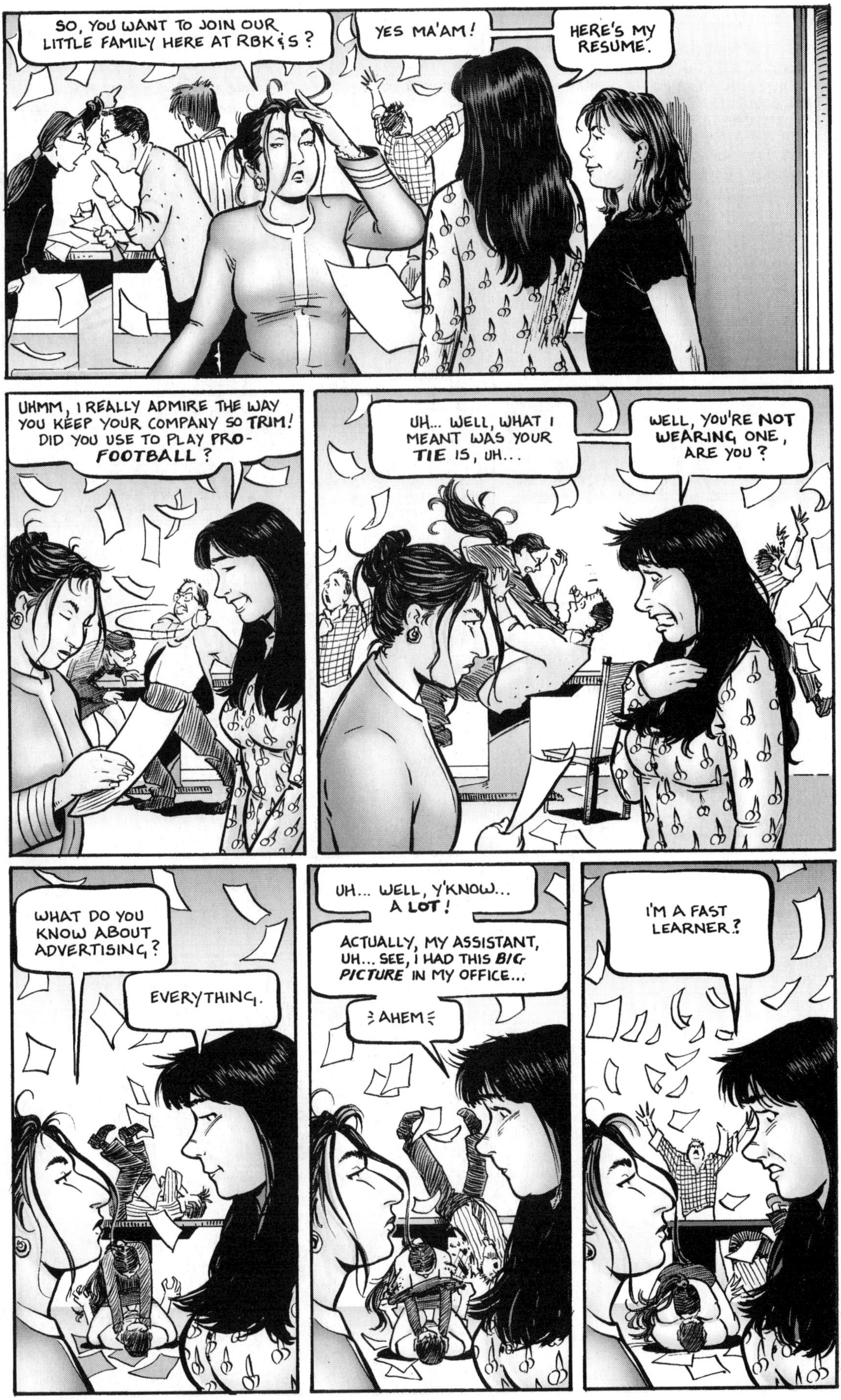
SO, YOU WANT TO JOIN OUR LITTLE FAMILY HERE AT RBK&S?
YES MA'AM!
HERE'S MY RESUME.
UHMM, I REALLY ADMIRE THE WAY YOU KEEP YOUR COMPANY SO TRIM! DID YOU USE TO PLAY PRO-FOOTBALL?
UH... WELL, WHAT I MEANT WAS YOUR TIE IS, UH...
WELL, YOU'RE NOT WEARING ONE, ARE YOU?
WHAT DO YOU KNOW ABOUT ADVERTISING?
EVERYTHING.
UH... WELL, Y'KNOW... A LOT!
ACTUALLY, MY ASSISTANT, UH... SEE, I HAD THIS BIG PICTURE IN MY OFFICE...
AHEM
I'M A FAST LEARNER?

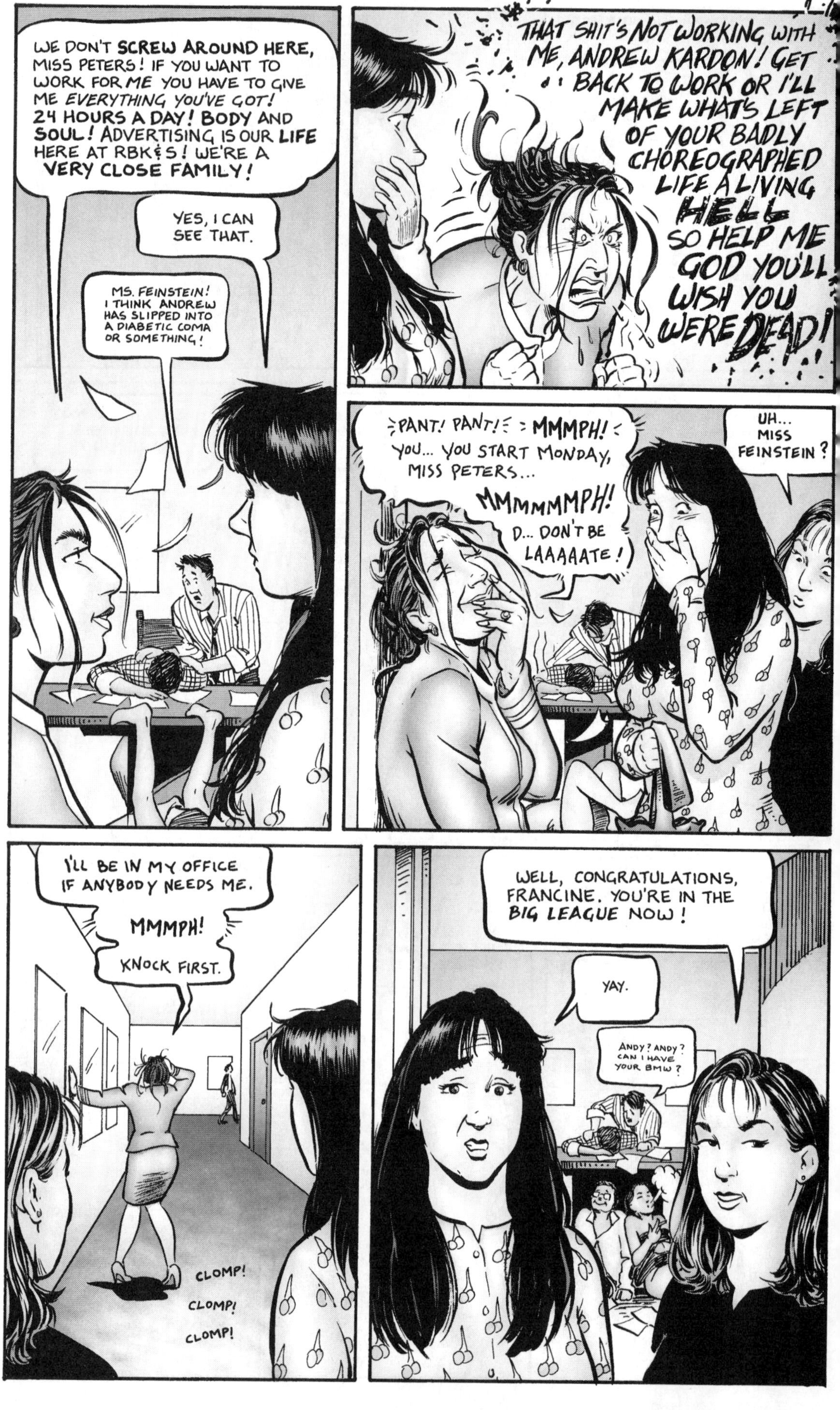
WE DON'T SCREW AROUND HERE, MISS PETERS! IF YOU WANT TO WORK FOR ME YOU HAVE TO GIVE ME EVERYTHING YOU'VE GOT! 24 HOURS A DAY! BODY AND SOUL! ADVERTISING IS OUR LIFE HERE AT RBK&S! WE'RE A VERY CLOSE FAMILY!
YES, I CAN SEE THAT.
MS. FEINSTEIN! I THINK ANDREW HAS SLIPPED INTO A DIABETIC COMA OR SOMETHING!
THAT SHIT'S NOT WORKING WITH ME, ANDREW KARDON! GET BACK TO WORK OR I'LL MAKE WHAT'S LEFT OF YOUR BADLY CHOREOGRAPHED LIFE A LIVING HELL SO HELP ME GOD YOU'LL WISH YOU WERE DEAD!
PANT! PANT! MMMPH! YOU... YOU START MONDAY, MISS PETERS... MMMMMMPH! D... DON'T BE LAAAAATE!
UH... MISS FEINSTEIN?
I'LL BE IN MY OFFICE IF ANYBODY NEEDS ME. MMMPH! KNOCK FIRST.
CLOMP!
CLOMP!
CLOMP!
WELL, CONGRATULATIONS, FRANCINE. YOU'RE IN THE BIG LEAGUE NOW!
YAY.
ANDY? ANDY? CAN I HAVE YOUR BMW?

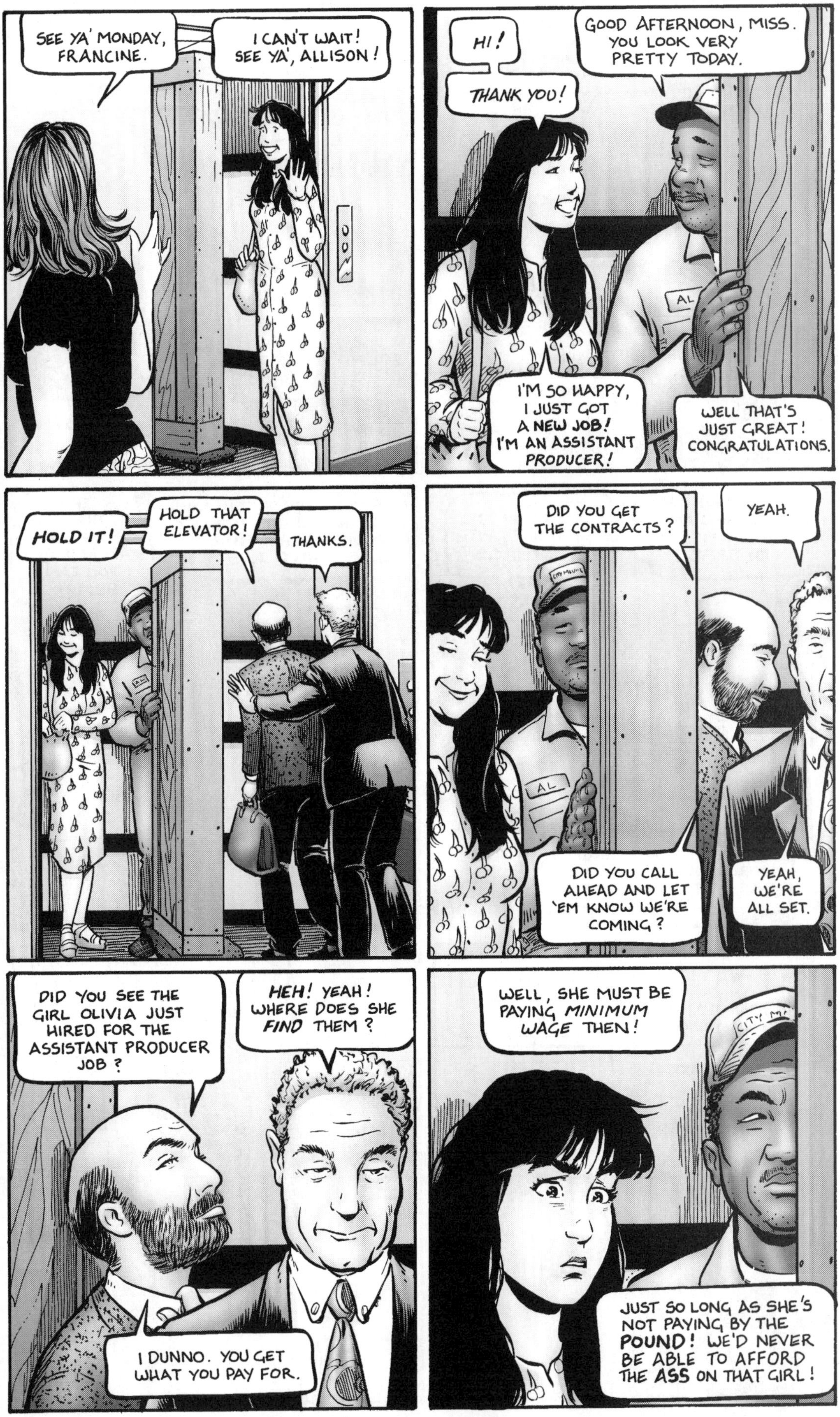
SEE YA' MONDAY, FRANCINE.
I CAN'T WAIT! SEE YA', ALLISON!
HI!
THANK YOU!
GOOD AFTERNOON, MISS. YOU LOOK VERY PRETTY TODAY.
I'M SO HAPPY, I JUST GOT A NEW JOB! I'M AN ASSISTANT PRODUCER!
WELL THAT'S JUST GREAT! CONGRATULATIONS.
HOLD IT!
HOLD THAT ELEVATOR!
THANKS.
DID YOU GET THE CONTRACTS?
YEAH.
DID YOU CALL AHEAD AND LET 'EM KNOW WE'RE COMING?
YEAH, WE'RE ALL SET.
DID YOU SEE THE GIRL OLIVIA JUST HIRED FOR THE ASSISTANT PRODUCER JOB?
HEH! YEAH! WHERE DOES SHE FIND THEM?
I DUNNO. YOU GET WHAT YOU PAY FOR.
WELL, SHE MUST BE PAYING MINIMUM WAGE THEN!
JUST SO LONG AS SHE'S NOT PAYING BY THE POUND! WE'D NEVER BE ABLE TO AFFORD THE ASS ON THAT GIRL!

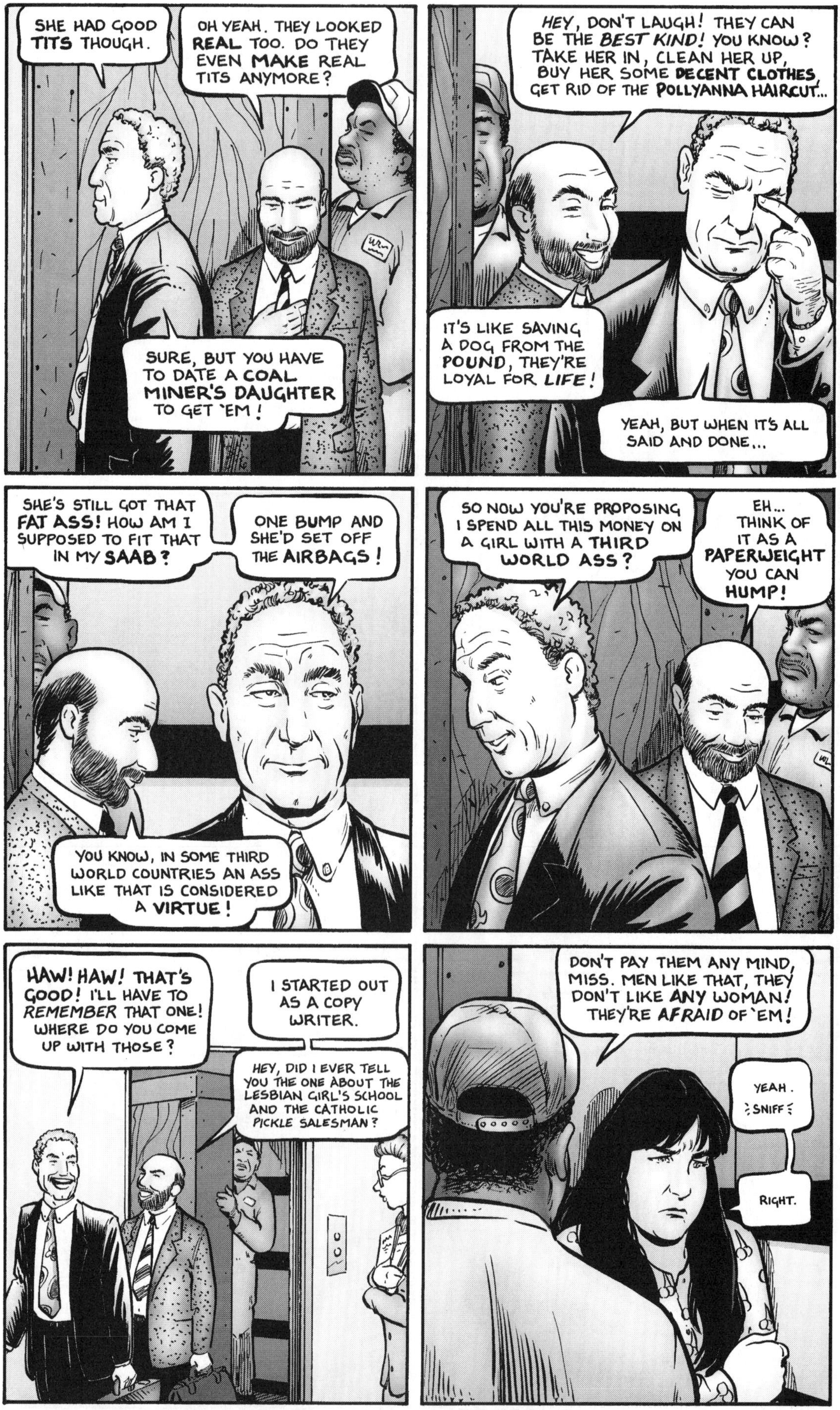

SHE HAD GOOD TITS THOUGH.
OH YEAH. THEY LOOKED REAL TOO. DO THEY EVEN MAKE REAL TITS ANYMORE?
SURE, BUT YOU HAVE TO DATE A COAL MINER'S DAUGHTER TO GET 'EM!
HEY, DON'T LAUGH! THEY CAN BE THE BEST KIND! YOU KNOW? TAKE HER IN, CLEAN HER UP, BUY HER SOME DECENT CLOTHES, GET RID OF THE POLLYANNA HAIRCUT...
IT'S LIKE SAVING A DOG FROM THE POUND, THEY'RE LOYAL FOR LIFE!
YEAH, BUT WHEN IT'S ALL SAID AND DONE...
SHE'S STILL GOT THAT FAT ASS! HOW AM I SUPPOSED TO FIT THAT IN MY SAAB?
ONE BUMP AND SHE'D SET OFF THE AIRBAGS!
YOU KNOW, IN SOME THIRD WORLD COUNTRIES AN ASS LIKE THAT IS CONSIDERED A VIRTUE!
SO NOW YOU'RE PROPOSING I SPEND ALL THIS MONEY ON A GIRL WITH A THIRD WORLD ASS?
EH... THINK OF IT AS A PAPERWEIGHT YOU CAN HUMP!
HAW! HAW! THAT'S GOOD! I'LL HAVE TO REMEMBER THAT ONE! WHERE DO YOU COME UP WITH THOSE?
I STARTED OUT AS A COPY WRITER.
HEY, DID I EVER TELL YOU THE ONE ABOUT THE LESBIAN GIRL'S SCHOOL AND THE CATHOLIC PICKLE SALESMAN?
DON'T PAY THEM ANY MIND, MISS. MEN LIKE THAT, THEY DON'T LIKE ANY WOMAN! THEY'RE AFRAID OF 'EM!
YEAH. SNIFF
RIGHT.

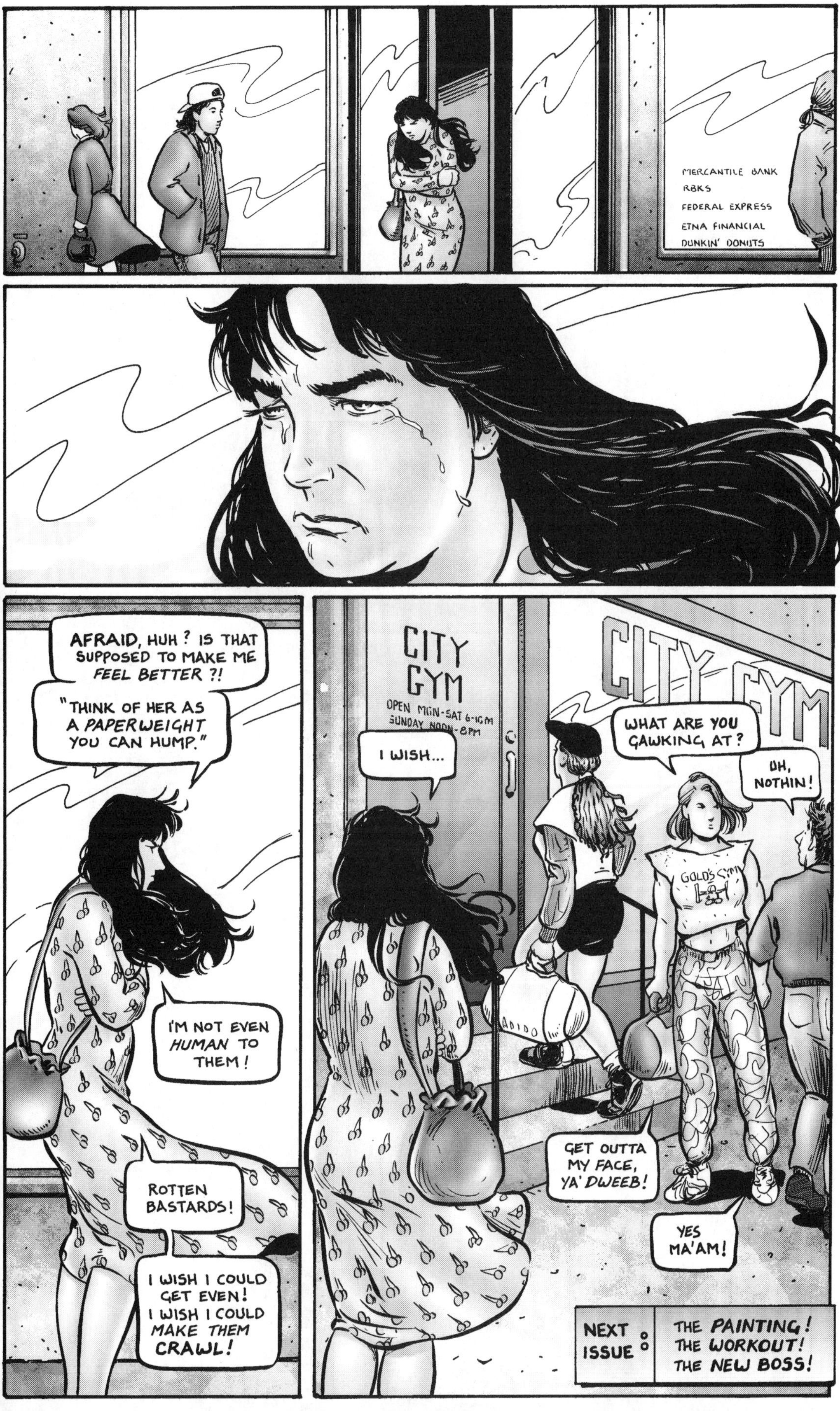

MERCANTILE BANK
RBKS
FEDERAL EXPRESS
ETNA FINANCIAL
DUNKIN' DONUTS
AFRAID, HUH? IS THAT SUPPOSED TO MAKE ME *FEEL BETTER*?!
"THINK OF HER AS A *PAPERWEIGHT* YOU CAN HUMP."
I'M NOT EVEN *HUMAN* TO THEM!
ROTTEN BASTARDS!
I WISH I COULD GET EVEN! I WISH I COULD *MAKE THEM* **CRAWL**!
CITY GYM
OPEN MON-SAT 6-10PM
SUNDAY NOON-8PM
CITY GYM
I WISH...
WHAT ARE YOU GAWKING AT?
UH, NOTHIN!
GOLD'S GYM
GET OUTTA MY FACE, YA' *DWEEB*!
YES MA'AM!
NEXT ISSUE: THE *PAINTING*! THE *WORKOUT*! THE *NEW BOSS*!

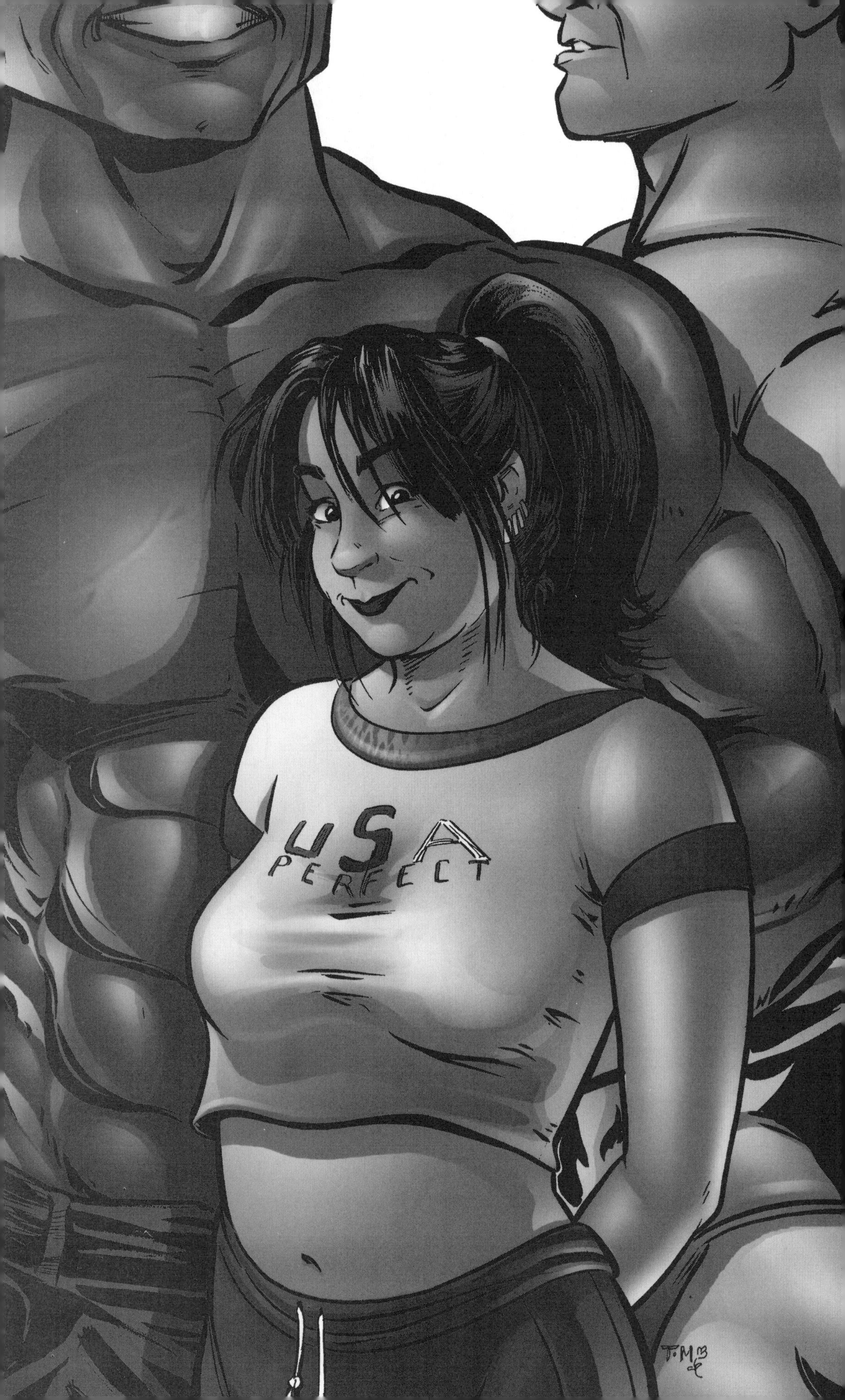
USA
PERFECT

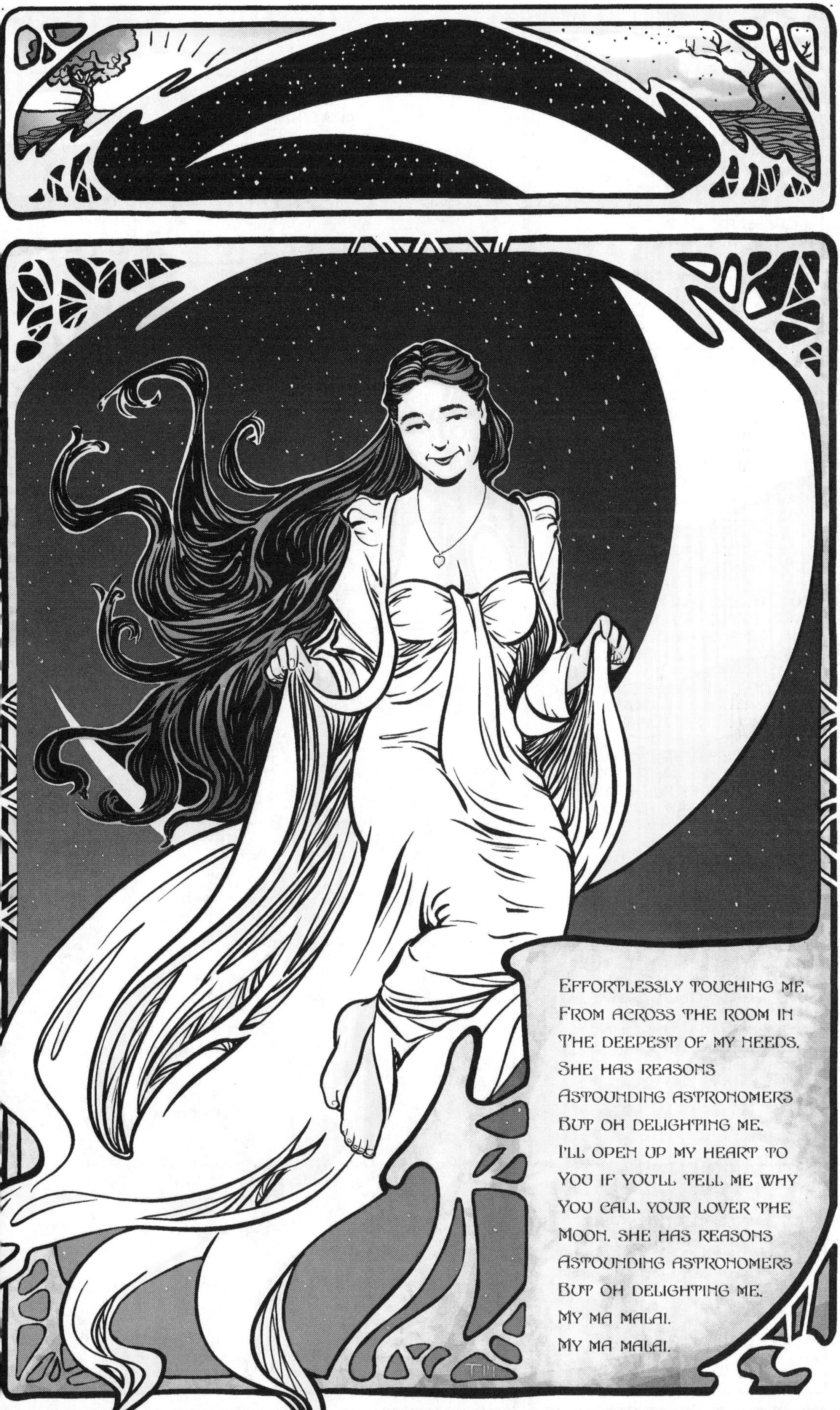
Effortlessly touching me
From across the room in
The deepest of my needs.
She has reasons
Astounding astronomers
But oh delighting me.
I'll open up my heart to
You if you'll tell me why
You call your lover the
Moon. She has reasons
Astounding astronomers
But oh delighting me.
My ma malai.
My ma malai.

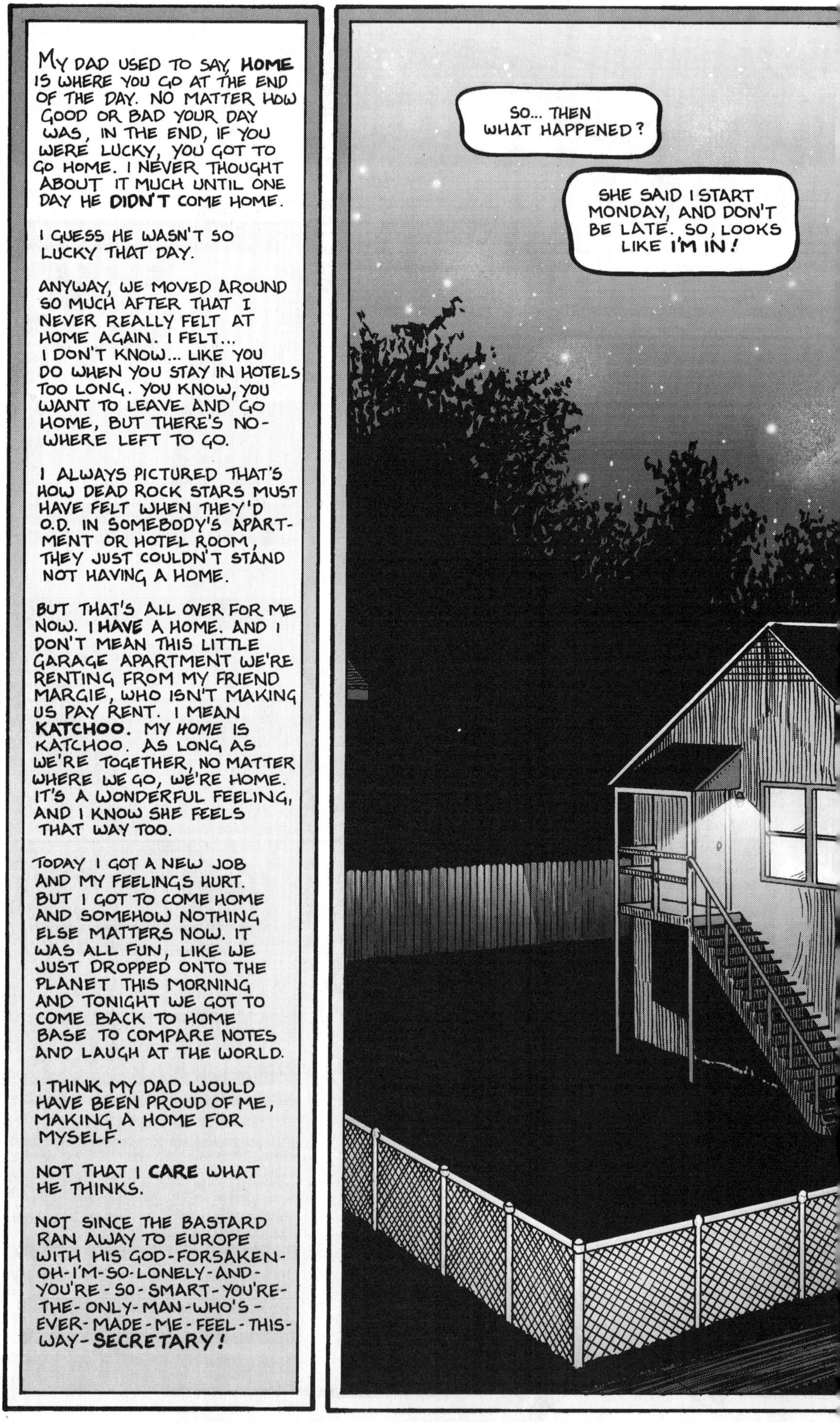
MY DAD USED TO SAY, **HOME** IS WHERE YOU GO AT THE END OF THE DAY. NO MATTER HOW GOOD OR BAD YOUR DAY WAS, IN THE END, IF YOU WERE LUCKY, YOU GOT TO GO HOME. I NEVER THOUGHT ABOUT IT MUCH UNTIL ONE DAY HE **DIDN'T** COME HOME.
I GUESS HE WASN'T SO LUCKY THAT DAY.
ANYWAY, WE MOVED AROUND SO MUCH AFTER THAT I NEVER REALLY FELT AT HOME AGAIN. I FELT... I DON'T KNOW... LIKE YOU DO WHEN YOU STAY IN HOTELS TOO LONG. YOU KNOW, YOU WANT TO LEAVE AND GO HOME, BUT THERE'S NO-WHERE LEFT TO GO.
I ALWAYS PICTURED THAT'S HOW DEAD ROCK STARS MUST HAVE FELT WHEN THEY'D O.D. IN SOMEBODY'S APART-MENT OR HOTEL ROOM, THEY JUST COULDN'T STAND NOT HAVING A HOME.
BUT THAT'S ALL OVER FOR ME NOW. I **HAVE** A HOME. AND I DON'T MEAN THIS LITTLE GARAGE APARTMENT WE'RE RENTING FROM MY FRIEND MARGIE, WHO ISN'T MAKING US PAY RENT. I MEAN **KATCHOO.** MY *HOME* IS KATCHOO. AS LONG AS WE'RE TOGETHER, NO MATTER WHERE WE GO, WE'RE HOME. IT'S A WONDERFUL FEELING, AND I KNOW SHE FEELS THAT WAY TOO.
TODAY I GOT A NEW JOB AND MY FEELINGS HURT. BUT I GOT TO COME HOME AND SOMEHOW NOTHING ELSE MATTERS NOW. IT WAS ALL FUN, LIKE WE JUST DROPPED ONTO THE PLANET THIS MORNING AND TONIGHT WE GOT TO COME BACK TO HOME BASE TO COMPARE NOTES AND LAUGH AT THE WORLD.
I THINK MY DAD WOULD HAVE BEEN PROUD OF ME, MAKING A HOME FOR MYSELF.
NOT THAT I **CARE** WHAT HE THINKS.
NOT SINCE THE BASTARD RAN AWAY TO EUROPE WITH HIS GOD-FORSAKEN-OH-I'M-SO-LONELY-AND-YOU'RE-SO-SMART-YOU'RE-THE-ONLY-MAN-WHO'S-EVER-MADE-ME-FEEL-THIS-WAY-**SECRETARY!**
SO... THEN WHAT HAPPENED?
SHE SAID I START MONDAY, AND DON'T BE LATE. SO, LOOKS LIKE **I'M IN!**

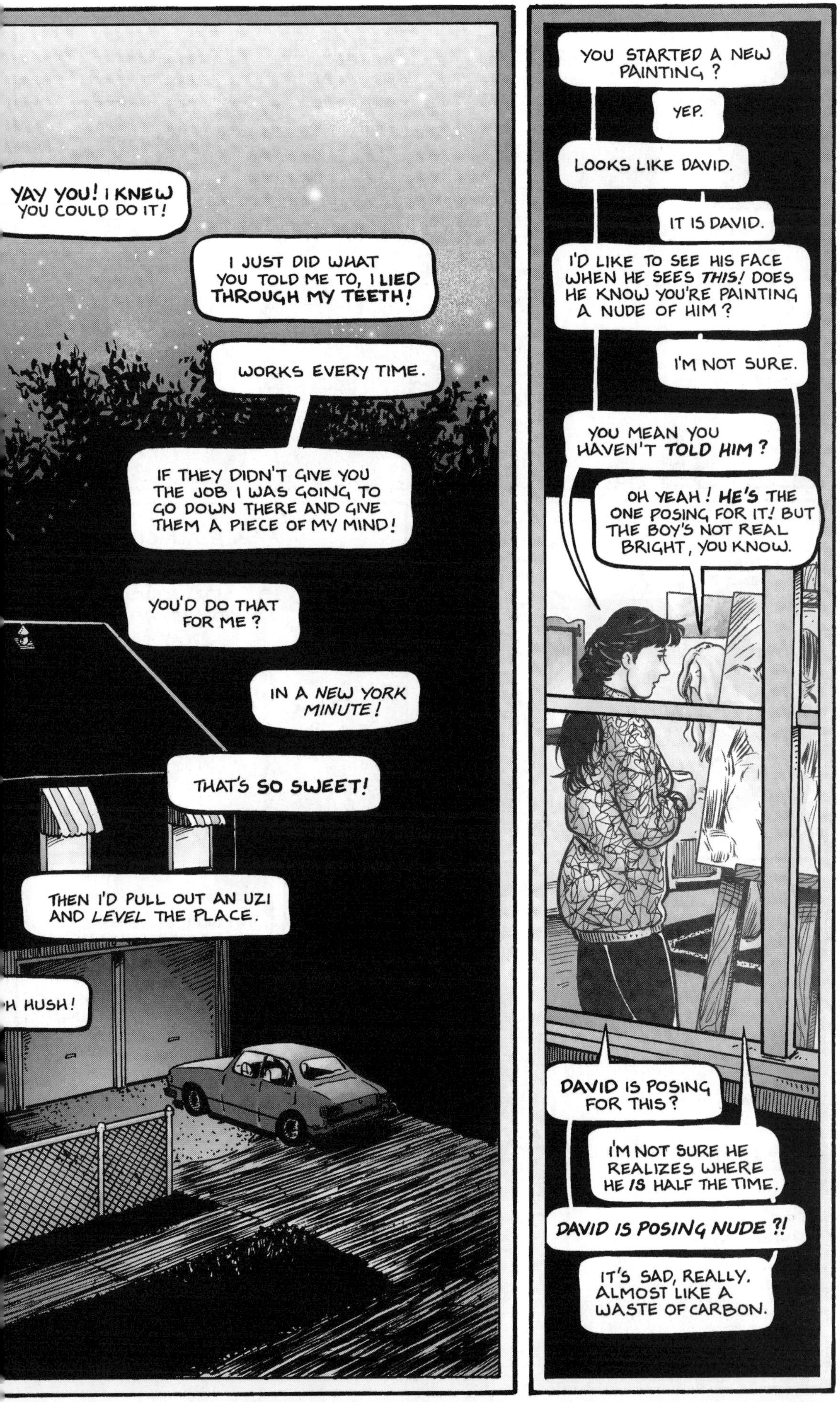

YAY YOU! I KNEW YOU COULD DO IT!
I JUST DID WHAT YOU TOLD ME TO, I LIED THROUGH MY TEETH!
WORKS EVERY TIME.
IF THEY DIDN'T GIVE YOU THE JOB I WAS GOING TO GO DOWN THERE AND GIVE THEM A PIECE OF MY MIND!
YOU'D DO THAT FOR ME?
IN A NEW YORK MINUTE!
THAT'S SO SWEET!
THEN I'D PULL OUT AN UZI AND LEVEL THE PLACE.
H HUSH!
YOU STARTED A NEW PAINTING?
YEP.
LOOKS LIKE DAVID.
IT IS DAVID.
I'D LIKE TO SEE HIS FACE WHEN HE SEES THIS! DOES HE KNOW YOU'RE PAINTING A NUDE OF HIM?
I'M NOT SURE.
YOU MEAN YOU HAVEN'T TOLD HIM?
OH YEAH! HE'S THE ONE POSING FOR IT! BUT THE BOY'S NOT REAL BRIGHT, YOU KNOW.
DAVID IS POSING FOR THIS?
I'M NOT SURE HE REALIZES WHERE HE IS HALF THE TIME.
DAVID IS POSING NUDE?!
IT'S SAD, REALLY. ALMOST LIKE A WASTE OF CARBON.

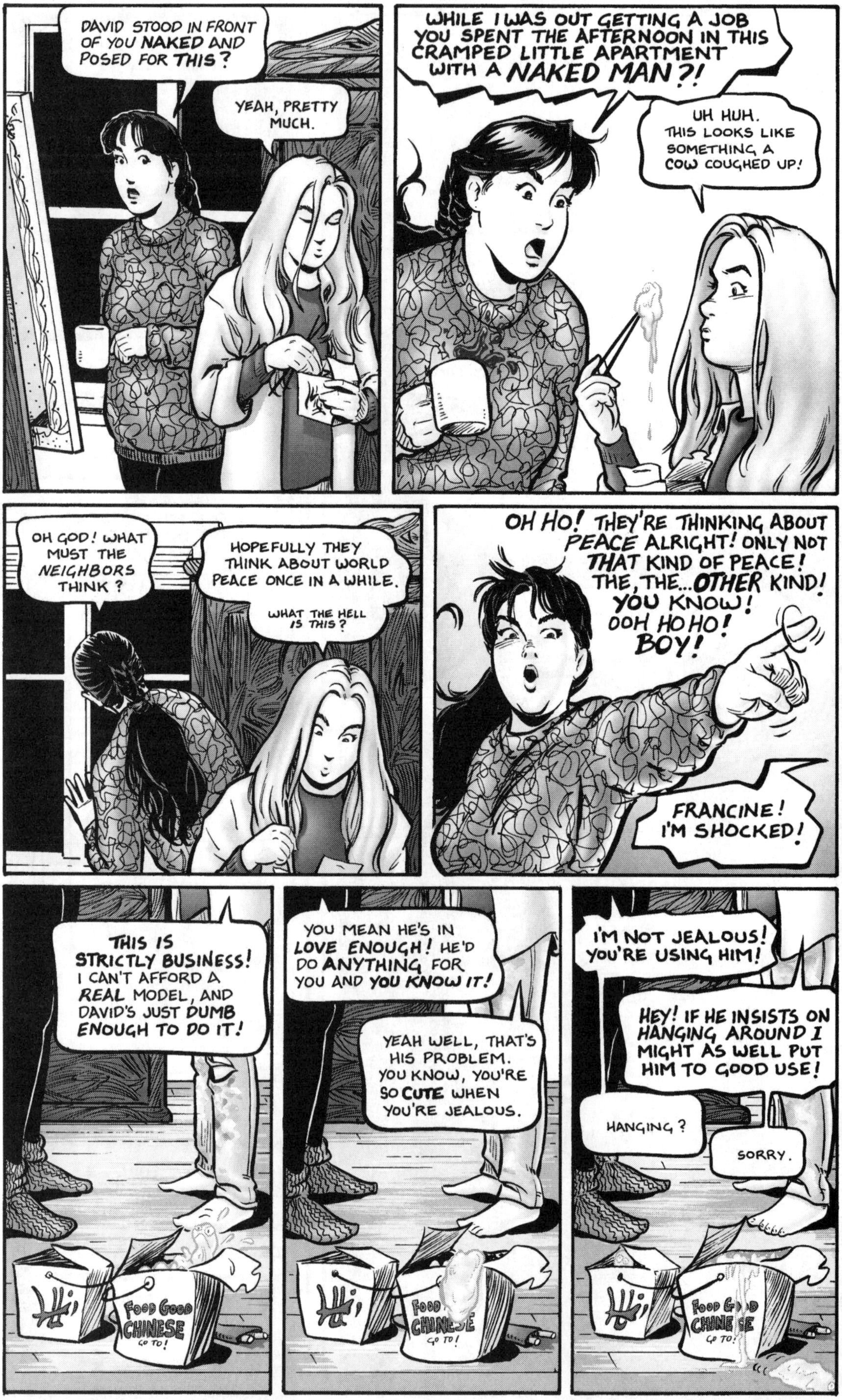
DAVID STOOD IN FRONT OF YOU NAKED AND POSED FOR THIS?
YEAH, PRETTY MUCH.
WHILE I WAS OUT GETTING A JOB YOU SPENT THE AFTERNOON IN THIS CRAMPED LITTLE APARTMENT WITH A NAKED MAN?!
UH HUH. THIS LOOKS LIKE SOMETHING A COW COUGHED UP!
OH GOD! WHAT MUST THE NEIGHBORS THINK?
HOPEFULLY THEY THINK ABOUT WORLD PEACE ONCE IN A WHILE.
WHAT THE HELL IS THIS?
OH HO! THEY'RE THINKING ABOUT PEACE ALRIGHT! ONLY NOT THAT KIND OF PEACE! THE, THE...OTHER KIND! YOU KNOW! OOH HO HO! BOY!
FRANCINE! I'M SHOCKED!
THIS IS STRICTLY BUSINESS! I CAN'T AFFORD A REAL MODEL, AND DAVID'S JUST DUMB ENOUGH TO DO IT!
Hi,
FOOD GOOD CHINESE GO TO!
YOU MEAN HE'S IN LOVE ENOUGH! HE'D DO ANYTHING FOR YOU AND YOU KNOW IT!
YEAH WELL, THAT'S HIS PROBLEM. YOU KNOW, YOU'RE SO CUTE WHEN YOU'RE JEALOUS.
I'M NOT JEALOUS! YOU'RE USING HIM!
HEY! IF HE INSISTS ON HANGING AROUND I MIGHT AS WELL PUT HIM TO GOOD USE!
HANGING?
SORRY.

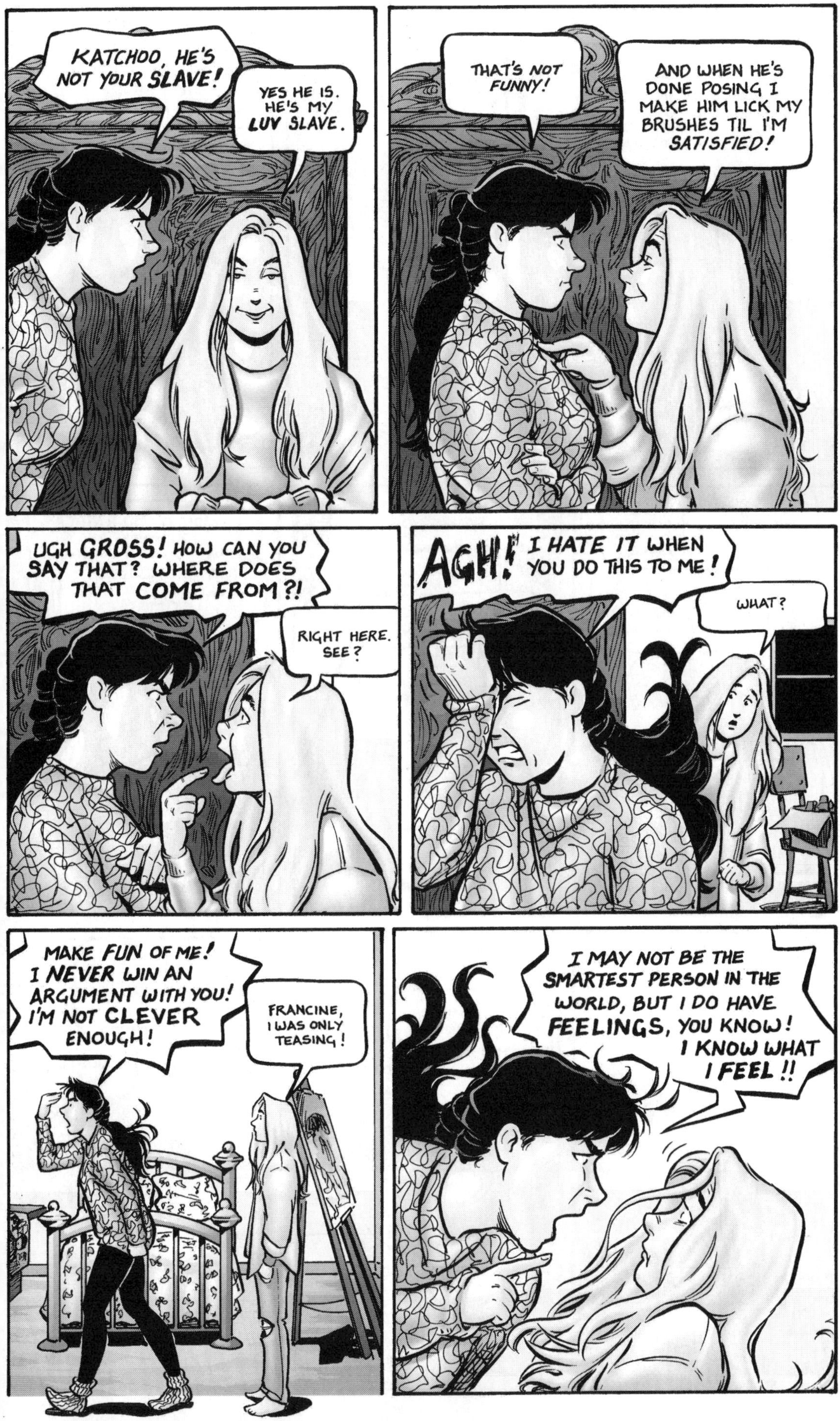
KATCHOO, HE'S NOT YOUR SLAVE!
YES HE IS. HE'S MY LUV SLAVE.
THAT'S NOT FUNNY!
AND WHEN HE'S DONE POSING I MAKE HIM LICK MY BRUSHES TIL I'M SATISFIED!
UGH GROSS! HOW CAN YOU SAY THAT? WHERE DOES THAT COME FROM?!
RIGHT HERE. SEE?
AGH! I HATE IT WHEN YOU DO THIS TO ME!
WHAT?
MAKE FUN OF ME! I NEVER WIN AN ARGUMENT WITH YOU! I'M NOT CLEVER ENOUGH!
FRANCINE, I WAS ONLY TEASING!
I MAY NOT BE THE SMARTEST PERSON IN THE WORLD, BUT I DO HAVE FEELINGS, YOU KNOW! I KNOW WHAT I FEEL!!

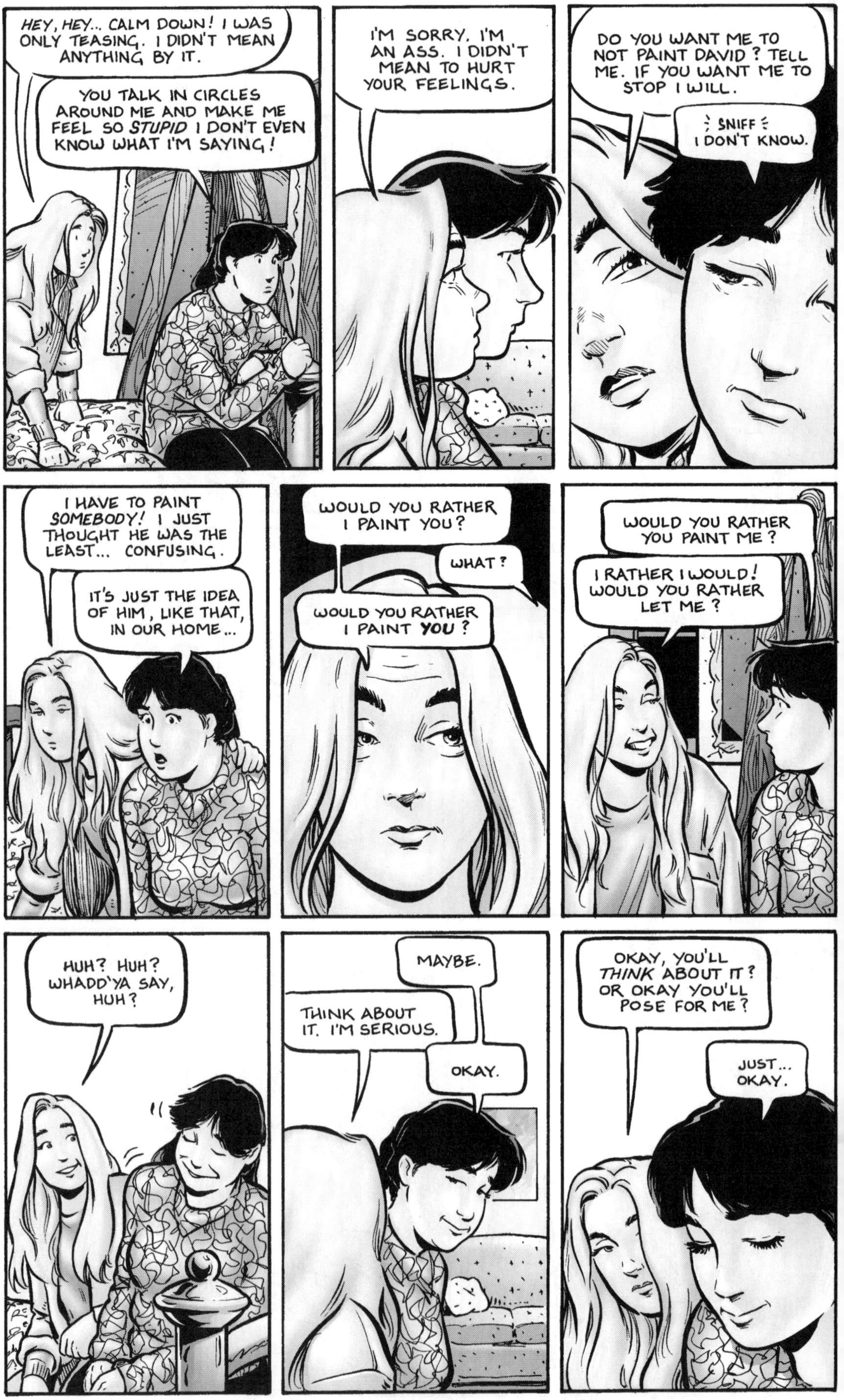
HEY, HEY... CALM DOWN! I WAS ONLY TEASING. I DIDN'T MEAN ANYTHING BY IT.
YOU TALK IN CIRCLES AROUND ME AND MAKE ME FEEL SO *STUPID* I DON'T EVEN KNOW WHAT I'M SAYING!
I'M SORRY. I'M AN ASS. I DIDN'T MEAN TO HURT YOUR FEELINGS.
DO YOU WANT ME TO NOT PAINT DAVID? TELL ME. IF YOU WANT ME TO STOP I WILL.
SNIFF
I DON'T KNOW.
I HAVE TO PAINT *SOMEBODY*! I JUST THOUGHT HE WAS THE LEAST... CONFUSING.
IT'S JUST THE IDEA OF HIM, LIKE THAT, IN OUR HOME...
WOULD YOU RATHER I PAINT YOU?
WHAT?
WOULD YOU RATHER I PAINT **YOU**?
WOULD YOU RATHER YOU PAINT ME?
I RATHER I WOULD! WOULD YOU RATHER LET ME?
HUH? HUH? WHADD'YA SAY, HUH?
MAYBE.
THINK ABOUT IT. I'M SERIOUS.
OKAY.
OKAY, YOU'LL *THINK* ABOUT IT? OR OKAY YOU'LL POSE FOR ME?
JUST... OKAY.

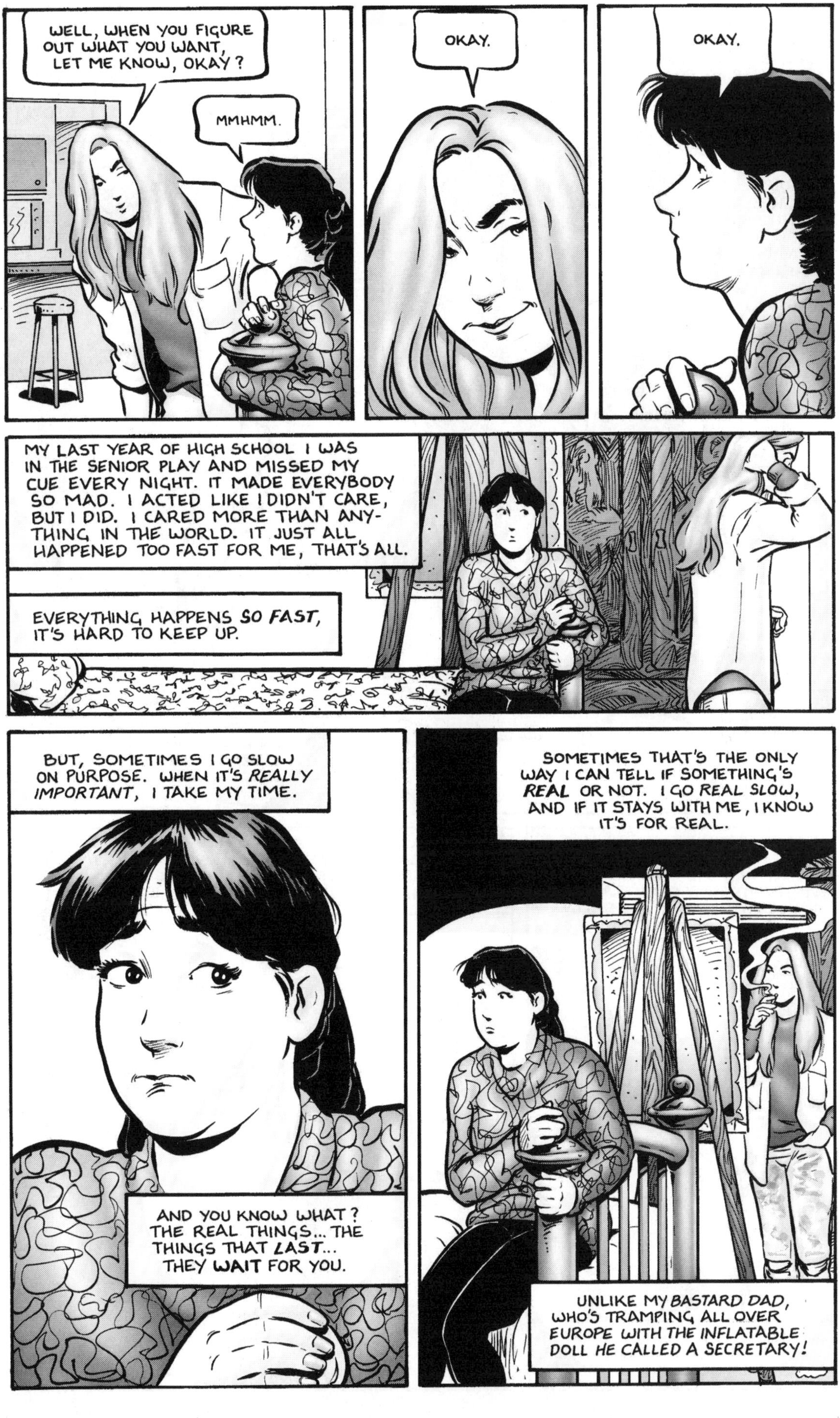

WELL, WHEN YOU FIGURE OUT WHAT YOU WANT, LET ME KNOW, OKAY?
MMHMM.
OKAY.
OKAY.
MY LAST YEAR OF HIGH SCHOOL I WAS IN THE SENIOR PLAY AND MISSED MY CUE EVERY NIGHT. IT MADE EVERYBODY SO MAD. I ACTED LIKE I DIDN'T CARE, BUT I DID. I CARED MORE THAN ANYTHING IN THE WORLD. IT JUST ALL HAPPENED TOO FAST FOR ME, THAT'S ALL.
EVERYTHING HAPPENS SO FAST, IT'S HARD TO KEEP UP.
BUT, SOMETIMES I GO SLOW ON PURPOSE. WHEN IT'S REALLY IMPORTANT, I TAKE MY TIME.
AND YOU KNOW WHAT? THE REAL THINGS... THE THINGS THAT LAST... THEY WAIT FOR YOU.
SOMETIMES THAT'S THE ONLY WAY I CAN TELL IF SOMETHING'S REAL OR NOT. I GO REAL SLOW, AND IF IT STAYS WITH ME, I KNOW IT'S FOR REAL.
UNLIKE MY BASTARD DAD, WHO'S TRAMPING ALL OVER EUROPE WITH THE INFLATABLE DOLL HE CALLED A SECRETARY!

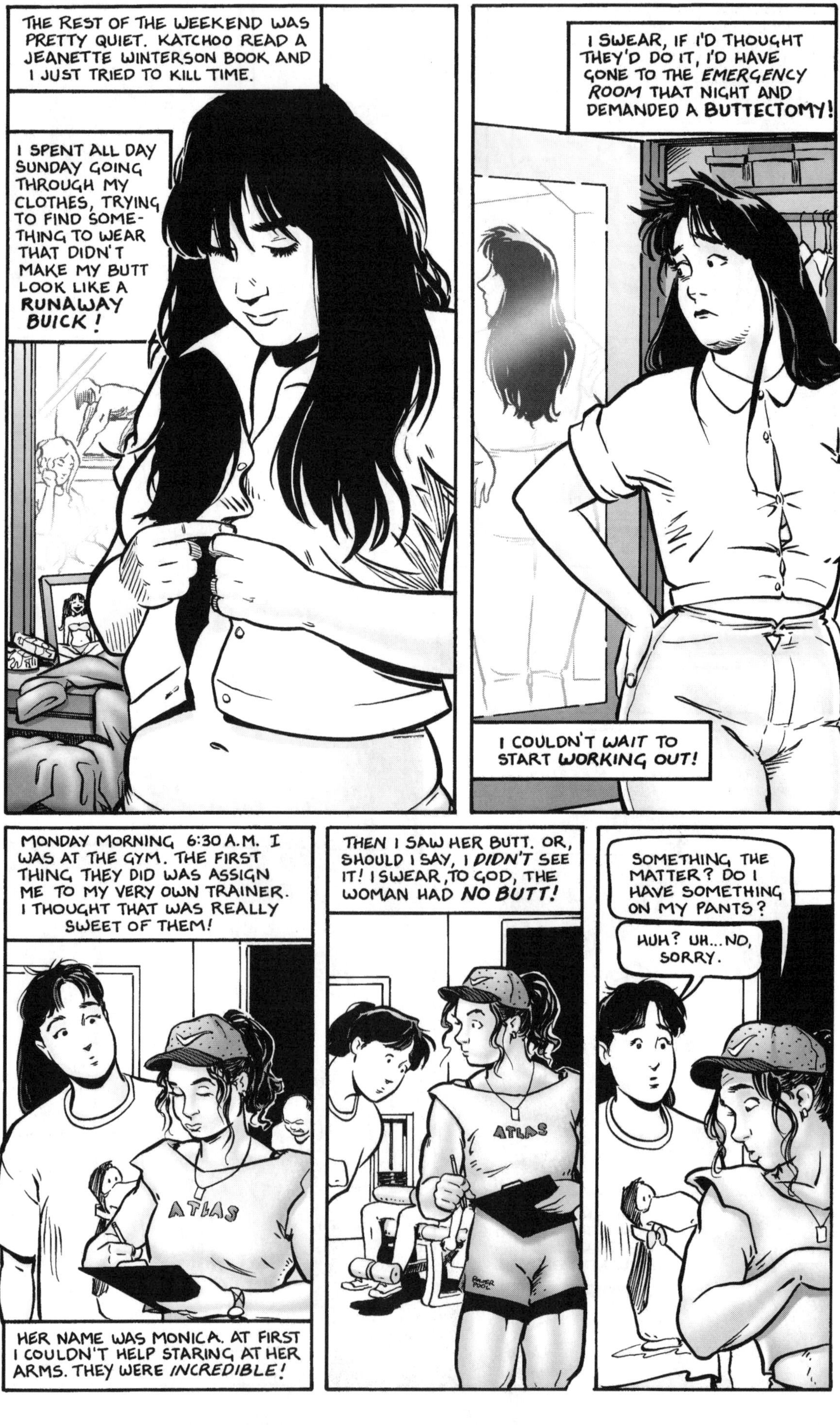
THE REST OF THE WEEKEND WAS PRETTY QUIET. KATCHOO READ A JEANETTE WINTERSON BOOK AND I JUST TRIED TO KILL TIME.
I SPENT ALL DAY SUNDAY GOING THROUGH MY CLOTHES, TRYING TO FIND SOME-THING TO WEAR THAT DIDN'T MAKE MY BUTT LOOK LIKE A RUNAWAY BUICK!
I SWEAR, IF I'D THOUGHT THEY'D DO IT, I'D HAVE GONE TO THE EMERGENCY ROOM THAT NIGHT AND DEMANDED A BUTTECTOMY!
I COULDN'T WAIT TO START WORKING OUT!
MONDAY MORNING 6:30 A.M. I WAS AT THE GYM. THE FIRST THING THEY DID WAS ASSIGN ME TO MY VERY OWN TRAINER. I THOUGHT THAT WAS REALLY SWEET OF THEM!
ATLAS
HER NAME WAS MONICA. AT FIRST I COULDN'T HELP STARING AT HER ARMS. THEY WERE INCREDIBLE!
THEN I SAW HER BUTT. OR, SHOULD I SAY, I DIDN'T SEE IT! I SWEAR, TO GOD, THE WOMAN HAD NO BUTT!
ATLAS
SOMETHING THE MATTER? DO I HAVE SOMETHING ON MY PANTS?
HUH? UH... NO, SORRY.

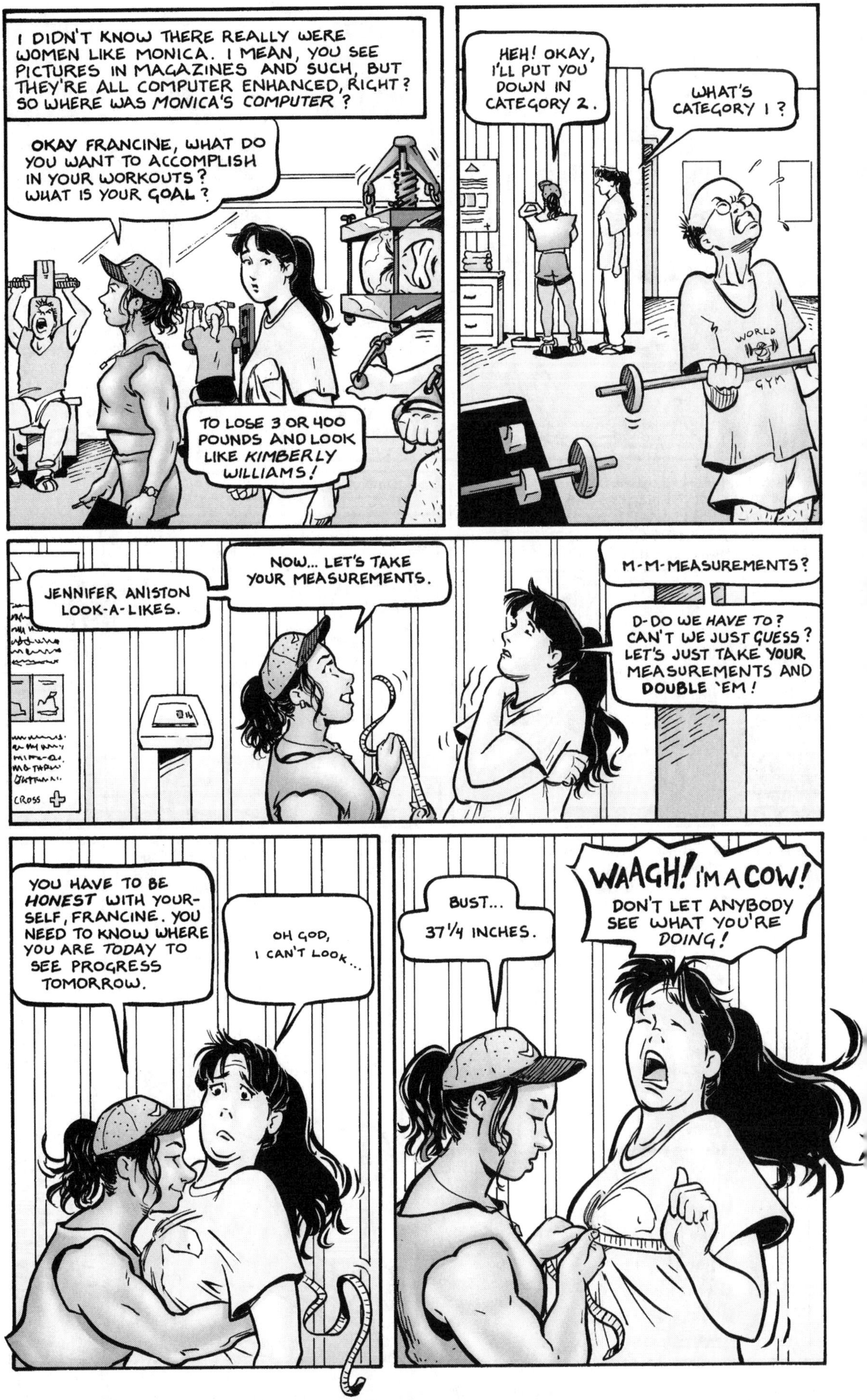
I DIDN'T KNOW THERE REALLY WERE WOMEN LIKE MONICA. I MEAN, YOU SEE PICTURES IN MAGAZINES AND SUCH, BUT THEY'RE ALL COMPUTER ENHANCED, RIGHT? SO WHERE WAS *MONICA'S COMPUTER*?
OKAY FRANCINE, WHAT DO YOU WANT TO ACCOMPLISH IN YOUR WORKOUTS? WHAT IS YOUR GOAL?
TO LOSE 3 OR 400 POUNDS AND LOOK LIKE *KIMBERLY WILLIAMS*!
HEH! OKAY, I'LL PUT YOU DOWN IN CATEGORY 2.
WHAT'S CATEGORY 1?
WORLD GYM
JENNIFER ANISTON LOOK-A-LIKES.
NOW... LET'S TAKE YOUR MEASUREMENTS.
M-M-MEASUREMENTS?
D-DO WE *HAVE TO*? CAN'T WE JUST *GUESS*? LET'S JUST TAKE **YOUR** MEASUREMENTS AND **DOUBLE** 'EM!
CROSS
YOU HAVE TO BE *HONEST* WITH YOURSELF, FRANCINE. YOU NEED TO KNOW WHERE YOU ARE *TODAY* TO SEE PROGRESS TOMORROW.
OH GOD, I CAN'T LOOK...
BUST... 37 1/4 INCHES.
WAAGH! I'M A COW!
DON'T LET ANYBODY SEE WHAT YOU'RE *DOING*!

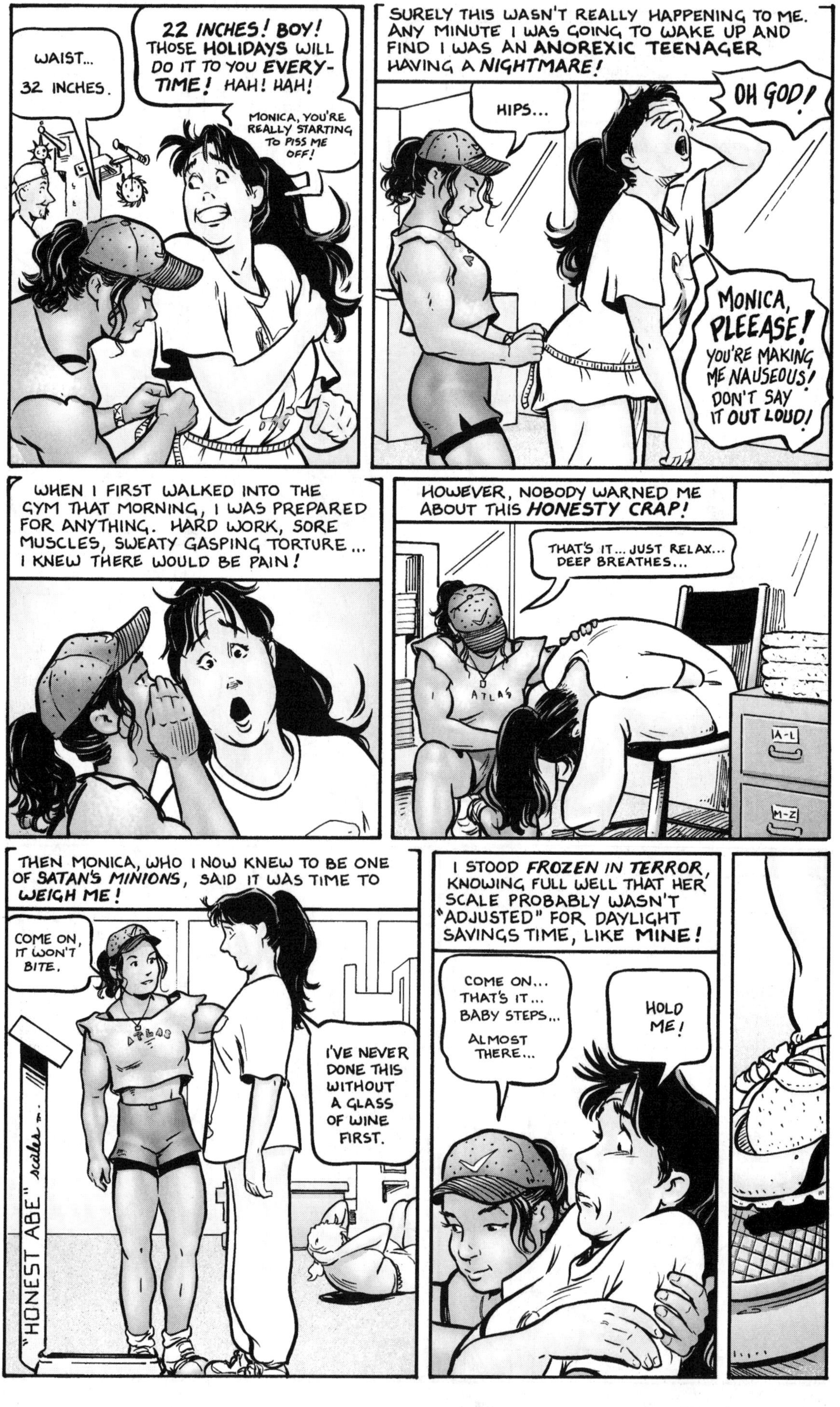

WAIST... 32 INCHES.
22 INCHES! BOY! THOSE HOLIDAYS WILL DO IT TO YOU EVERY-TIME! HAH! HAH!
MONICA, YOU'RE REALLY STARTING TO PISS ME OFF!
SURELY THIS WASN'T REALLY HAPPENING TO ME. ANY MINUTE I WAS GOING TO WAKE UP AND FIND I WAS AN ANOREXIC TEENAGER HAVING A NIGHTMARE!
HIPS...
OH GOD!
MONICA, PLEEASE! YOU'RE MAKING ME NAUSEOUS! DON'T SAY IT OUT LOUD!
WHEN I FIRST WALKED INTO THE GYM THAT MORNING, I WAS PREPARED FOR ANYTHING. HARD WORK, SORE MUSCLES, SWEATY GASPING TORTURE... I KNEW THERE WOULD BE PAIN!
HOWEVER, NOBODY WARNED ME ABOUT THIS HONESTY CRAP!
THAT'S IT... JUST RELAX... DEEP BREATHES...
ATLAS
A-L
M-Z
THEN MONICA, WHO I NOW KNEW TO BE ONE OF SATAN'S MINIONS, SAID IT WAS TIME TO WEIGH ME!
COME ON, IT WON'T BITE.
ATLAS
I'VE NEVER DONE THIS WITHOUT A GLASS OF WINE FIRST.
"HONEST ABE" scales
I STOOD FROZEN IN TERROR, KNOWING FULL WELL THAT HER SCALE PROBABLY WASN'T "ADJUSTED" FOR DAYLIGHT SAVINGS TIME, LIKE MINE!
COME ON... THAT'S IT... BABY STEPS... ALMOST THERE...
HOLD ME!

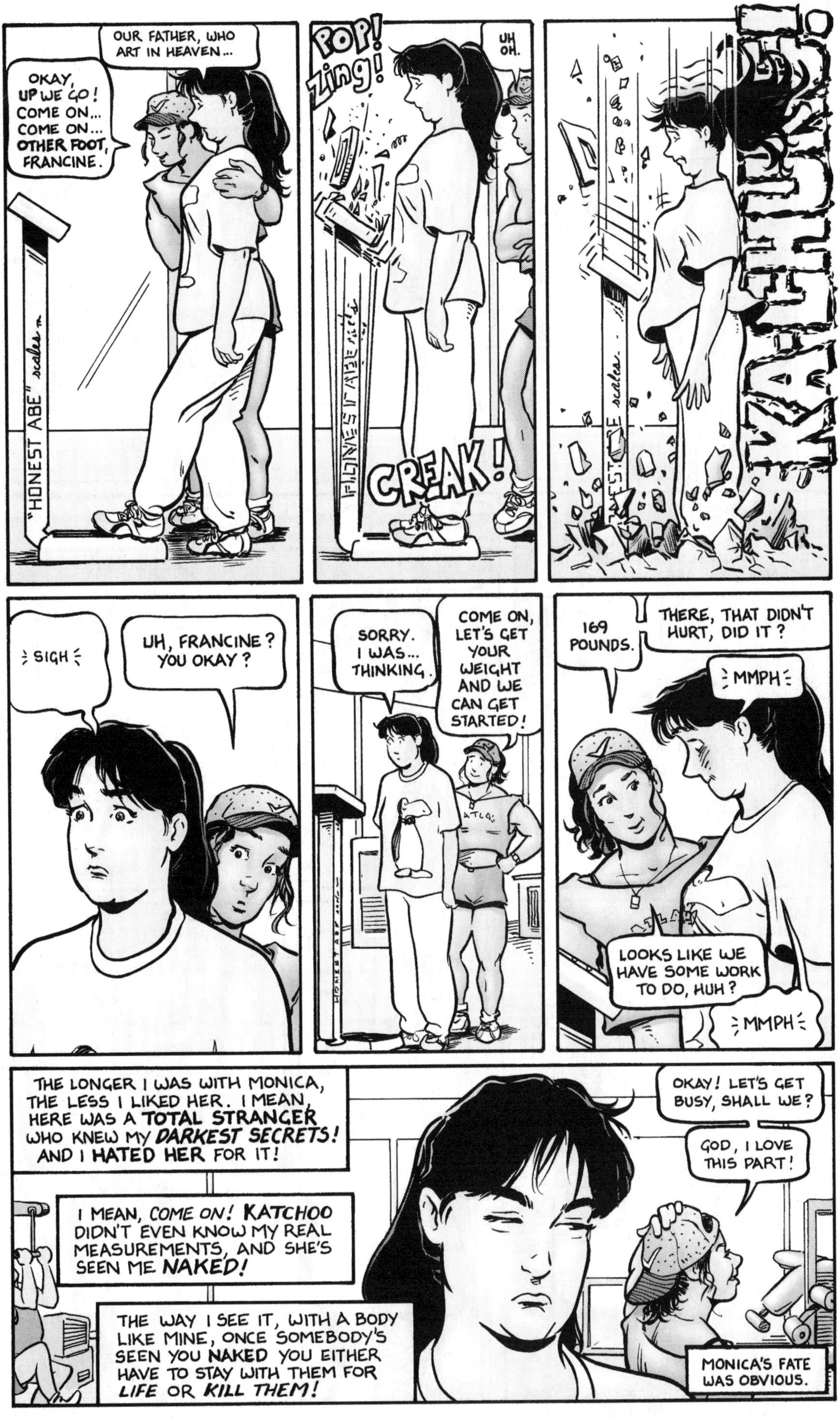
OUR FATHER, WHO ART IN HEAVEN...
OKAY, UP WE GO! COME ON... COME ON... OTHER FOOT, FRANCINE.
"HONEST ABE" scales
POP! zing!
UH OH.
CREAK!
KA-CHUNK!
SIGH
UH, FRANCINE? YOU OKAY?
SORRY. I WAS... THINKING.
COME ON, LET'S GET YOUR WEIGHT AND WE CAN GET STARTED!
169 POUNDS.
THERE, THAT DIDN'T HURT, DID IT?
MMPH
LOOKS LIKE WE HAVE SOME WORK TO DO, HUH?
MMPH
THE LONGER I WAS WITH MONICA, THE LESS I LIKED HER. I MEAN, HERE WAS A TOTAL STRANGER WHO KNEW MY DARKEST SECRETS! AND I HATED HER FOR IT!
I MEAN, COME ON! KATCHOO DIDN'T EVEN KNOW MY REAL MEASUREMENTS, AND SHE'S SEEN ME NAKED!
THE WAY I SEE IT, WITH A BODY LIKE MINE, ONCE SOMEBODY'S SEEN YOU NAKED YOU EITHER HAVE TO STAY WITH THEM FOR LIFE OR KILL THEM!
OKAY! LET'S GET BUSY, SHALL WE?
GOD, I LOVE THIS PART!
MONICA'S FATE WAS OBVIOUS.

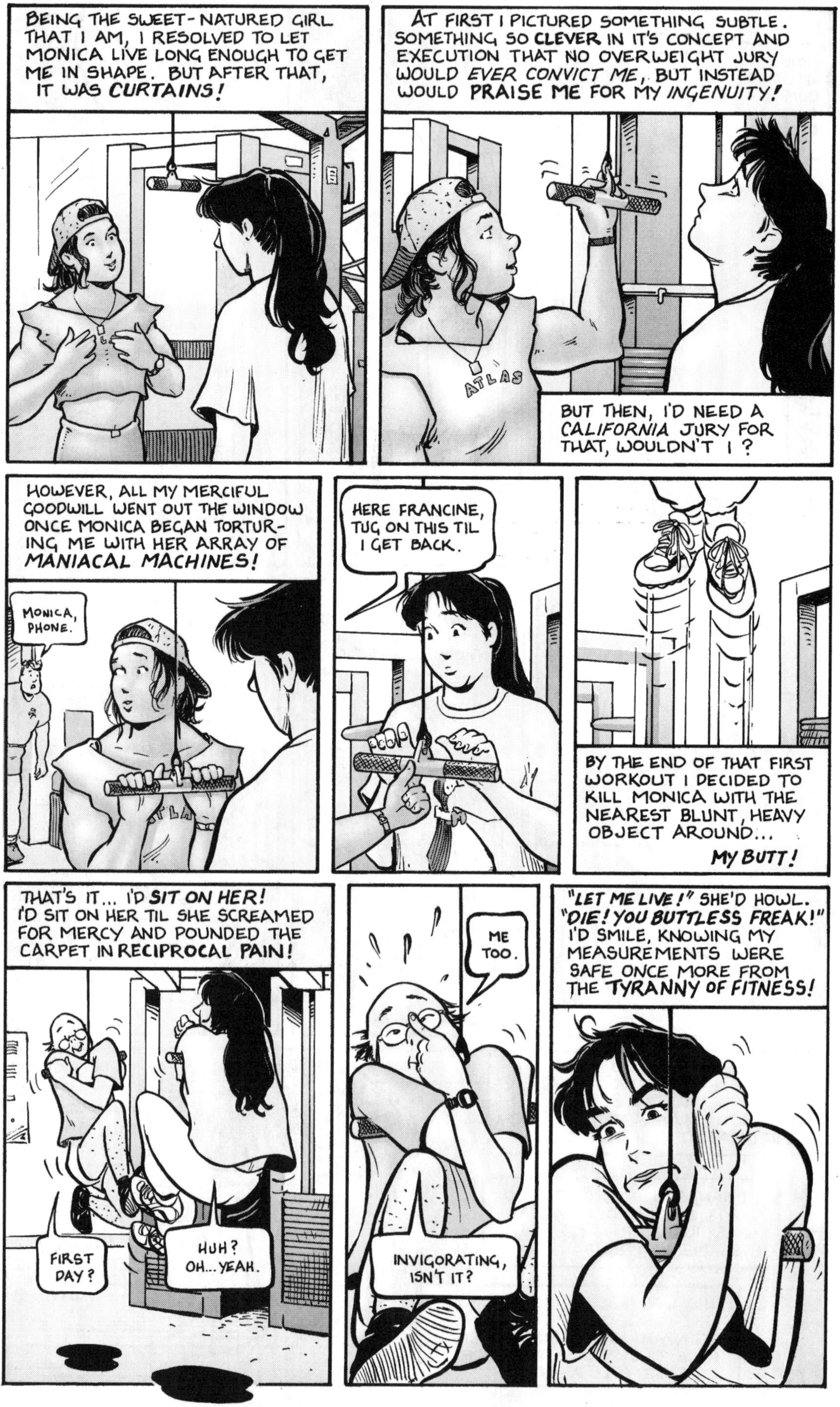
BEING THE SWEET-NATURED GIRL THAT I AM, I RESOLVED TO LET MONICA LIVE LONG ENOUGH TO GET ME IN SHAPE. BUT AFTER THAT, IT WAS CURTAINS!
AT FIRST I PICTURED SOMETHING SUBTLE. SOMETHING SO CLEVER IN IT'S CONCEPT AND EXECUTION THAT NO OVERWEIGHT JURY WOULD EVER CONVICT ME, BUT INSTEAD WOULD PRAISE ME FOR MY INGENUITY!
ATLAS
BUT THEN, I'D NEED A CALIFORNIA JURY FOR THAT, WOULDN'T I?
HOWEVER, ALL MY MERCIFUL GOODWILL WENT OUT THE WINDOW ONCE MONICA BEGAN TORTURING ME WITH HER ARRAY OF MANIACAL MACHINES!
MONICA, PHONE.
HERE FRANCINE, TUG ON THIS TIL I GET BACK.
BY THE END OF THAT FIRST WORKOUT I DECIDED TO KILL MONICA WITH THE NEAREST BLUNT, HEAVY OBJECT AROUND...
MY BUTT!
THAT'S IT... I'D SIT ON HER! I'D SIT ON HER TIL SHE SCREAMED FOR MERCY AND POUNDED THE CARPET IN RECIPROCAL PAIN!
FIRST DAY?
HUH? OH... YEAH.
ME TOO.
INVIGORATING, ISN'T IT?
"LET ME LIVE!" SHE'D HOWL. "DIE! YOU BUTTLESS FREAK!" I'D SMILE, KNOWING MY MEASUREMENTS WERE SAFE ONCE MORE FROM THE TYRANNY OF FITNESS!

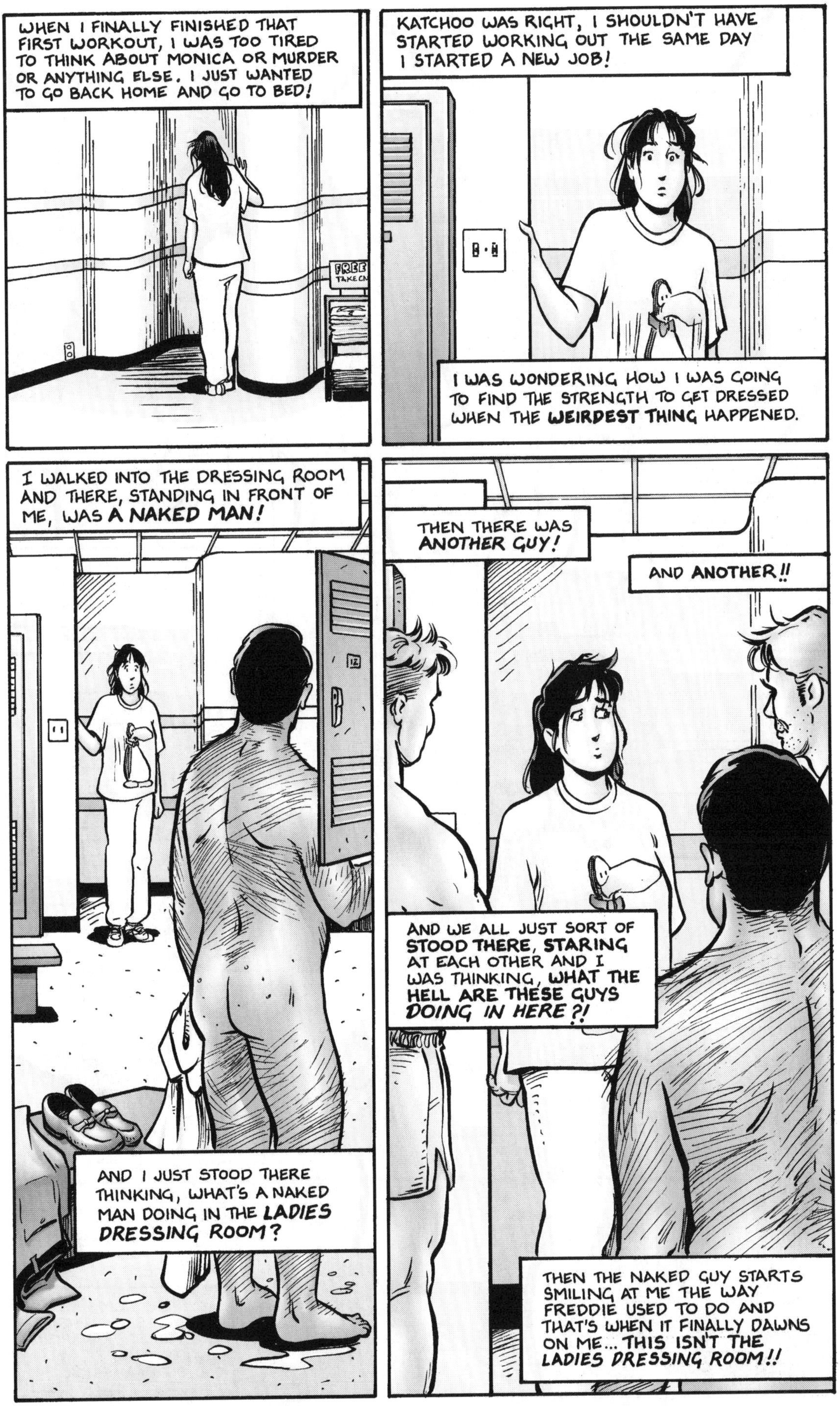
WHEN I FINALLY FINISHED THAT FIRST WORKOUT, I WAS TOO TIRED TO THINK ABOUT MONICA OR MURDER OR ANYTHING ELSE. I JUST WANTED TO GO BACK HOME AND GO TO BED!
KATCHOO WAS RIGHT, I SHOULDN'T HAVE STARTED WORKING OUT THE SAME DAY I STARTED A NEW JOB!
I WAS WONDERING HOW I WAS GOING TO FIND THE STRENGTH TO GET DRESSED WHEN THE **WEIRDEST THING** HAPPENED.
I WALKED INTO THE DRESSING ROOM AND THERE, STANDING IN FRONT OF ME, WAS **A NAKED MAN!**
AND I JUST STOOD THERE THINKING, WHAT'S A NAKED MAN DOING IN THE ***LADIES DRESSING ROOM***?
THEN THERE WAS ***ANOTHER GUY!***
AND **ANOTHER!!**
AND WE ALL JUST SORT OF **STOOD THERE, STARING** AT EACH OTHER AND I WAS THINKING, **WHAT THE HELL ARE THESE GUYS *DOING IN HERE?!***
THEN THE NAKED GUY STARTS SMILING AT ME THE WAY FREDDIE USED TO DO AND THAT'S WHEN IT FINALLY DAWNS ON ME... **THIS ISN'T THE *LADIES DRESSING ROOM!!***

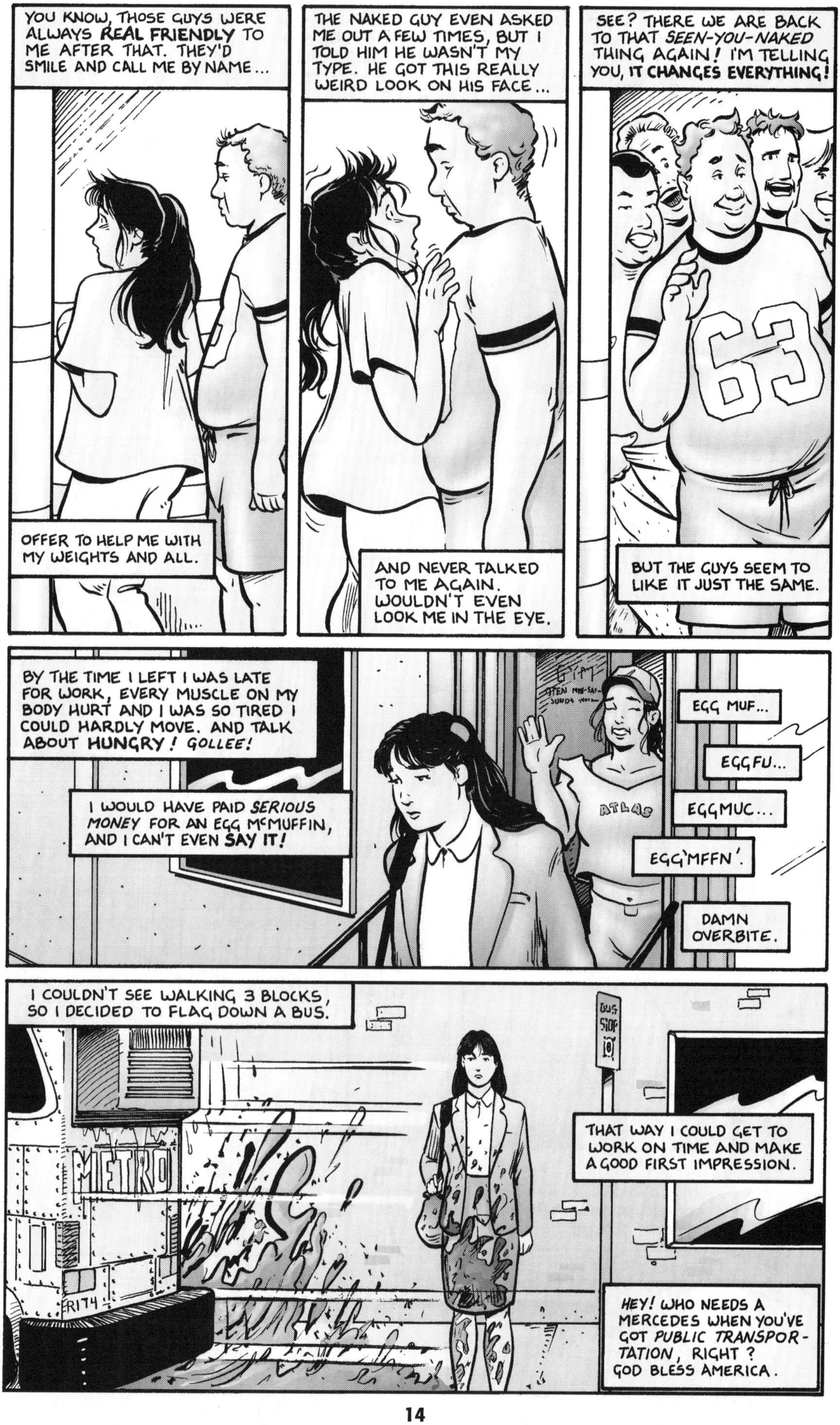
YOU KNOW, THOSE GUYS WERE ALWAYS REAL FRIENDLY TO ME AFTER THAT. THEY'D SMILE AND CALL ME BY NAME...
OFFER TO HELP ME WITH MY WEIGHTS AND ALL.
THE NAKED GUY EVEN ASKED ME OUT A FEW TIMES, BUT I TOLD HIM HE WASN'T MY TYPE. HE GOT THIS REALLY WEIRD LOOK ON HIS FACE...
AND NEVER TALKED TO ME AGAIN. WOULDN'T EVEN LOOK ME IN THE EYE.
SEE? THERE WE ARE BACK TO THAT SEEN-YOU-NAKED THING AGAIN! I'M TELLING YOU, IT CHANGES EVERYTHING!
63
BUT THE GUYS SEEM TO LIKE IT JUST THE SAME.
BY THE TIME I LEFT I WAS LATE FOR WORK, EVERY MUSCLE ON MY BODY HURT AND I WAS SO TIRED I COULD HARDLY MOVE. AND TALK ABOUT HUNGRY! GOLLEE!
GYM
ATLAS
I WOULD HAVE PAID SERIOUS MONEY FOR AN EGG McMUFFIN, AND I CAN'T EVEN SAY IT!
EGG MUF...
EGGFU...
EGGMUC...
EGG'MFFN'.
DAMN OVERBITE.
I COULDN'T SEE WALKING 3 BLOCKS, SO I DECIDED TO FLAG DOWN A BUS.
BUS STOP
METRO
R174
THAT WAY I COULD GET TO WORK ON TIME AND MAKE A GOOD FIRST IMPRESSION.
HEY! WHO NEEDS A MERCEDES WHEN YOU'VE GOT PUBLIC TRANSPORTATION, RIGHT? GOD BLESS AMERICA.

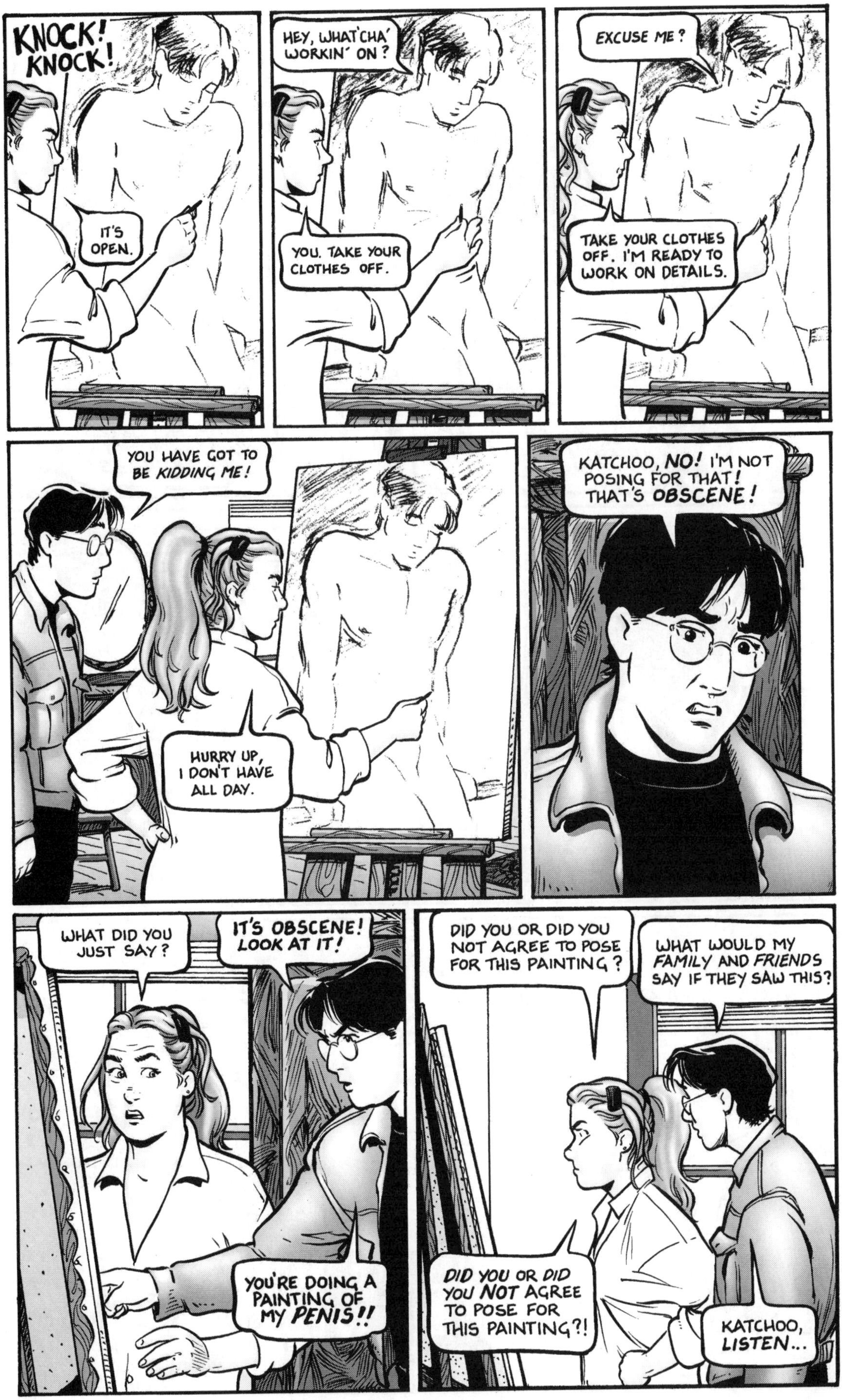
KNOCK! KNOCK!
IT'S OPEN.
HEY, WHAT'CHA' WORKIN' ON?
YOU. TAKE YOUR CLOTHES OFF.
EXCUSE ME?
TAKE YOUR CLOTHES OFF. I'M READY TO WORK ON DETAILS.
YOU HAVE GOT TO BE KIDDING ME!
HURRY UP, I DON'T HAVE ALL DAY.
KATCHOO, NO! I'M NOT POSING FOR THAT! THAT'S OBSCENE!
WHAT DID YOU JUST SAY?
IT'S OBSCENE! LOOK AT IT!
YOU'RE DOING A PAINTING OF MY PENIS!!
DID YOU OR DID YOU NOT AGREE TO POSE FOR THIS PAINTING?
WHAT WOULD MY FAMILY AND FRIENDS SAY IF THEY SAW THIS?
DID YOU OR DID YOU NOT AGREE TO POSE FOR THIS PAINTING?!
KATCHOO, LISTEN...

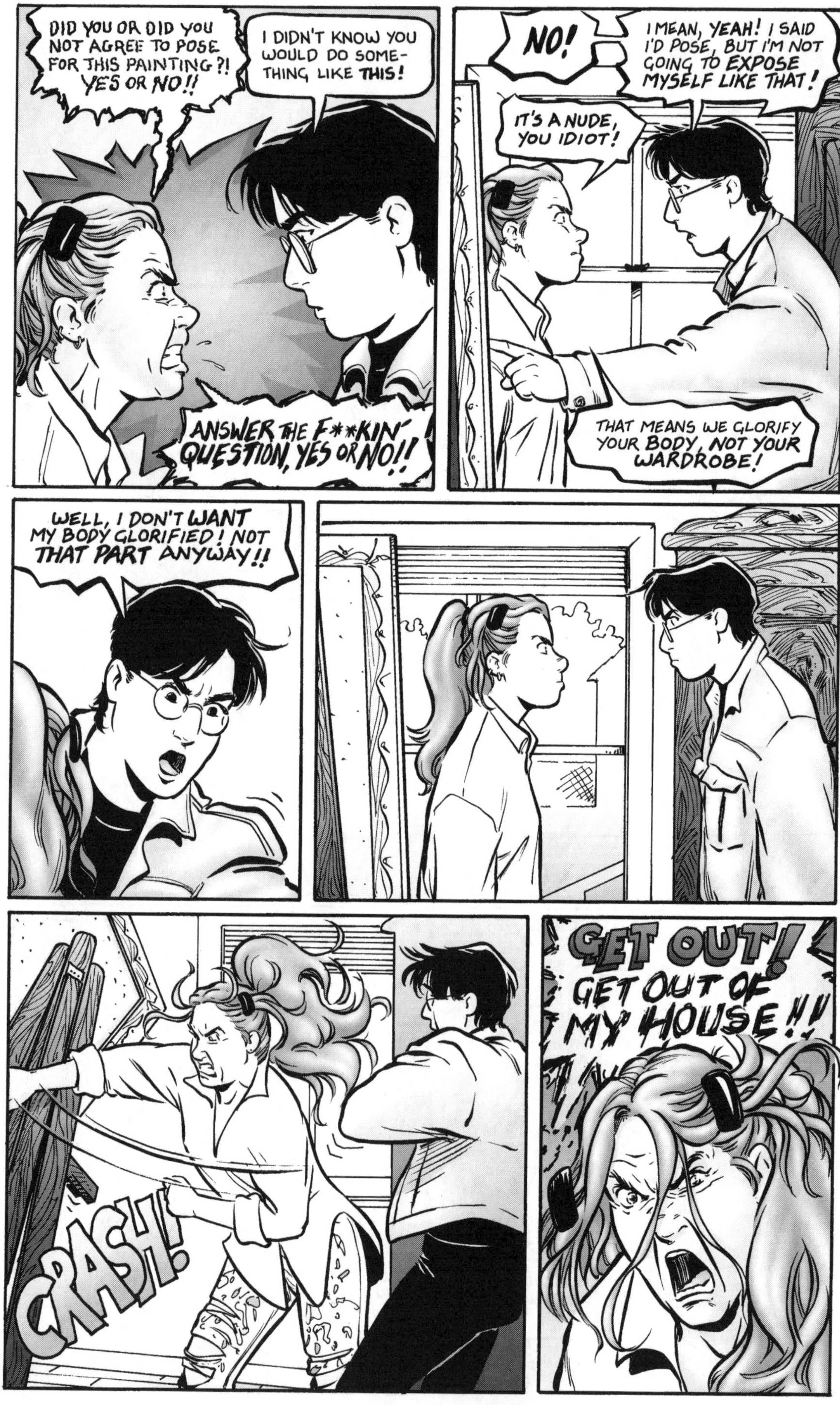
DID YOU OR DID YOU NOT AGREE TO POSE FOR THIS PAINTING?! YES OR NO!!
I DIDN'T KNOW YOU WOULD DO SOMETHING LIKE THIS!
ANSWER THE F**KIN' QUESTION, YES OR NO!!
NO!
I MEAN, YEAH! I SAID I'D POSE, BUT I'M NOT GOING TO EXPOSE MYSELF LIKE THAT!
IT'S A NUDE, YOU IDIOT!
THAT MEANS WE GLORIFY YOUR BODY, NOT YOUR WARDROBE!
WELL, I DON'T WANT MY BODY GLORIFIED! NOT THAT PART ANYWAY!!
CRASH!
GET OUT!
GET OUT OF MY HOUSE!!!

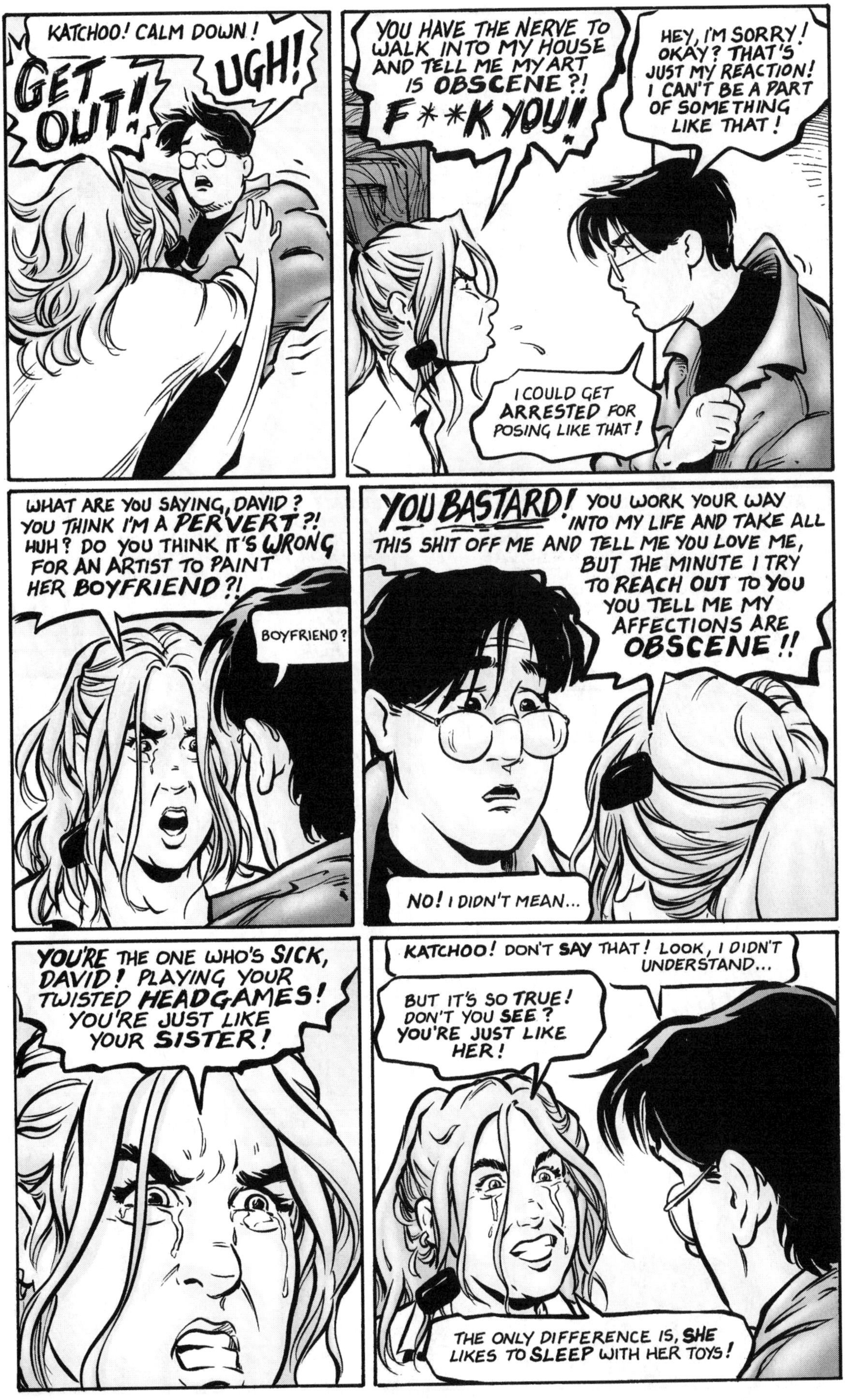
KATCHOO! CALM DOWN!
GET OUT!
UGH!
YOU HAVE THE NERVE TO WALK INTO MY HOUSE AND TELL ME MY ART IS OBSCENE?! F**K YOU!!
HEY, I'M SORRY! OKAY? THAT'S JUST MY REACTION! I CAN'T BE A PART OF SOMETHING LIKE THAT!
I COULD GET ARRESTED FOR POSING LIKE THAT!
WHAT ARE YOU SAYING, DAVID? YOU THINK I'M A PERVERT?! HUH? DO YOU THINK IT'S WRONG FOR AN ARTIST TO PAINT HER BOYFRIEND?!
BOYFRIEND?
YOU BASTARD! YOU WORK YOUR WAY INTO MY LIFE AND TAKE ALL THIS SHIT OFF ME AND TELL ME YOU LOVE ME, BUT THE MINUTE I TRY TO REACH OUT TO YOU YOU TELL ME MY AFFECTIONS ARE OBSCENE!!
NO! I DIDN'T MEAN...
YOU'RE THE ONE WHO'S SICK, DAVID! PLAYING YOUR TWISTED HEADGAMES! YOU'RE JUST LIKE YOUR SISTER!
KATCHOO! DON'T SAY THAT! LOOK, I DIDN'T UNDERSTAND...
BUT IT'S SO TRUE! DON'T YOU SEE? YOU'RE JUST LIKE HER!
THE ONLY DIFFERENCE IS, SHE LIKES TO SLEEP WITH HER TOYS!

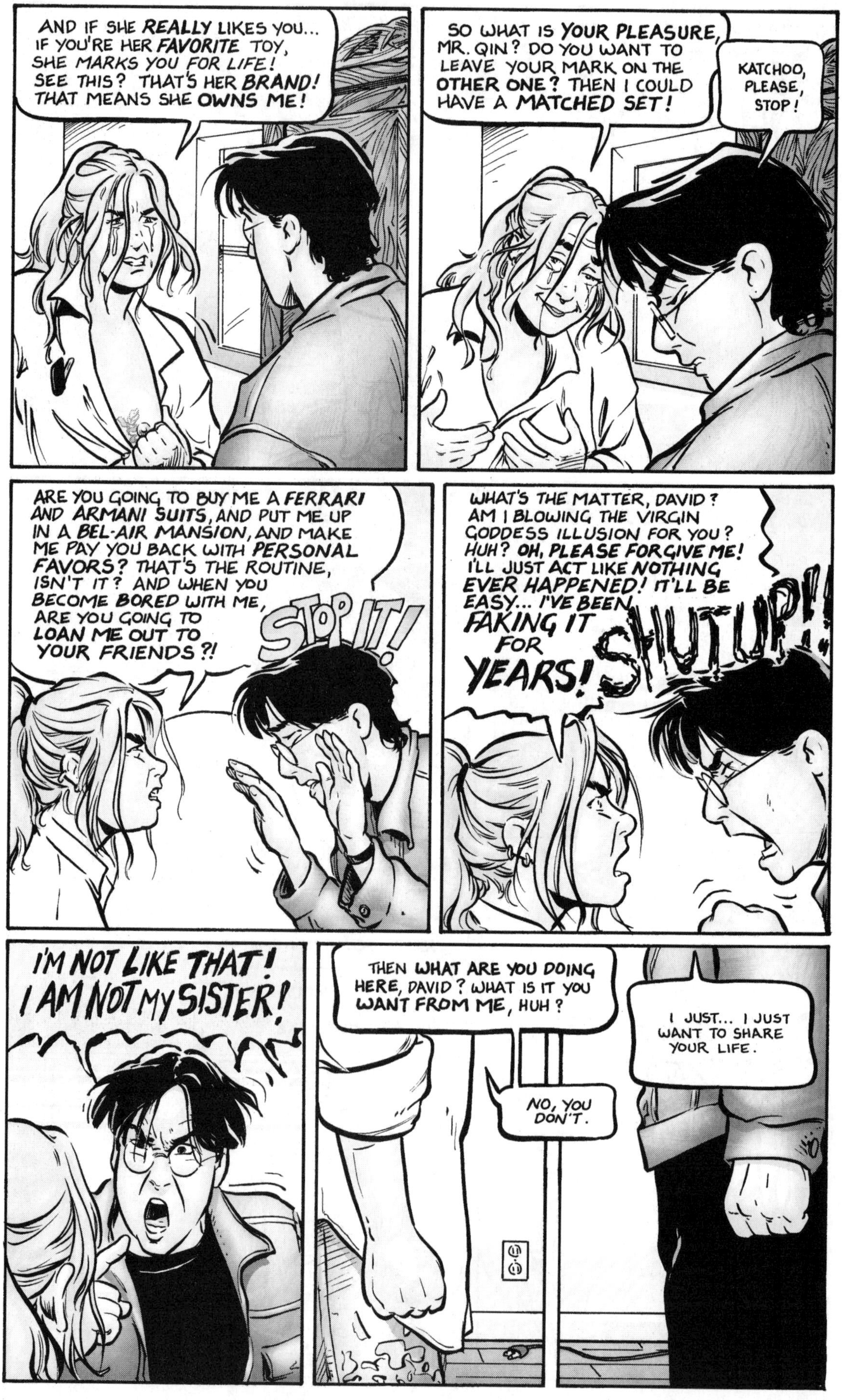
AND IF SHE REALLY LIKES YOU... IF YOU'RE HER FAVORITE TOY, SHE MARKS YOU FOR LIFE! SEE THIS? THAT'S HER BRAND! THAT MEANS SHE OWNS ME!
SO WHAT IS YOUR PLEASURE, MR. QIN? DO YOU WANT TO LEAVE YOUR MARK ON THE OTHER ONE? THEN I COULD HAVE A MATCHED SET!
KATCHOO, PLEASE, STOP!
ARE YOU GOING TO BUY ME A FERRARI AND ARMANI SUITS, AND PUT ME UP IN A BEL-AIR MANSION, AND MAKE ME PAY YOU BACK WITH PERSONAL FAVORS? THAT'S THE ROUTINE, ISN'T IT? AND WHEN YOU BECOME BORED WITH ME, ARE YOU GOING TO LOAN ME OUT TO YOUR FRIENDS?!
STOP IT!
WHAT'S THE MATTER, DAVID? AM I BLOWING THE VIRGIN GODDESS ILLUSION FOR YOU? HUH? OH, PLEASE FORGIVE ME! I'LL JUST ACT LIKE NOTHING EVER HAPPENED! IT'LL BE EASY... I'VE BEEN FAKING IT FOR YEARS!
SHUT UP!!
I'M NOT LIKE THAT! I AM NOT MY SISTER!
THEN WHAT ARE YOU DOING HERE, DAVID? WHAT IS IT YOU WANT FROM ME, HUH?
I JUST... I JUST WANT TO SHARE YOUR LIFE.
NO, YOU DON'T.

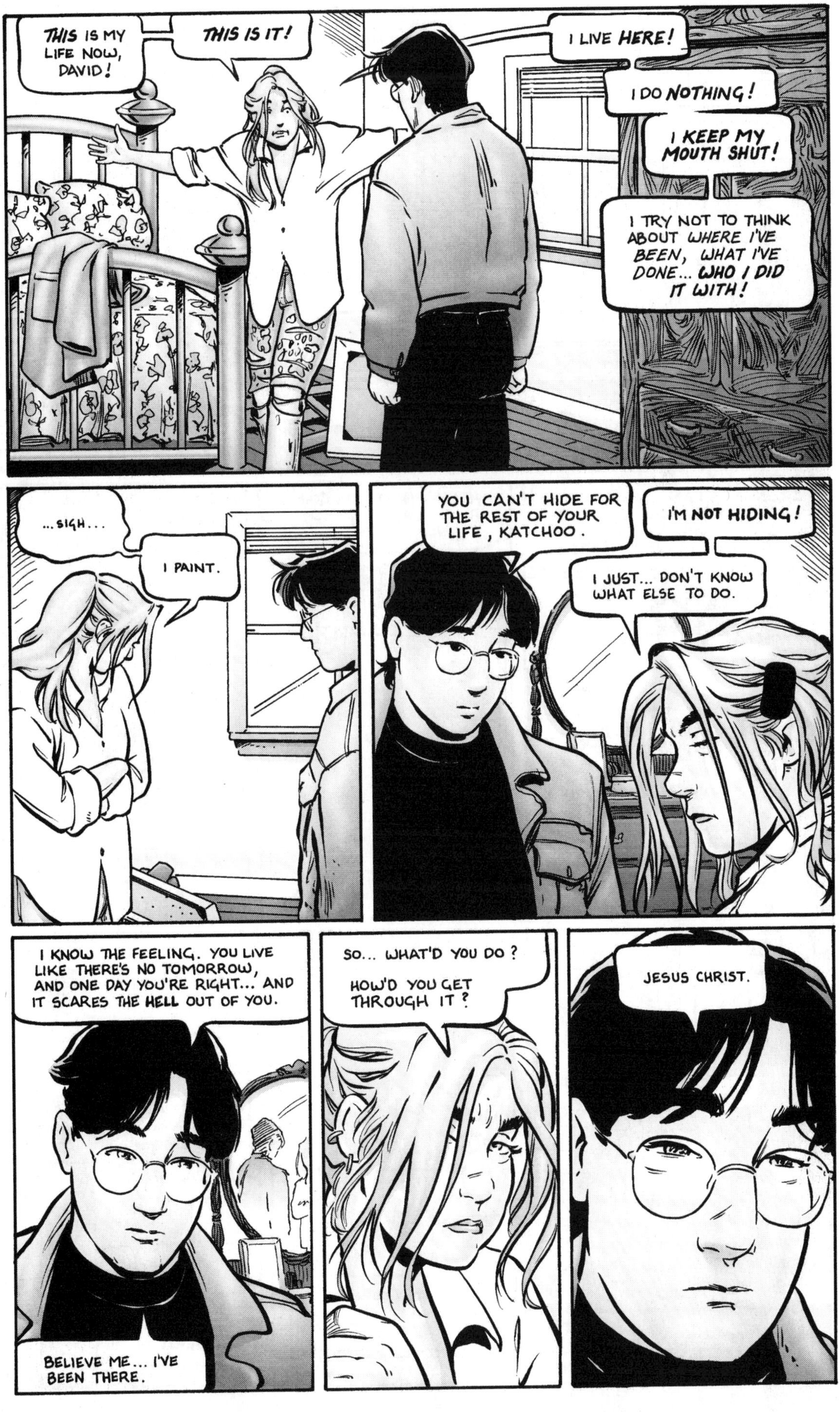
THIS IS MY LIFE NOW, DAVID!
THIS IS IT!
I LIVE HERE!
I DO NOTHING!
I KEEP MY MOUTH SHUT!
I TRY NOT TO THINK ABOUT WHERE I'VE BEEN, WHAT I'VE DONE... WHO I DID IT WITH!
...SIGH...
I PAINT.
YOU CAN'T HIDE FOR THE REST OF YOUR LIFE, KATCHOO.
I'M NOT HIDING!
I JUST... DON'T KNOW WHAT ELSE TO DO.
I KNOW THE FEELING. YOU LIVE LIKE THERE'S NO TOMORROW, AND ONE DAY YOU'RE RIGHT... AND IT SCARES THE HELL OUT OF YOU.
BELIEVE ME... I'VE BEEN THERE.
SO... WHAT'D YOU DO?
HOW'D YOU GET THROUGH IT?
JESUS CHRIST.

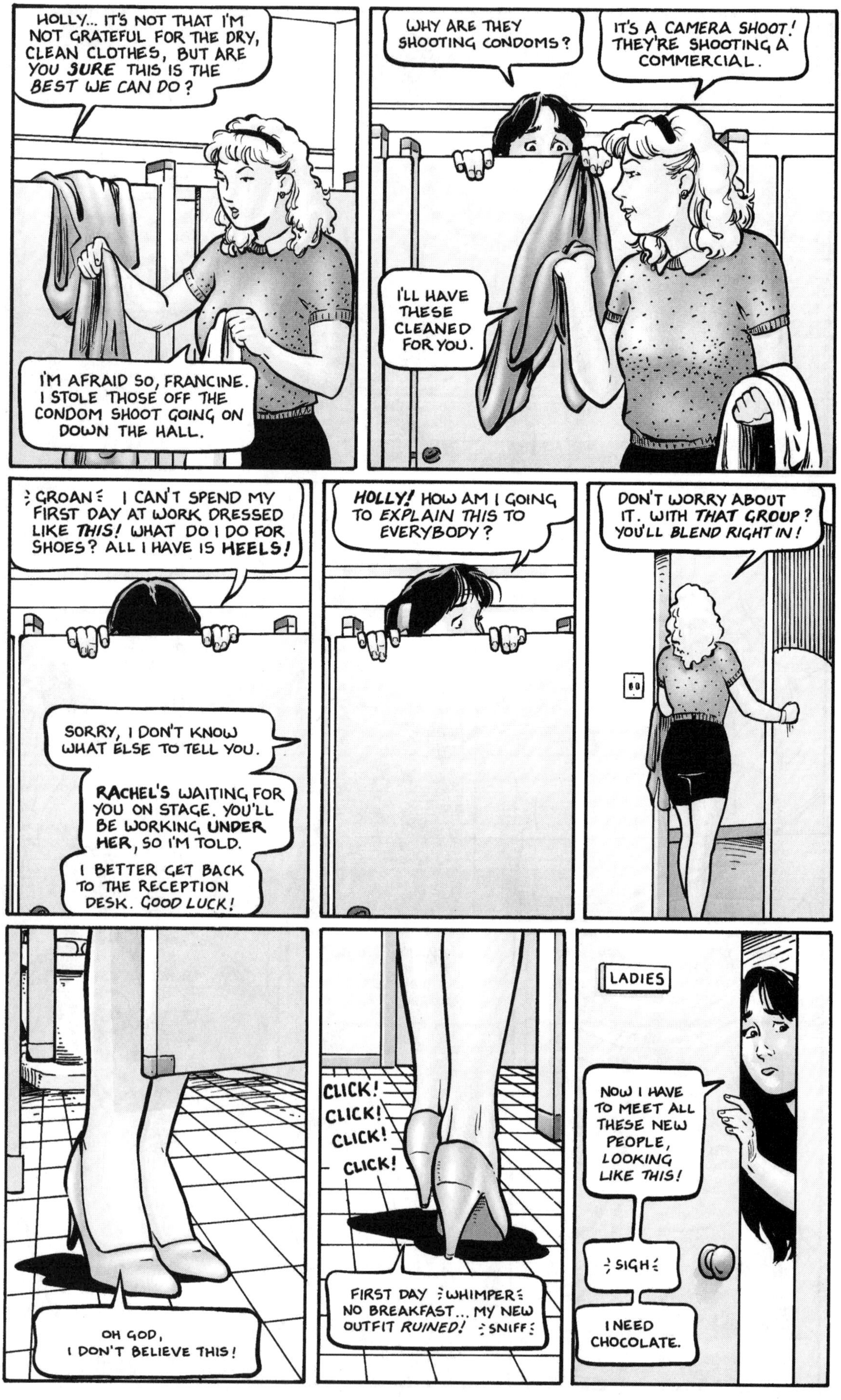
HOLLY... IT'S NOT THAT I'M NOT GRATEFUL FOR THE DRY, CLEAN CLOTHES, BUT ARE YOU SURE THIS IS THE BEST WE CAN DO?
I'M AFRAID SO, FRANCINE. I STOLE THOSE OFF THE CONDOM SHOOT GOING ON DOWN THE HALL.
WHY ARE THEY SHOOTING CONDOMS?
IT'S A CAMERA SHOOT! THEY'RE SHOOTING A COMMERCIAL.
I'LL HAVE THESE CLEANED FOR YOU.
GROAN I CAN'T SPEND MY FIRST DAY AT WORK DRESSED LIKE THIS! WHAT DO I DO FOR SHOES? ALL I HAVE IS HEELS!
SORRY, I DON'T KNOW WHAT ELSE TO TELL YOU.
RACHEL'S WAITING FOR YOU ON STAGE. YOU'LL BE WORKING UNDER HER, SO I'M TOLD.
I BETTER GET BACK TO THE RECEPTION DESK. GOOD LUCK!
HOLLY! HOW AM I GOING TO EXPLAIN THIS TO EVERYBODY?
DON'T WORRY ABOUT IT. WITH THAT GROUP? YOU'LL BLEND RIGHT IN!
OH GOD, I DON'T BELIEVE THIS!
CLICK! CLICK! CLICK! CLICK!
FIRST DAY WHIMPER NO BREAKFAST... MY NEW OUTFIT RUINED! SNIFF
LADIES
NOW I HAVE TO MEET ALL THESE NEW PEOPLE, LOOKING LIKE THIS!
SIGH
I NEED CHOCOLATE.

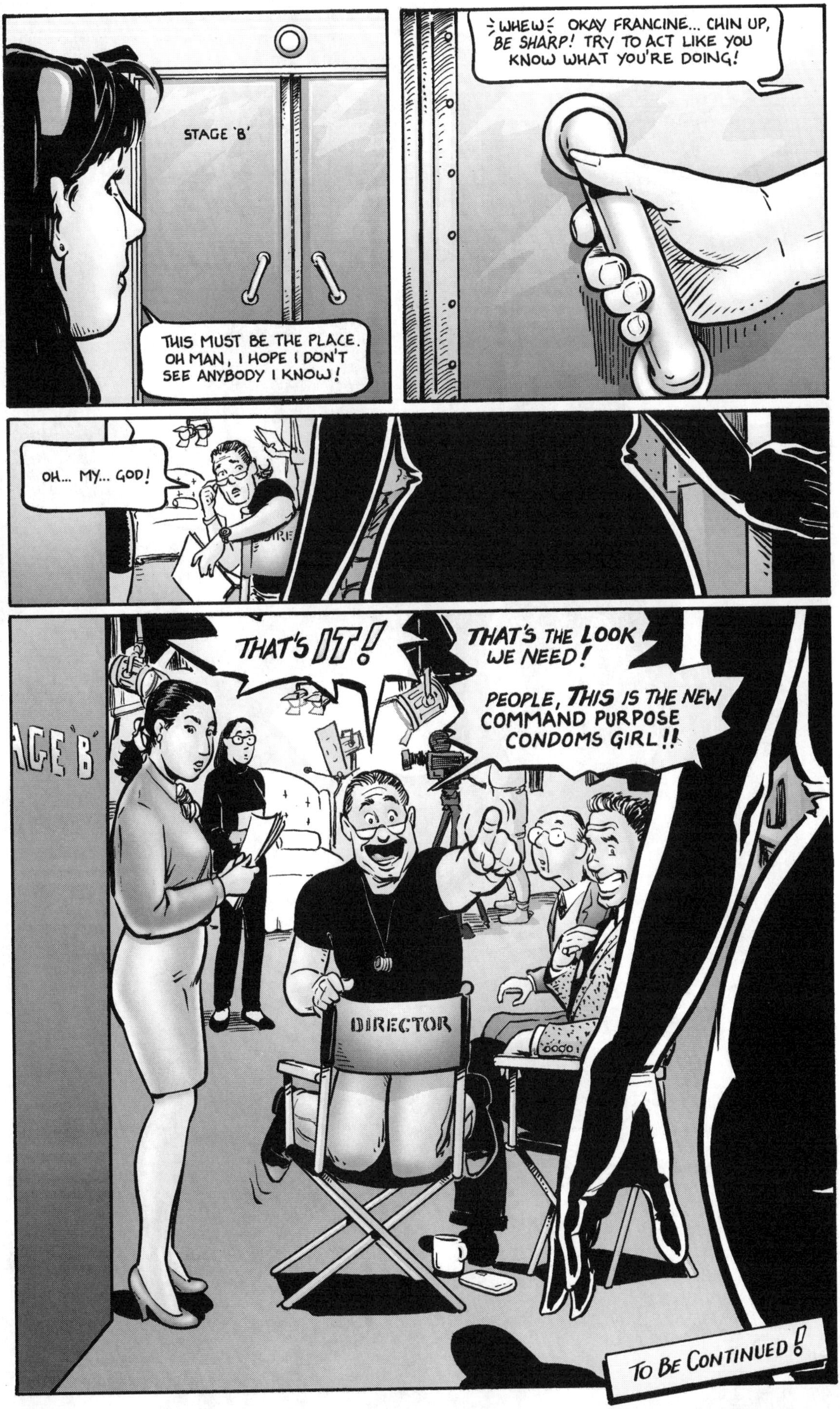
STAGE 'B'
THIS MUST BE THE PLACE. OH MAN, I HOPE I DON'T SEE ANYBODY I KNOW!
WHEW OKAY FRANCINE... CHIN UP, BE SHARP! TRY TO ACT LIKE YOU KNOW WHAT YOU'RE DOING!
OH... MY... GOD!
THAT'S IT!
THAT'S THE LOOK WE NEED!
PEOPLE, THIS IS THE NEW COMMAND PURPOSE CONDOMS GIRL!!
DIRECTOR
TO BE CONTINUED!

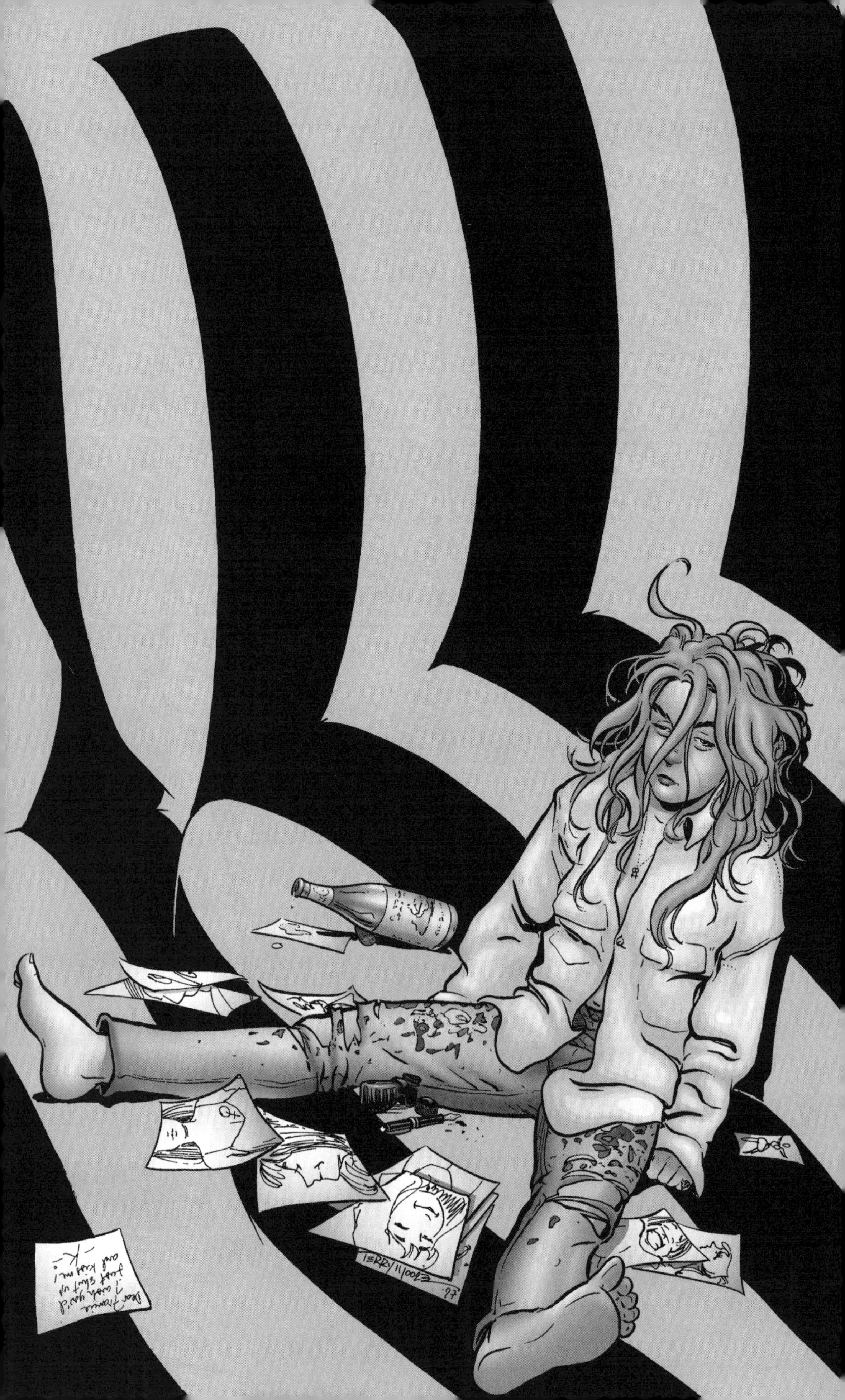
Dear Francine,
I wish you'd
just shut up
and kiss me!
—K—
TERRY 11/00

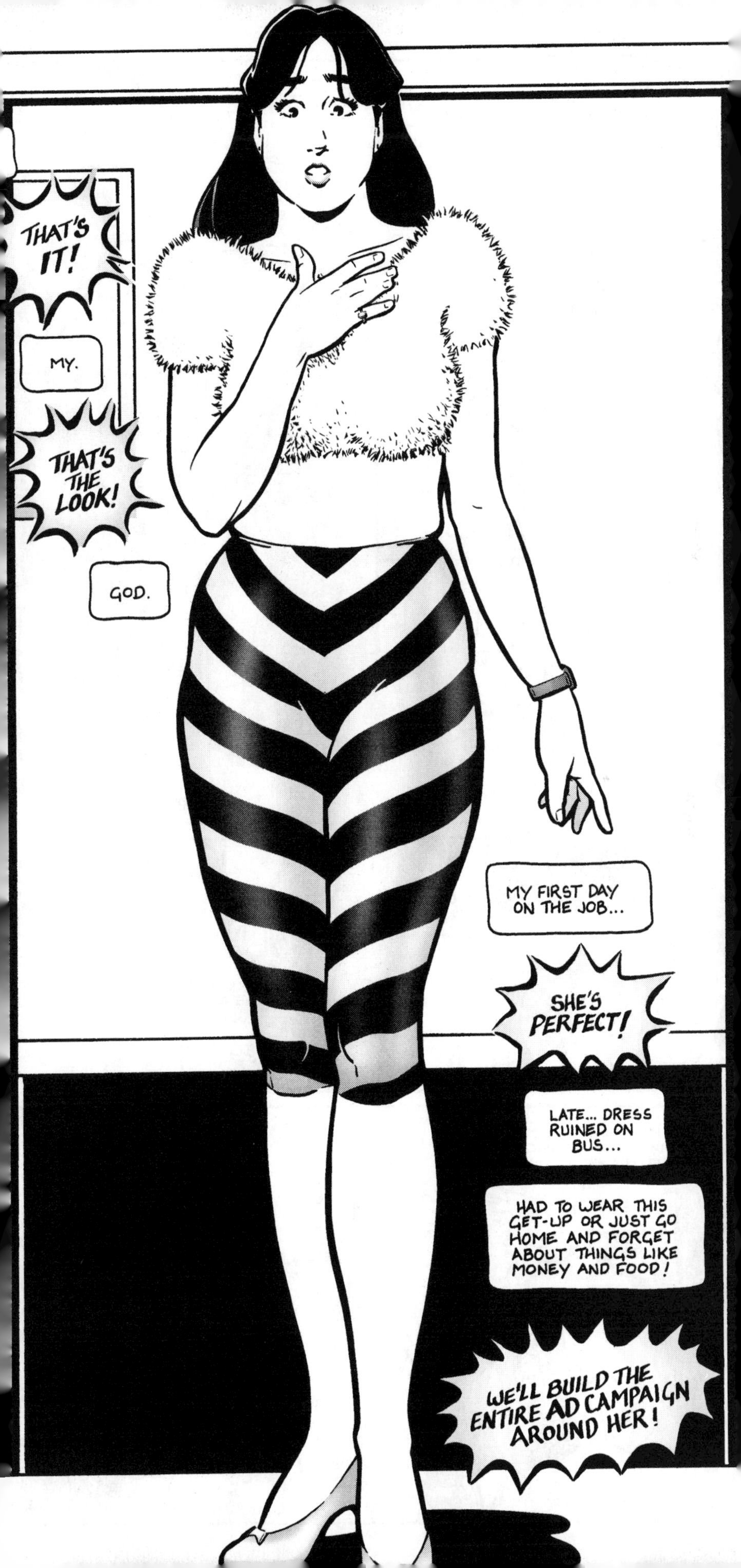
THAT'S IT!
MY.
THAT'S THE LOOK!
GOD.
MY FIRST DAY ON THE JOB...
SHE'S PERFECT!
LATE... DRESS RUINED ON BUS...
HAD TO WEAR THIS GET-UP OR JUST GO HOME AND FORGET ABOUT THINGS LIKE MONEY AND FOOD!
WE'LL BUILD THE ENTIRE AD CAMPAIGN AROUND HER!

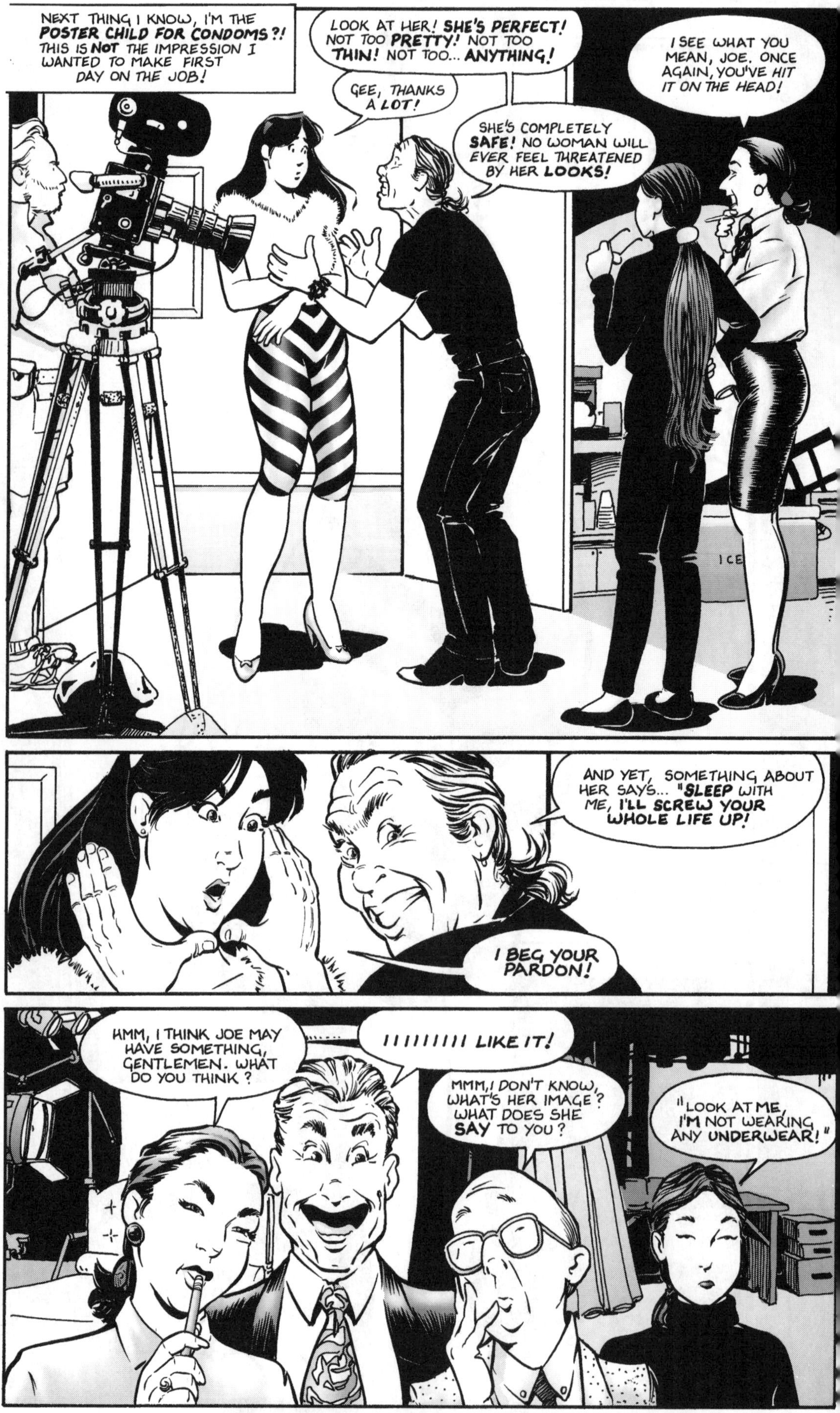
NEXT THING I KNOW, I'M THE POSTER CHILD FOR CONDOMS?! THIS IS NOT THE IMPRESSION I WANTED TO MAKE FIRST DAY ON THE JOB!
LOOK AT HER! SHE'S PERFECT! NOT TOO PRETTY! NOT TOO THIN! NOT TOO... ANYTHING!
GEE, THANKS A LOT!
SHE'S COMPLETELY SAFE! NO WOMAN WILL EVER FEEL THREATENED BY HER LOOKS!
I SEE WHAT YOU MEAN, JOE. ONCE AGAIN, YOU'VE HIT IT ON THE HEAD!
ICE
AND YET, SOMETHING ABOUT HER SAYS... "SLEEP WITH ME, I'LL SCREW YOUR WHOLE LIFE UP!
I BEG YOUR PARDON!
HMM, I THINK JOE MAY HAVE SOMETHING, GENTLEMEN. WHAT DO YOU THINK?
IIIIIIIII LIKE IT!
MMM, I DON'T KNOW, WHAT'S HER IMAGE? WHAT DOES SHE SAY TO YOU?
"LOOK AT ME, I'M NOT WEARING ANY UNDERWEAR!"

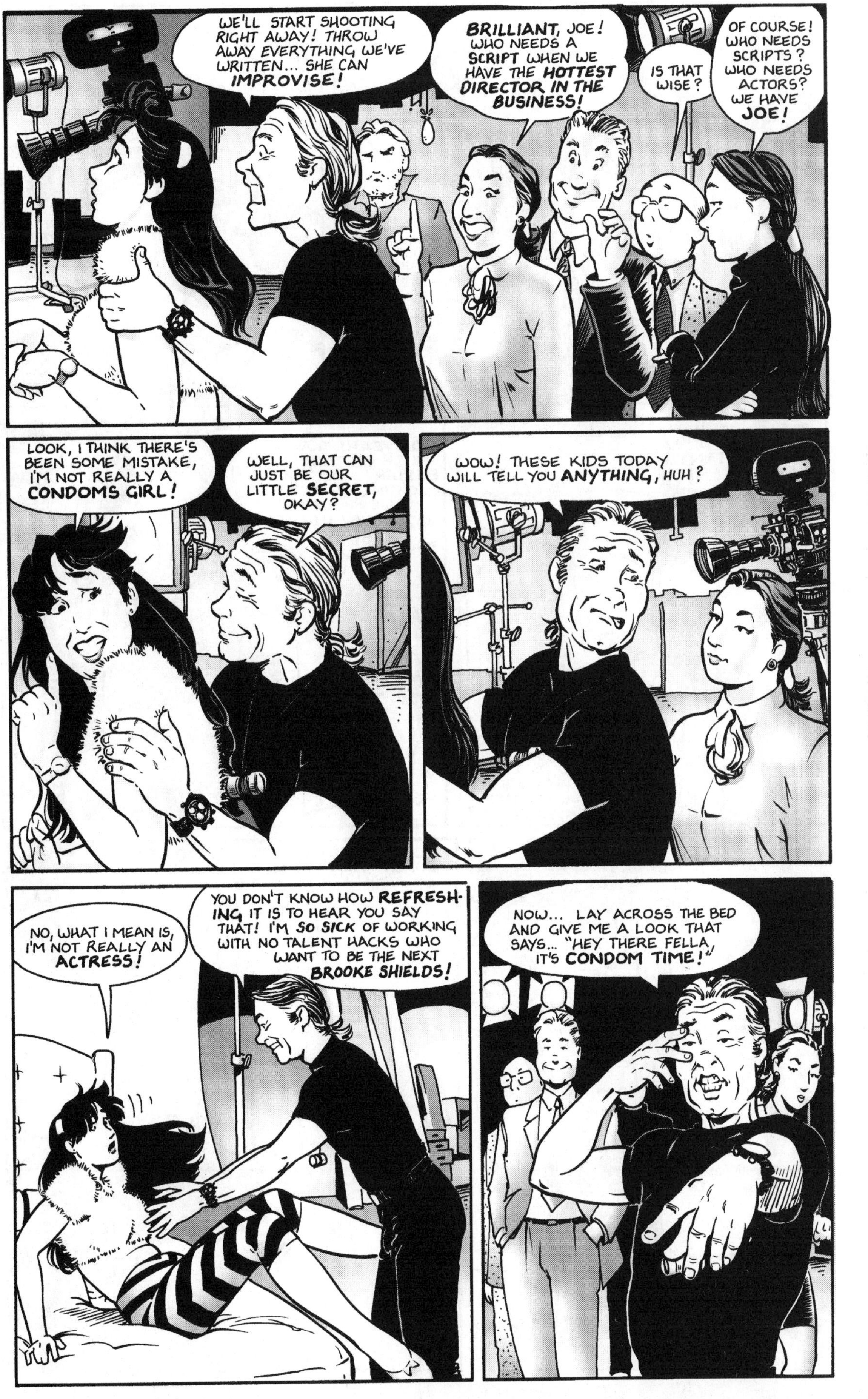
WE'LL START SHOOTING RIGHT AWAY! THROW AWAY EVERYTHING WE'VE WRITTEN... SHE CAN IMPROVISE!
BRILLIANT, JOE! WHO NEEDS A SCRIPT WHEN WE HAVE THE HOTTEST DIRECTOR IN THE BUSINESS!
IS THAT WISE?
OF COURSE! WHO NEEDS SCRIPTS? WHO NEEDS ACTORS? WE HAVE JOE!
LOOK, I THINK THERE'S BEEN SOME MISTAKE, I'M NOT REALLY A CONDOMS GIRL!
WELL, THAT CAN JUST BE OUR LITTLE SECRET, OKAY?
WOW! THESE KIDS TODAY WILL TELL YOU ANYTHING, HUH?
NO, WHAT I MEAN IS, I'M NOT REALLY AN ACTRESS!
YOU DON'T KNOW HOW REFRESHING IT IS TO HEAR YOU SAY THAT! I'M SO SICK OF WORKING WITH NO TALENT HACKS WHO WANT TO BE THE NEXT BROOKE SHIELDS!
NOW... LAY ACROSS THE BED AND GIVE ME A LOOK THAT SAYS... "HEY THERE FELLA, IT'S CONDOM TIME!"

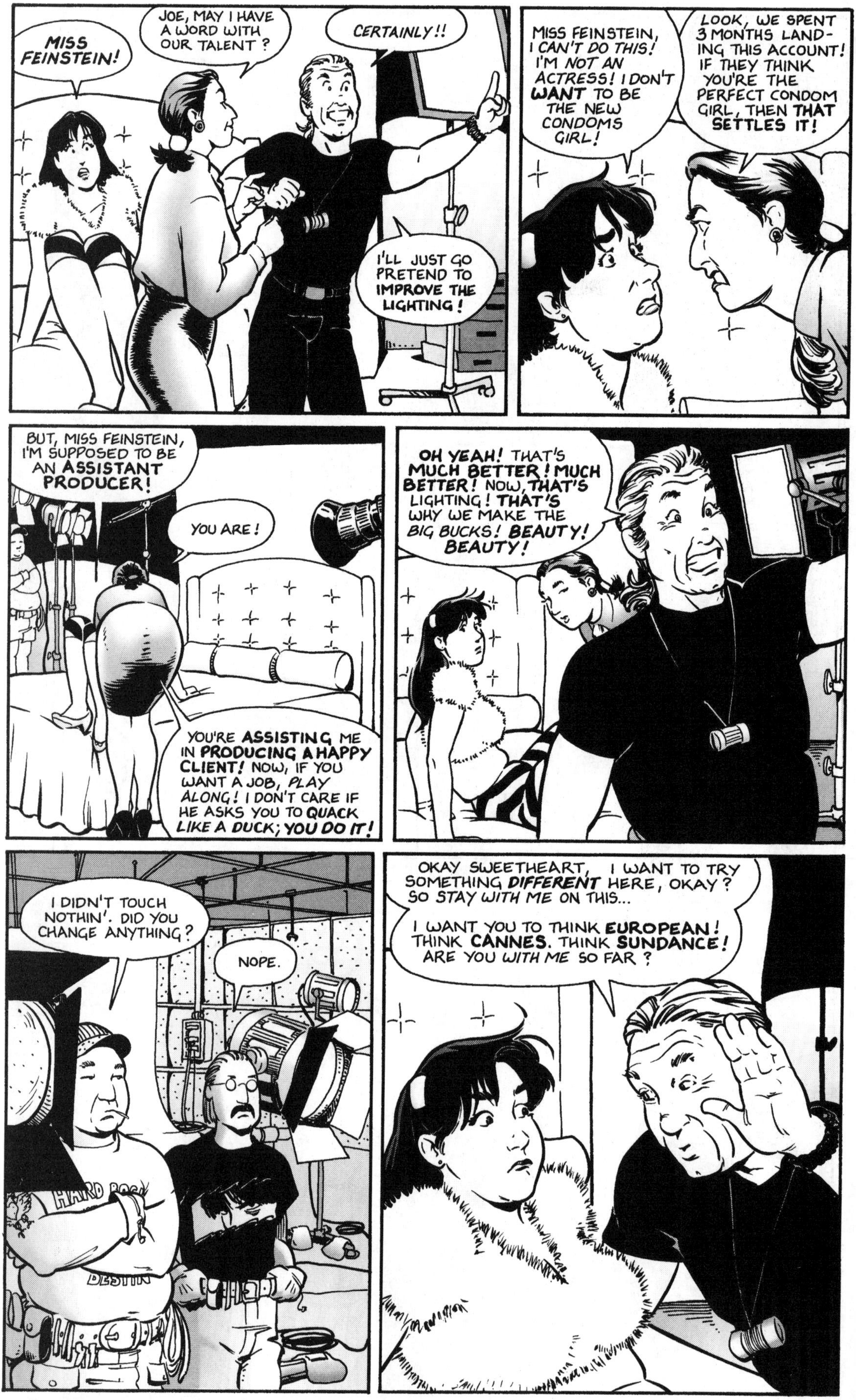
MISS FEINSTEIN!
JOE, MAY I HAVE A WORD WITH OUR TALENT?
CERTAINLY!!
I'LL JUST GO PRETEND TO IMPROVE THE LIGHTING!
MISS FEINSTEIN, I CAN'T DO THIS! I'M NOT AN ACTRESS! I DON'T WANT TO BE THE NEW CONDOMS GIRL!
LOOK, WE SPENT 3 MONTHS LANDING THIS ACCOUNT! IF THEY THINK YOU'RE THE PERFECT CONDOM GIRL, THEN THAT SETTLES IT!
BUT, MISS FEINSTEIN, I'M SUPPOSED TO BE AN ASSISTANT PRODUCER!
YOU ARE!
YOU'RE ASSISTING ME IN PRODUCING A HAPPY CLIENT! NOW, IF YOU WANT A JOB, PLAY ALONG! I DON'T CARE IF HE ASKS YOU TO QUACK LIKE A DUCK; YOU DO IT!
OH YEAH! THAT'S MUCH BETTER! MUCH BETTER! NOW, THAT'S LIGHTING! THAT'S WHY WE MAKE THE BIG BUCKS! BEAUTY! BEAUTY!
I DIDN'T TOUCH NOTHIN'. DID YOU CHANGE ANYTHING?
NOPE.
OKAY SWEETHEART, I WANT TO TRY SOMETHING DIFFERENT HERE, OKAY? SO STAY WITH ME ON THIS...
I WANT YOU TO THINK EUROPEAN! THINK CANNES. THINK SUNDANCE! ARE YOU WITH ME SO FAR?

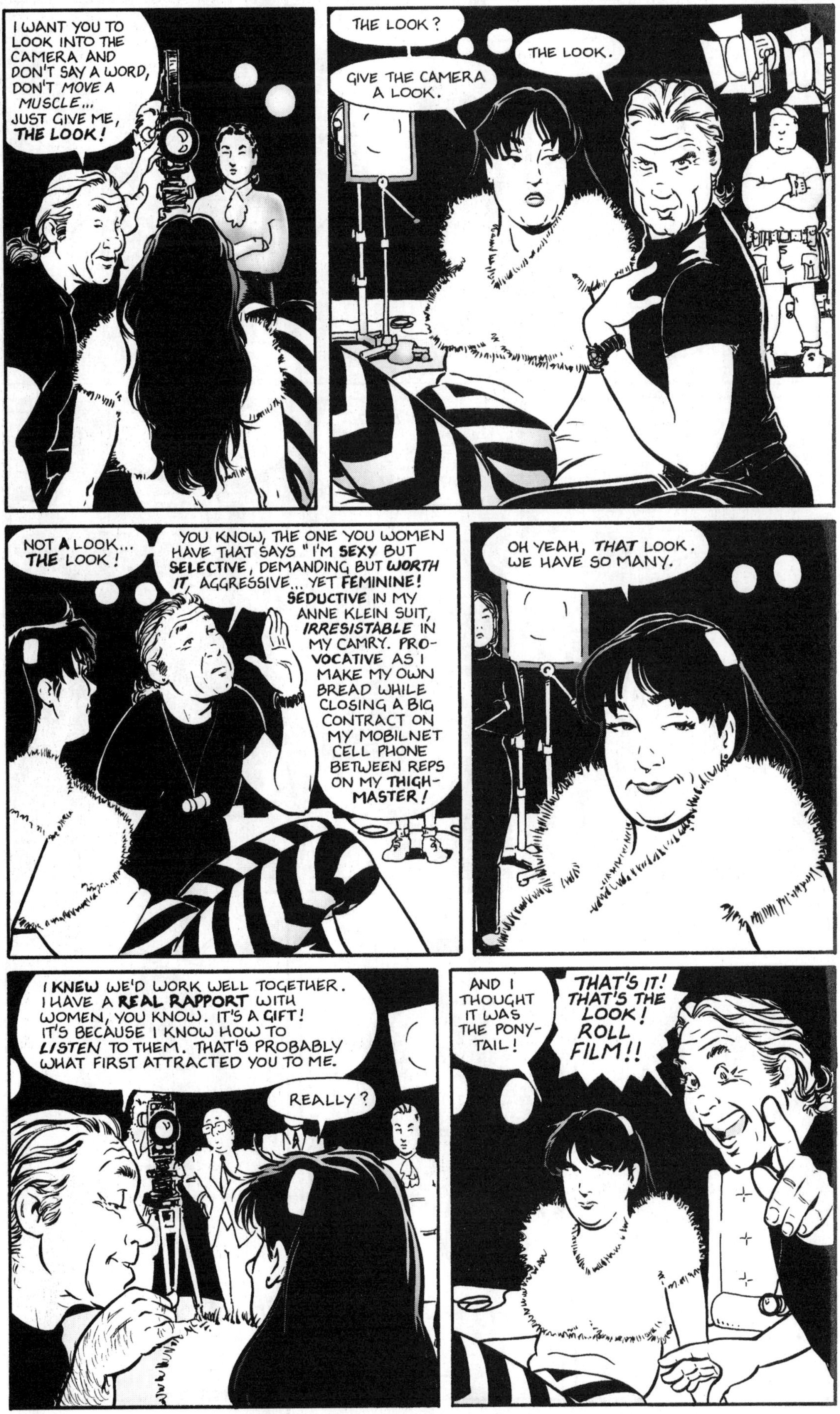
I WANT YOU TO LOOK INTO THE CAMERA AND DON'T SAY A WORD, DON'T MOVE A MUSCLE... JUST GIVE ME, THE LOOK!
THE LOOK?
GIVE THE CAMERA A LOOK.
THE LOOK.
NOT A LOOK... THE LOOK!
YOU KNOW, THE ONE YOU WOMEN HAVE THAT SAYS "I'M SEXY BUT SELECTIVE, DEMANDING BUT WORTH IT, AGGRESSIVE... YET FEMININE! SEDUCTIVE IN MY ANNE KLEIN SUIT, IRRESISTABLE IN MY CAMRY. PROVOCATIVE AS I MAKE MY OWN BREAD WHILE CLOSING A BIG CONTRACT ON MY MOBILNET CELL PHONE BETWEEN REPS ON MY THIGH-MASTER!
OH YEAH, THAT LOOK. WE HAVE SO MANY.
I KNEW WE'D WORK WELL TOGETHER. I HAVE A REAL RAPPORT WITH WOMEN, YOU KNOW. IT'S A GIFT! IT'S BECAUSE I KNOW HOW TO LISTEN TO THEM. THAT'S PROBABLY WHAT FIRST ATTRACTED YOU TO ME.
REALLY?
AND I THOUGHT IT WAS THE PONY-TAIL!
THAT'S IT! THAT'S THE LOOK! ROLL FILM!!

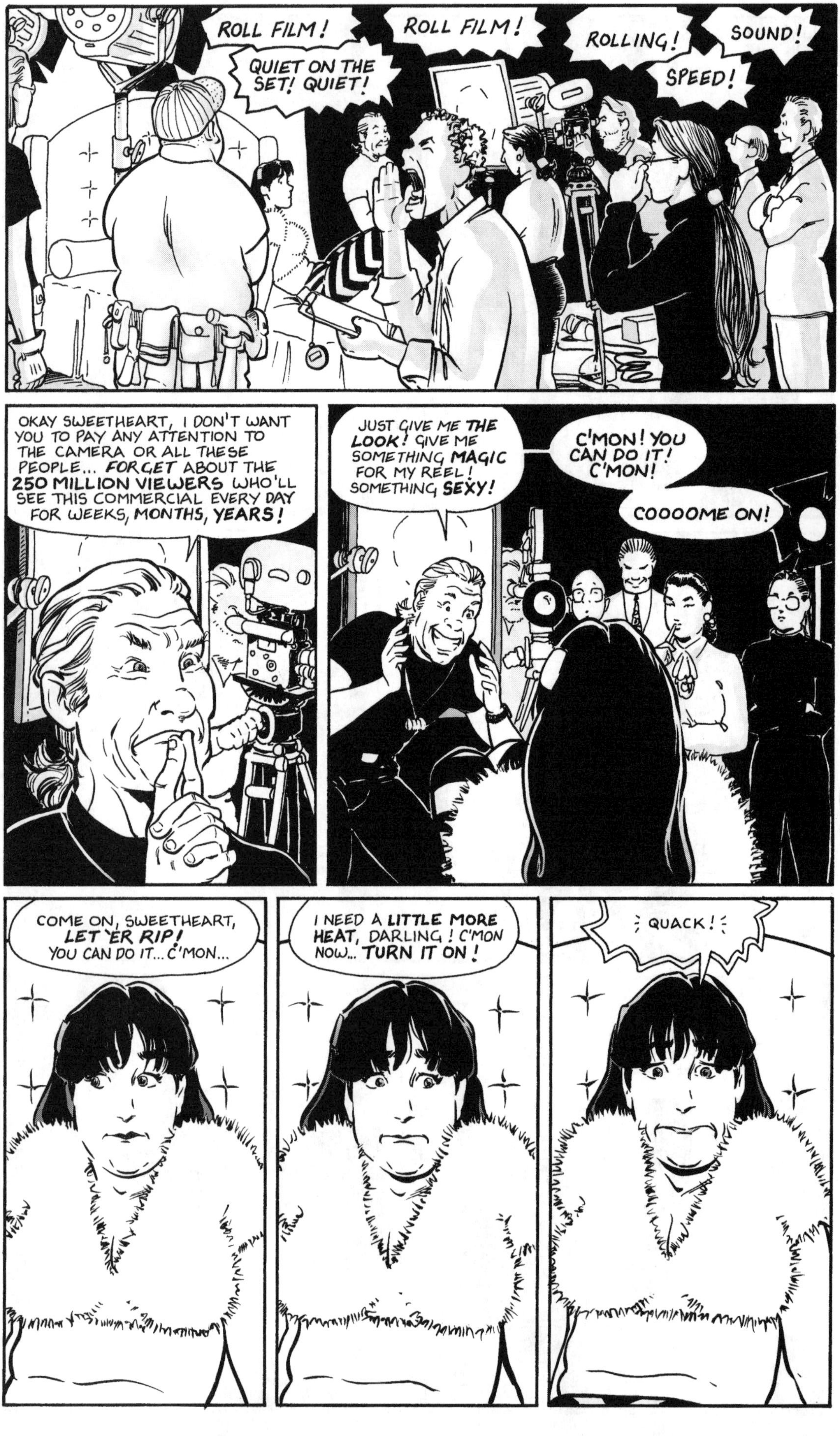
ROLL FILM!
QUIET ON THE SET! QUIET!
ROLL FILM!
ROLLING!
SOUND!
SPEED!
OKAY SWEETHEART, I DON'T WANT YOU TO PAY ANY ATTENTION TO THE CAMERA OR ALL THESE PEOPLE... FORGET ABOUT THE 250 MILLION VIEWERS WHO'LL SEE THIS COMMERCIAL EVERY DAY FOR WEEKS, MONTHS, YEARS!
JUST GIVE ME THE LOOK! GIVE ME SOMETHING MAGIC FOR MY REEL! SOMETHING SEXY!
C'MON! YOU CAN DO IT! C'MON!
COOOOME ON!
COME ON, SWEETHEART, LET 'ER RIP! YOU CAN DO IT... C'MON...
I NEED A LITTLE MORE HEAT, DARLING! C'MON NOW... TURN IT ON!
QUACK!

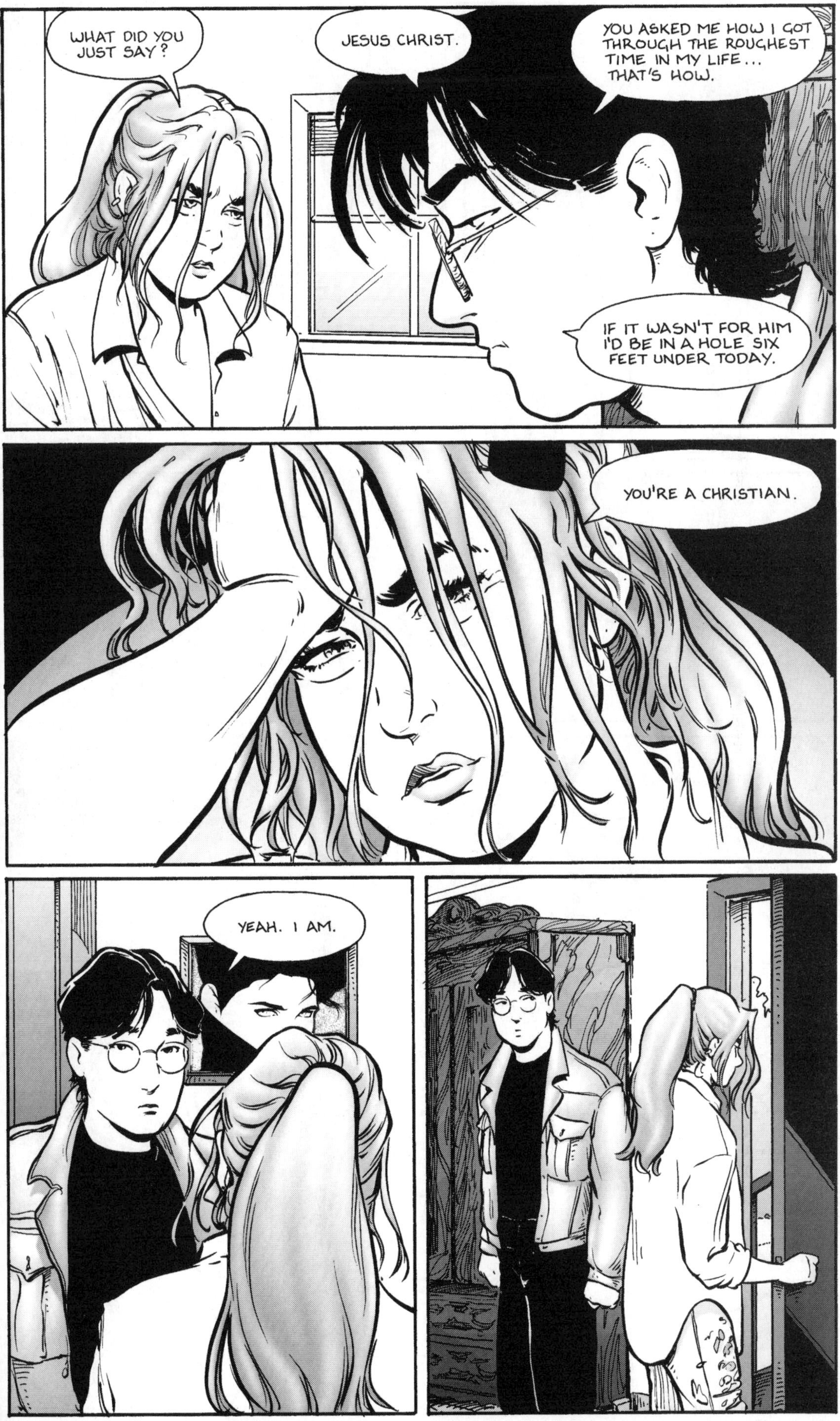
WHAT DID YOU JUST SAY?
JESUS CHRIST.
YOU ASKED ME HOW I GOT THROUGH THE ROUGHEST TIME IN MY LIFE... THAT'S HOW.
IF IT WASN'T FOR HIM I'D BE IN A HOLE SIX FEET UNDER TODAY.
YOU'RE A CHRISTIAN.
YEAH. I AM.

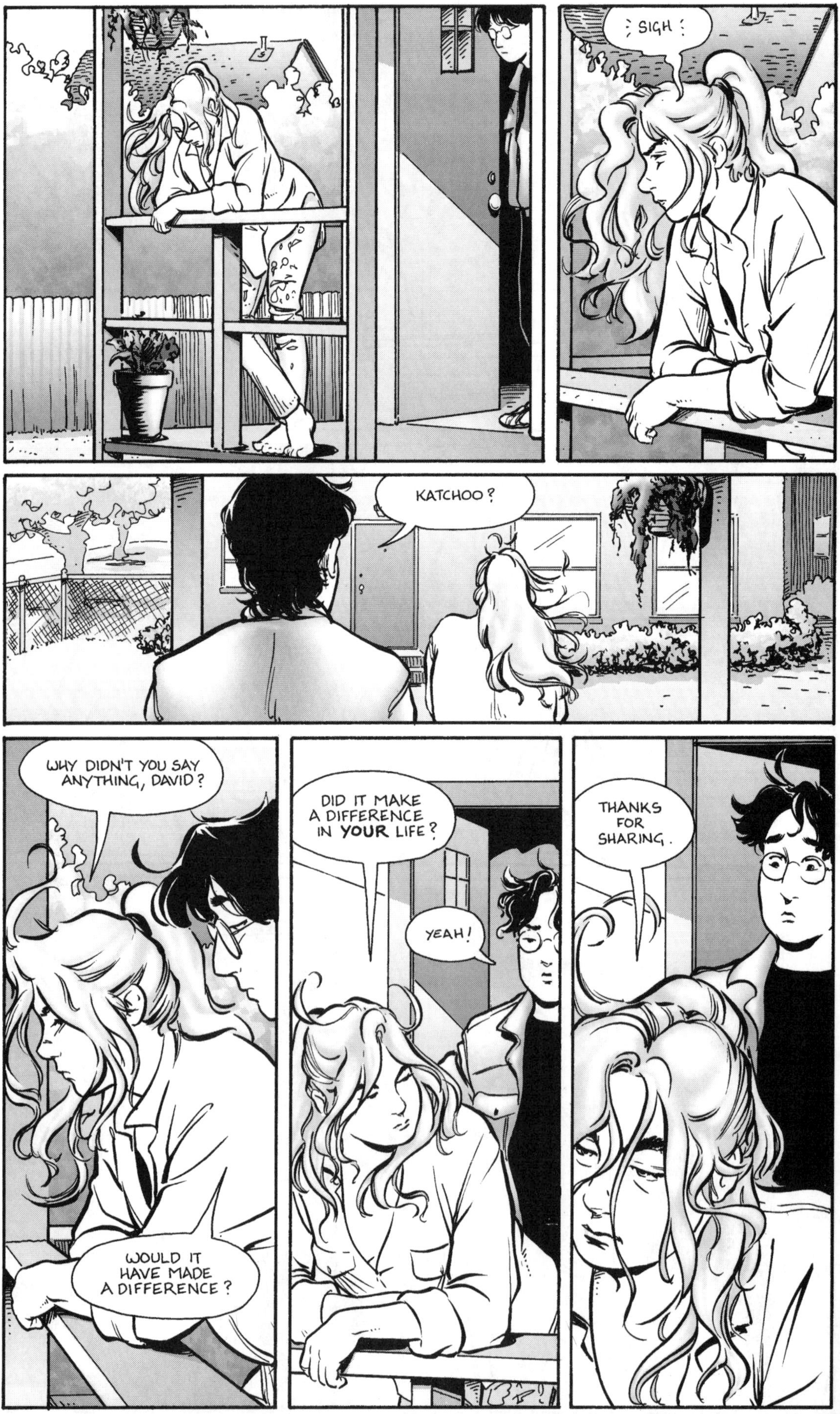

SIGH
KATCHOO?
WHY DIDN'T YOU SAY ANYTHING, DAVID?
WOULD IT HAVE MADE A DIFFERENCE?
DID IT MAKE A DIFFERENCE IN **YOUR** LIFE?
YEAH!
THANKS FOR SHARING.

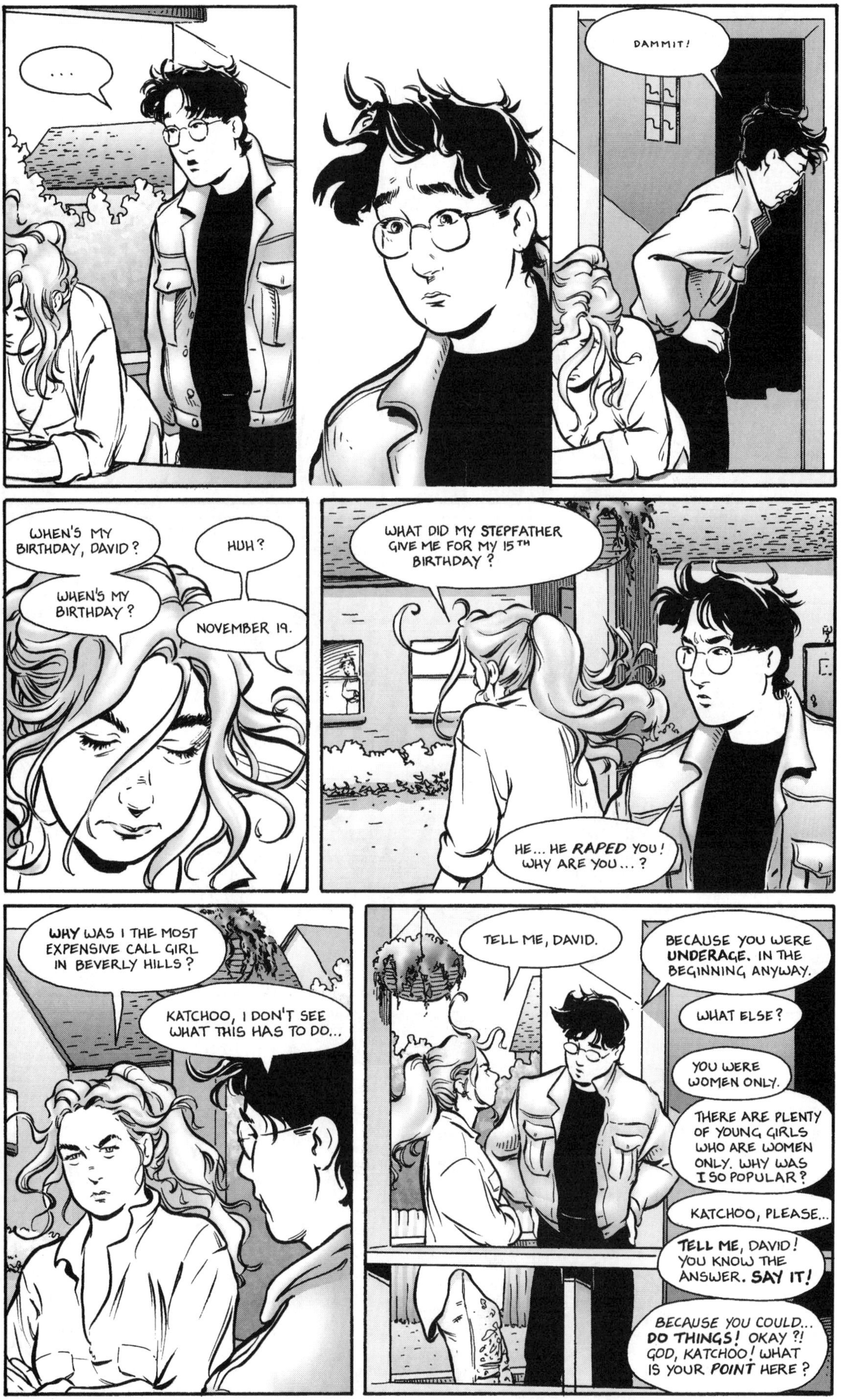
. . .
DAMMIT!
WHEN'S MY BIRTHDAY, DAVID?
HUH?
WHEN'S MY BIRTHDAY?
NOVEMBER 19.
WHAT DID MY STEPFATHER GIVE ME FOR MY 15TH BIRTHDAY?
HE... HE RAPED YOU! WHY ARE YOU...?
WHY WAS I THE MOST EXPENSIVE CALL GIRL IN BEVERLY HILLS?
KATCHOO, I DON'T SEE WHAT THIS HAS TO DO...
TELL ME, DAVID.
BECAUSE YOU WERE UNDERAGE. IN THE BEGINNING ANYWAY.
WHAT ELSE?
YOU WERE WOMEN ONLY.
THERE ARE PLENTY OF YOUNG GIRLS WHO ARE WOMEN ONLY. WHY WAS I SO POPULAR?
KATCHOO, PLEASE...
TELL ME, DAVID! YOU KNOW THE ANSWER. SAY IT!
BECAUSE YOU COULD... DO THINGS! OKAY?! GOD, KATCHOO! WHAT IS YOUR POINT HERE?

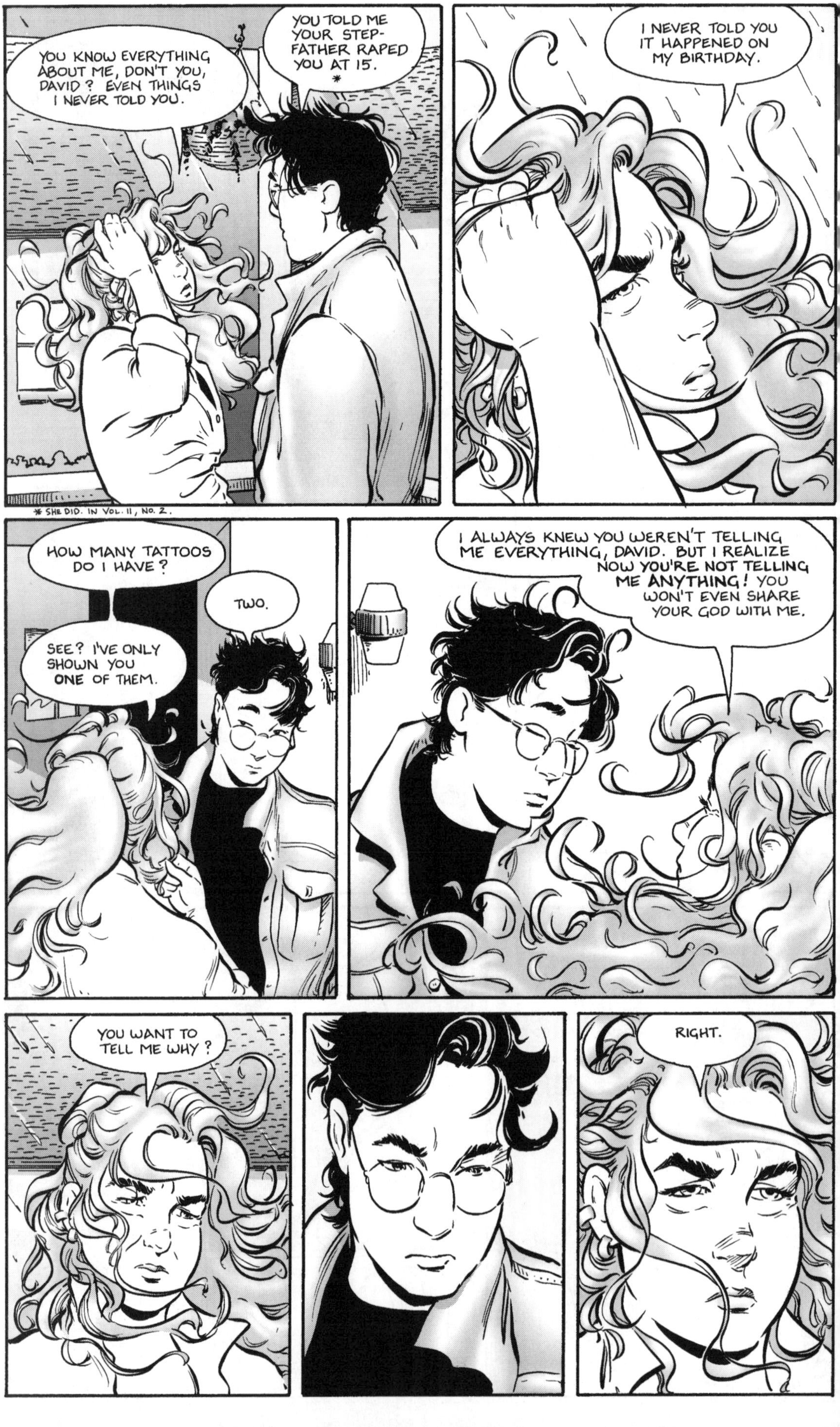
YOU KNOW EVERYTHING ABOUT ME, DON'T YOU, DAVID? EVEN THINGS I NEVER TOLD YOU.
YOU TOLD ME YOUR STEP-FATHER RAPED YOU AT 15. *
I NEVER TOLD YOU IT HAPPENED ON MY BIRTHDAY.
* SHE DID. IN VOL. II, NO. 2.
HOW MANY TATTOOS DO I HAVE?
TWO.
SEE? I'VE ONLY SHOWN YOU ONE OF THEM.
I ALWAYS KNEW YOU WEREN'T TELLING ME EVERYTHING, DAVID. BUT I REALIZE NOW YOU'RE NOT TELLING ME ANYTHING! YOU WON'T EVEN SHARE YOUR GOD WITH ME.
YOU WANT TO TELL ME WHY?
RIGHT.

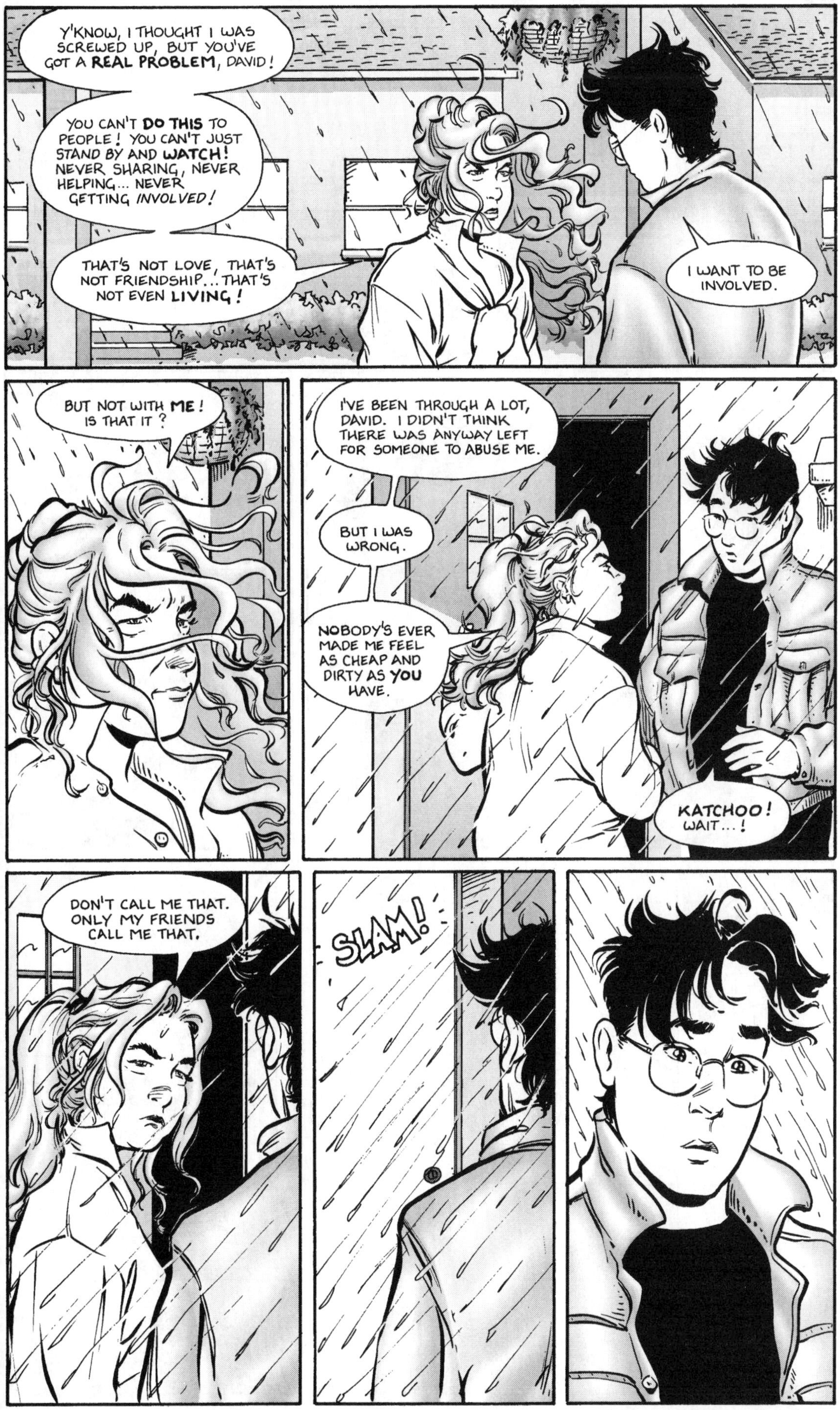

Y'KNOW, I THOUGHT I WAS SCREWED UP, BUT YOU'VE GOT A **REAL PROBLEM**, DAVID!
YOU CAN'T **DO THIS** TO PEOPLE! YOU CAN'T JUST STAND BY AND **WATCH**! NEVER SHARING, NEVER HELPING... NEVER GETTING *INVOLVED*!
THAT'S NOT LOVE, THAT'S NOT FRIENDSHIP... THAT'S NOT EVEN **LIVING**!
I WANT TO BE INVOLVED.
BUT NOT WITH **ME**! IS THAT IT?
I'VE BEEN THROUGH A LOT, DAVID. I DIDN'T THINK THERE WAS ANYWAY LEFT FOR SOMEONE TO ABUSE ME.
BUT I WAS WRONG.
NOBODY'S EVER MADE ME FEEL AS CHEAP AND DIRTY AS **YOU** HAVE.
KATCHOO! WAIT...!
DON'T CALL ME THAT. ONLY MY FRIENDS CALL ME THAT.
SLAM!

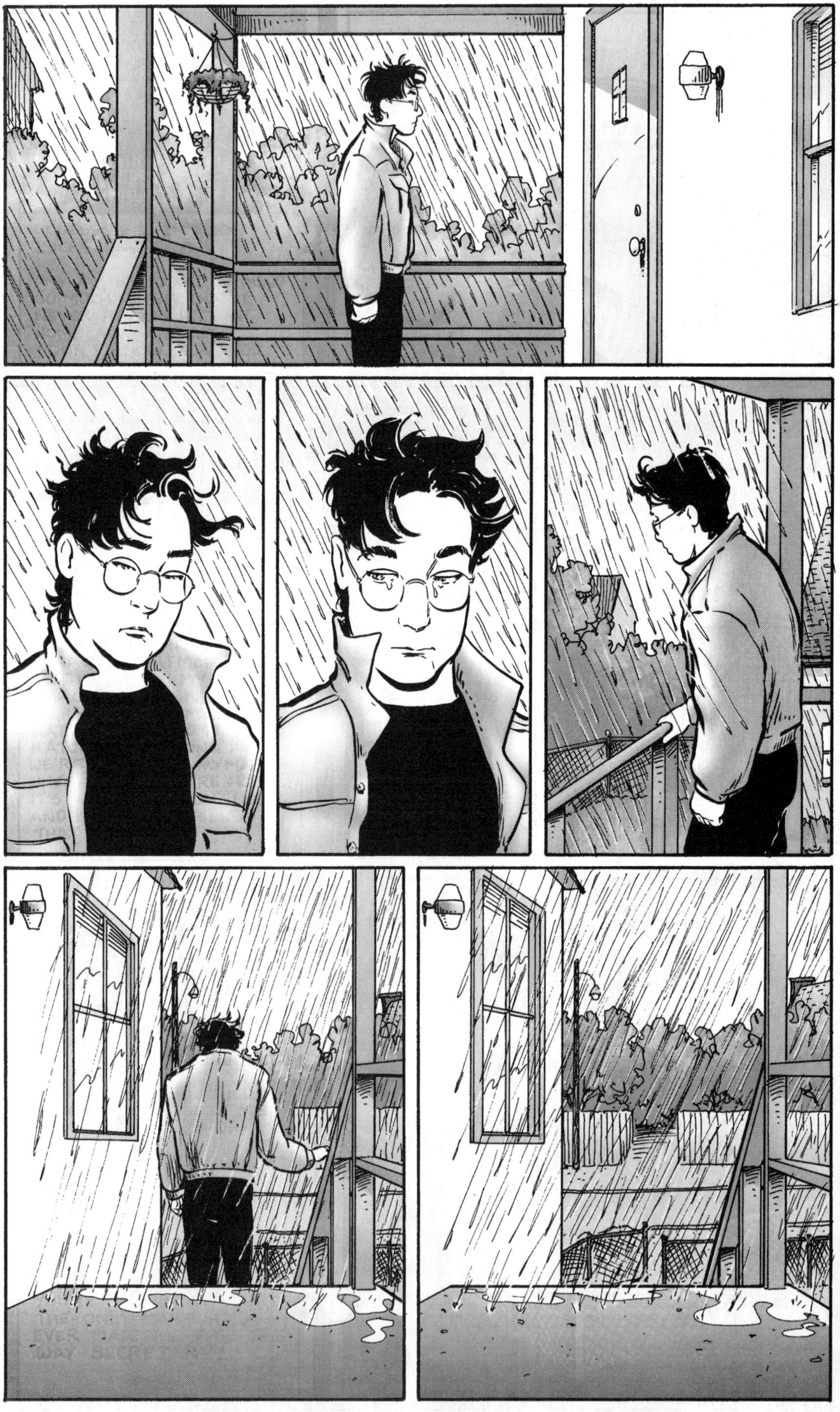

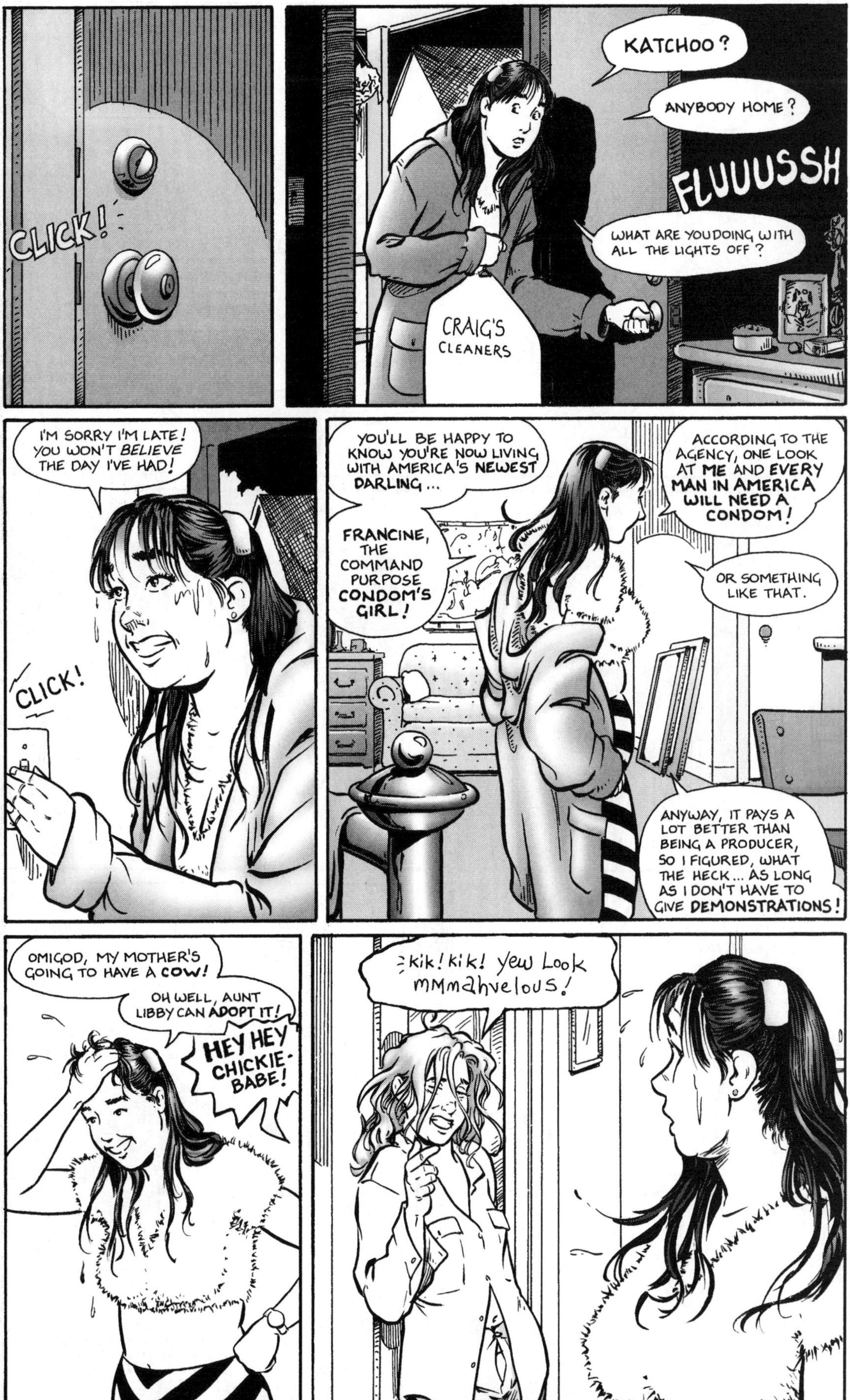
CLICK!
KATCHOO?
ANYBODY HOME?
FLUUUSSH
WHAT ARE YOU DOING WITH ALL THE LIGHTS OFF?
CRAIG'S CLEANERS
I'M SORRY I'M LATE! YOU WON'T BELIEVE THE DAY I'VE HAD!
CLICK!
YOU'LL BE HAPPY TO KNOW YOU'RE NOW LIVING WITH AMERICA'S NEWEST DARLING...
FRANCINE, THE COMMAND PURPOSE CONDOM'S GIRL!
ACCORDING TO THE AGENCY, ONE LOOK AT ME AND EVERY MAN IN AMERICA WILL NEED A CONDOM!
OR SOMETHING LIKE THAT.
ANYWAY, IT PAYS A LOT BETTER THAN BEING A PRODUCER, SO I FIGURED, WHAT THE HECK... AS LONG AS I DON'T HAVE TO GIVE DEMONSTRATIONS!
OMIGOD, MY MOTHER'S GOING TO HAVE A COW!
OH WELL, AUNT LIBBY CAN ADOPT IT!
HEY HEY CHICKIE-BABE!
kik! kik! yew Look mmmahvelous!

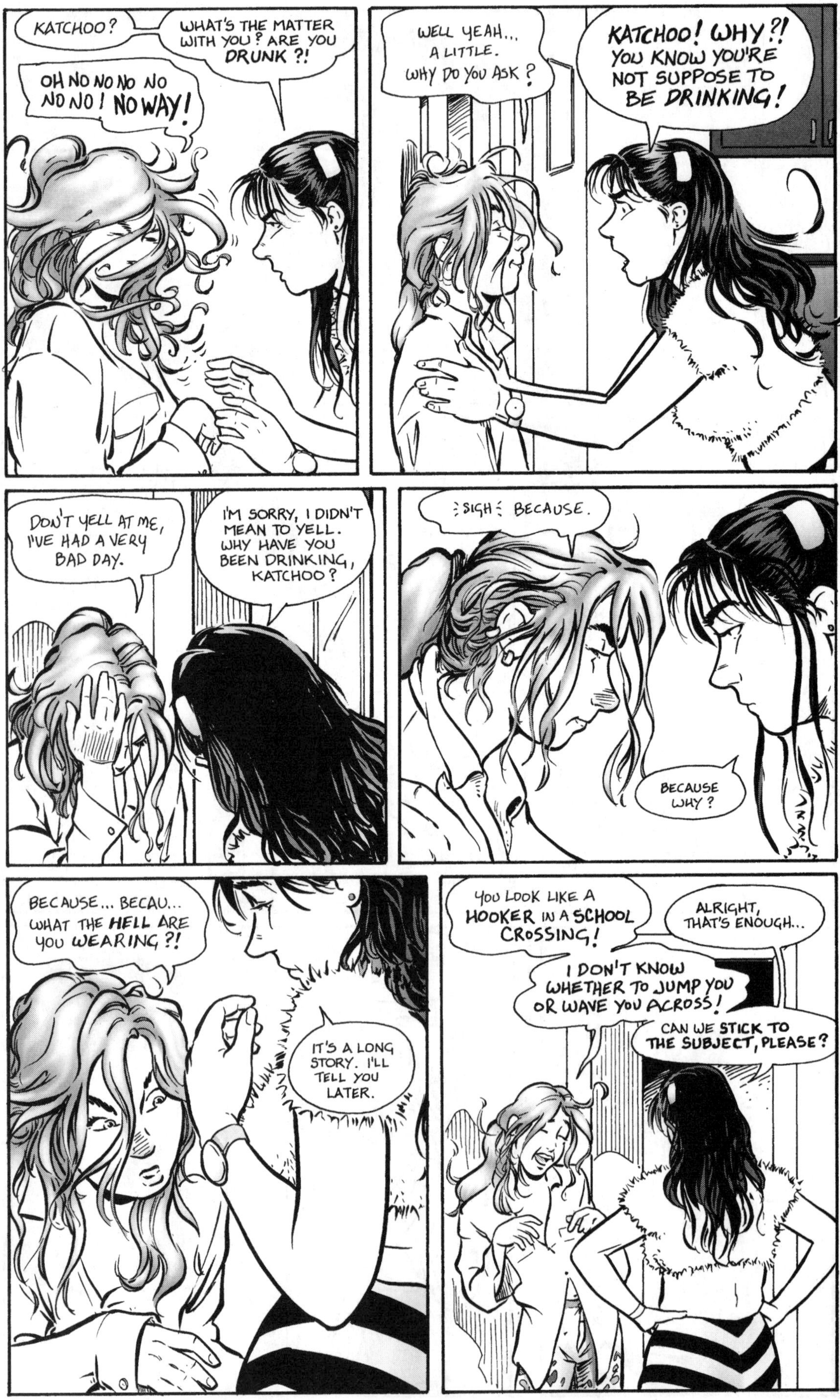
KATCHOO?
WHAT'S THE MATTER WITH YOU? ARE YOU DRUNK?!
OH NO NO NO NO NO NO! NO WAY!
WELL YEAH... A LITTLE. WHY DO YOU ASK?
KATCHOO! WHY?! YOU KNOW YOU'RE NOT SUPPOSE TO BE DRINKING!
DON'T YELL AT ME, I'VE HAD A VERY BAD DAY.
I'M SORRY, I DIDN'T MEAN TO YELL. WHY HAVE YOU BEEN DRINKING, KATCHOO?
SIGH BECAUSE.
BECAUSE WHY?
BECAUSE... BECAU... WHAT THE HELL ARE YOU WEARING?!
IT'S A LONG STORY. I'LL TELL YOU LATER.
YOU LOOK LIKE A HOOKER IN A SCHOOL CROSSING!
ALRIGHT, THAT'S ENOUGH...
I DON'T KNOW WHETHER TO JUMP YOU OR WAVE YOU ACROSS!
CAN WE STICK TO THE SUBJECT, PLEASE?

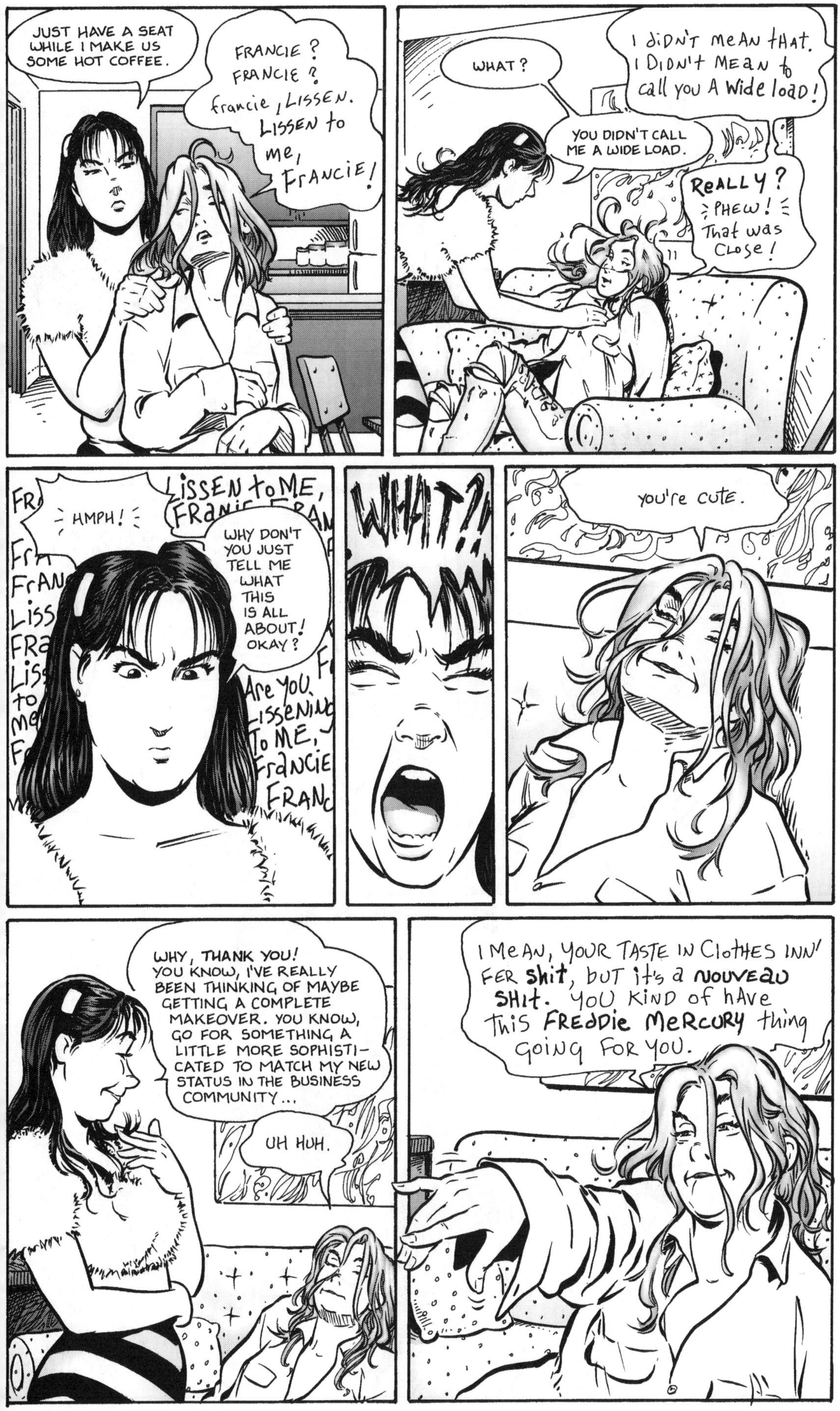
JUST HAVE A SEAT WHILE I MAKE US SOME HOT COFFEE.
FRANCIE? FRANCIE? francie, LISSEN. LISSEN to me, FRANCIE!
WHAT?
I DIDN'T MEAN THAT. I DIDN'T MEAN to call you A Wide load!
YOU DIDN'T CALL ME A WIDE LOAD.
REALLY? PHEW! That was Close!
HMPH!
LISSEN to ME,
WHY DON'T YOU JUST TELL ME WHAT THIS IS ALL ABOUT! OKAY?
Are you Lissening To ME,
WHAT?!!
you're cute.
WHY, THANK YOU! YOU KNOW, I'VE REALLY BEEN THINKING OF MAYBE GETTING A COMPLETE MAKEOVER. YOU KNOW, GO FOR SOMETHING A LITTLE MORE SOPHISTICATED TO MATCH MY NEW STATUS IN THE BUSINESS COMMUNITY...
UH HUH.
I MEAN, YOUR TASTE IN CLOTHES INN' FER SHIT, BUT IT'S A NOUVEAU SHIT. YOU KIND OF HAVE THIS FREDDIE MERCURY thing GOING FOR YOU.

I'LL MAKE THE COFFEE!

Y'KNOW... RUMOR HAS IT HE WAS HETOSEX... HERTEROSEX... HETO...

HE COULD'NT DANCE.

HE COMMITTED SUICIDE AFTER BEING UNJUSTLY ACCUSED OF NOT BEING A HOMOSEXUAL.*

WHAT THE...?

EUG!

*KATCHOO'S QUOTING NICHOLS AND MAY. SHE LOVES NICHOLS AND MAY. SO SHOULD YOU.

UH, KATCHOO...

YOU WANNA' TELL ME WHY YOUR PAINTING OF DAVID IS SMASHED INTO THE PANTRY?

FLOO

I DUNNO... SEEMED LIKE A SWELL IDEA AT THE TIME.

IS THAT WHAT THIS IS ALL ABOUT? DID YOU AND DAVID HAVE A FIGHT? IS THAT WHY YOU'VE BEEN DRINKING?

UHMMM...

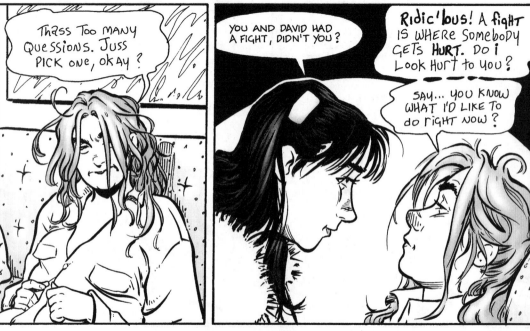

THASS TOO MANY QUESSIONS. JUSS PICK ONE, OKAY?

YOU AND DAVID HAD A FIGHT, DIDN'T YOU?

RIDIC'LOUS! A FIGHT IS WHERE SOMEBODY GETS HURT. DO I LOOK HURT TO YOU?

SAY... YOU KNOW WHAT I'D LIKE TO DO RIGHT NOW?

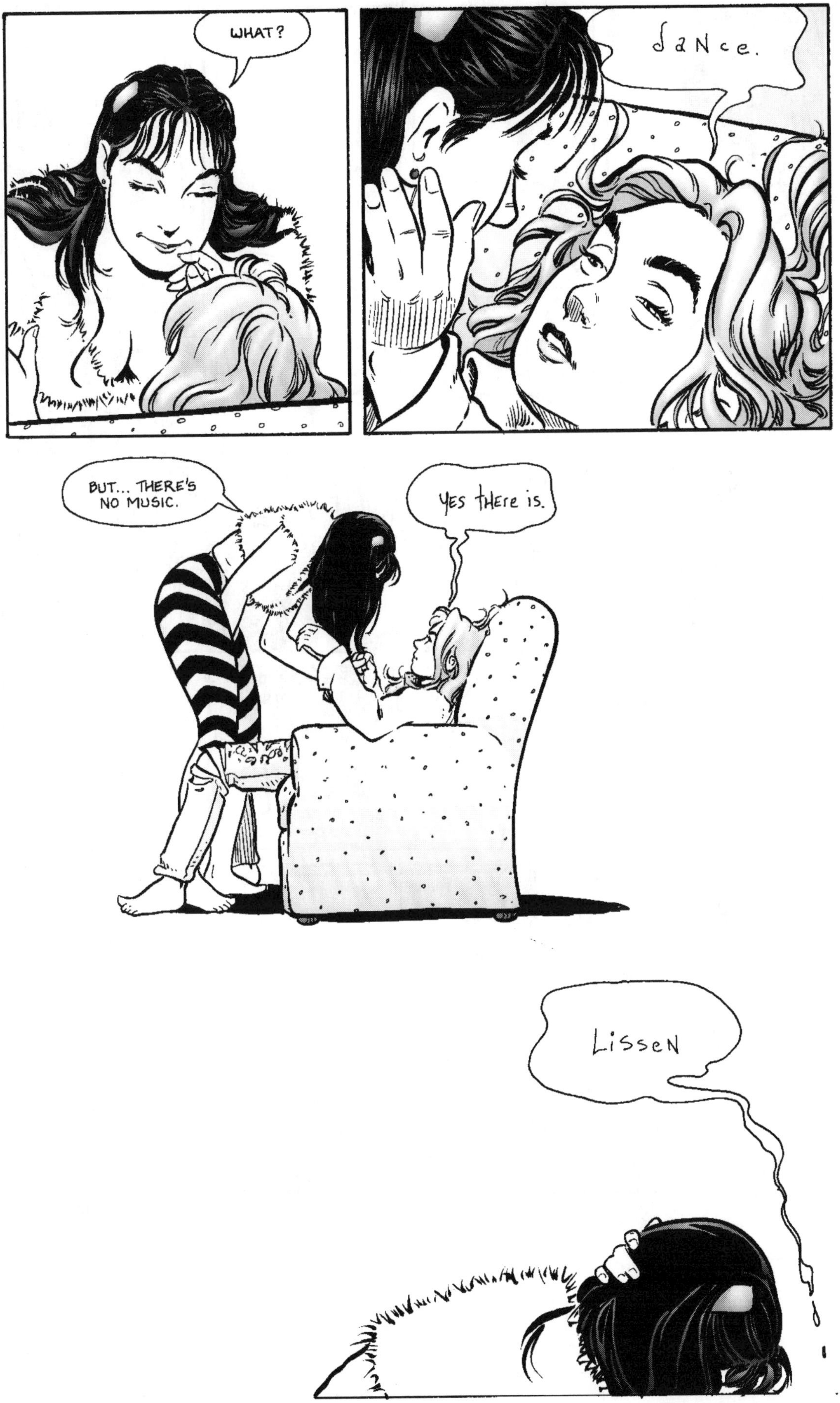
WHAT?
dance.
BUT... THERE'S NO MUSIC.
yes there is.
Lissen

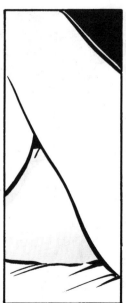

WHAT?
...OH YEAH.

COME ON BABY, COME ON. OH GOD, THAT FEELS SO GOOD. OH YES, LIKE THAT. THAT'S IT. OH GOD, YOU'RE AN ANIMAL. DO IT. YES. YES. YES.

OH YES, I'M CO...
YAWN!

OH GOD THAT WAS INCREDIBLE. IT'S NEVER FELT LIKE THAT BEFORE. I WON'T BE ABLE TO WALK FOR A WEEK.

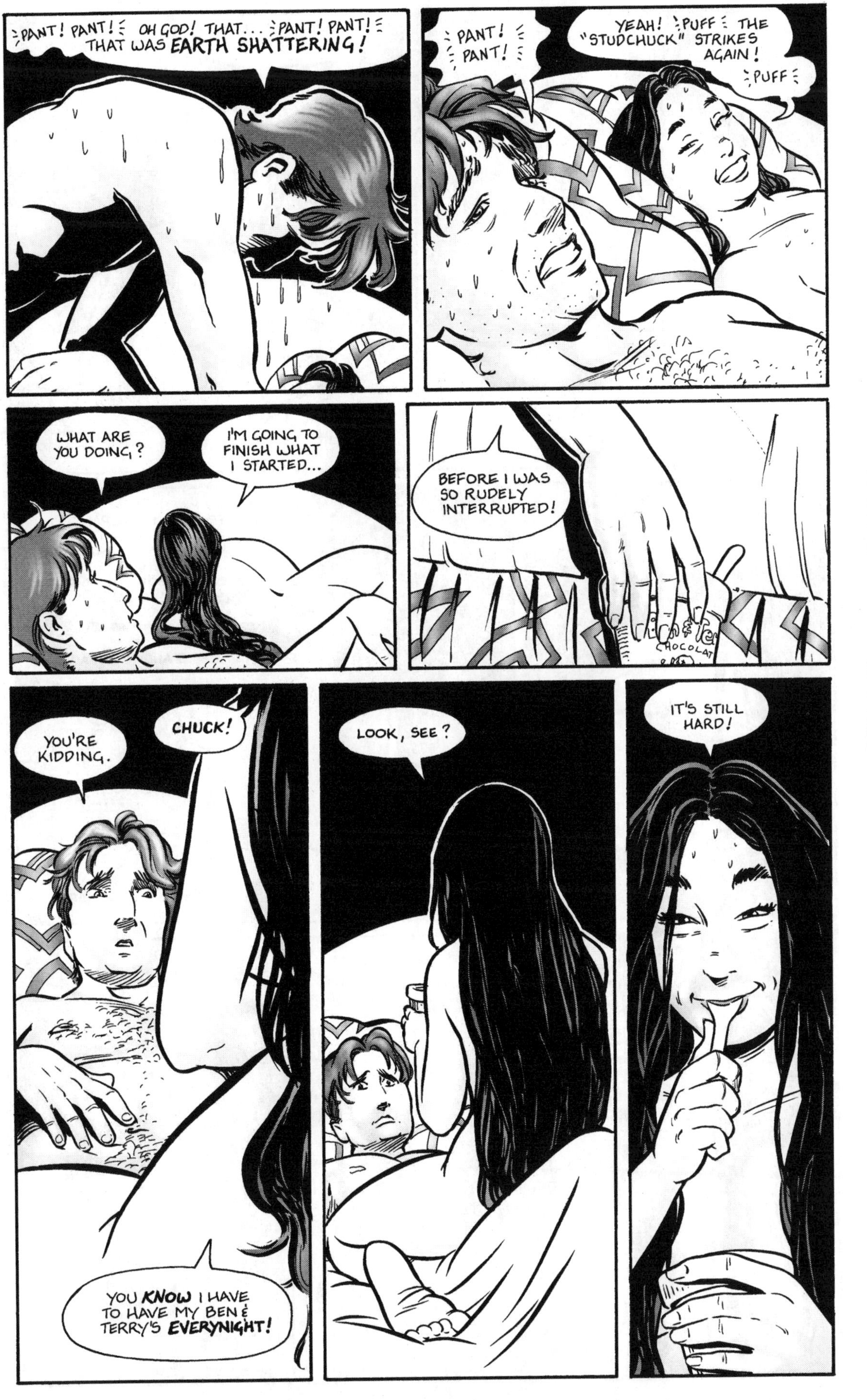
PANT! PANT! OH GOD! THAT... PANT! PANT! THAT WAS EARTH SHATTERING!
PANT! PANT!
YEAH! PUFF THE "STUDCHUCK" STRIKES AGAIN!
PUFF
WHAT ARE YOU DOING?
I'M GOING TO FINISH WHAT I STARTED...
BEFORE I WAS SO RUDELY INTERRUPTED!
CHOCOLAT
YOU'RE KIDDING.
CHUCK!
YOU KNOW I HAVE TO HAVE MY BEN & TERRY'S EVERYNIGHT!
LOOK, SEE?
IT'S STILL HARD!

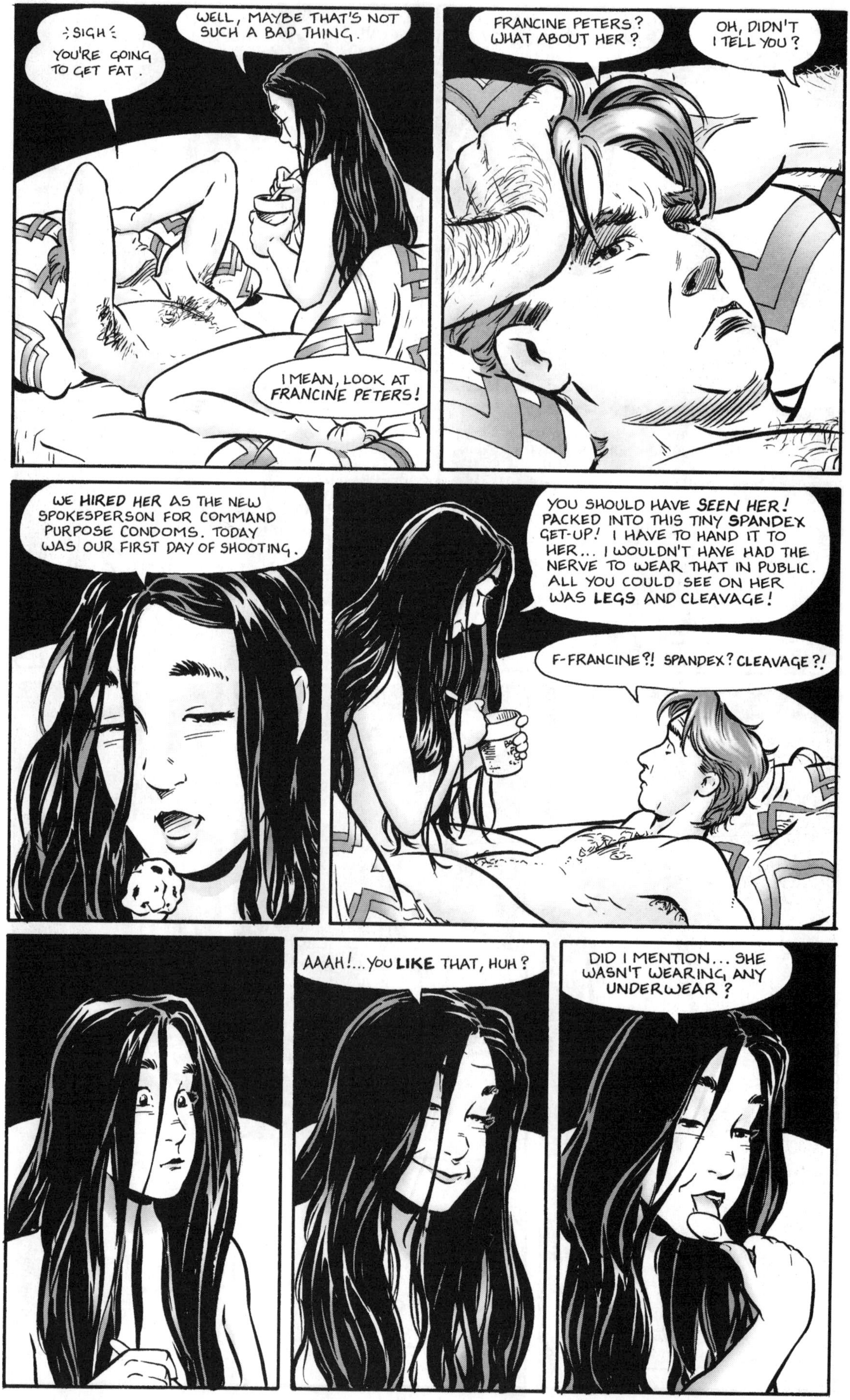

SIGH
YOU'RE GOING TO GET FAT.
WELL, MAYBE THAT'S NOT SUCH A BAD THING.
I MEAN, LOOK AT FRANCINE PETERS!
FRANCINE PETERS? WHAT ABOUT HER?
OH, DIDN'T I TELL YOU?
WE HIRED HER AS THE NEW SPOKESPERSON FOR COMMAND PURPOSE CONDOMS. TODAY WAS OUR FIRST DAY OF SHOOTING.
YOU SHOULD HAVE SEEN HER! PACKED INTO THIS TINY SPANDEX GET-UP! I HAVE TO HAND IT TO HER... I WOULDN'T HAVE HAD THE NERVE TO WEAR THAT IN PUBLIC. ALL YOU COULD SEE ON HER WAS LEGS AND CLEAVAGE!
F-FRANCINE?! SPANDEX? CLEAVAGE?!
AAAH!... YOU LIKE THAT, HUH?
DID I MENTION... SHE WASN'T WEARING ANY UNDERWEAR?

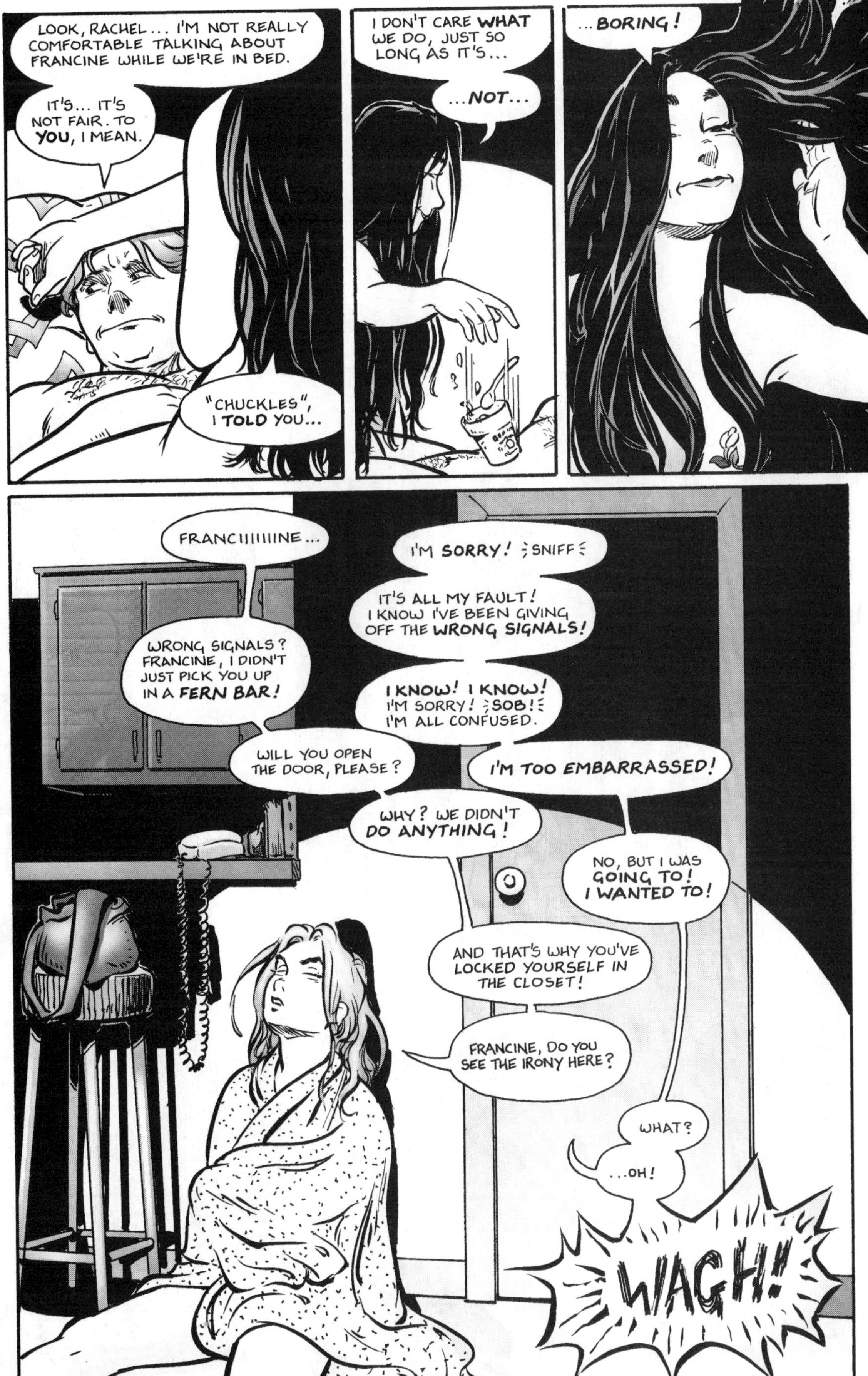
LOOK, RACHEL... I'M NOT REALLY COMFORTABLE TALKING ABOUT FRANCINE WHILE WE'RE IN BED.
IT'S... IT'S NOT FAIR. TO YOU, I MEAN.
"CHUCKLES", I TOLD YOU...
I DON'T CARE WHAT WE DO, JUST SO LONG AS IT'S...
...NOT...
...BORING!
FRANCIIIIIIINE...
I'M SORRY! ;SNIFF;
IT'S ALL MY FAULT! I KNOW I'VE BEEN GIVING OFF THE WRONG SIGNALS!
WRONG SIGNALS? FRANCINE, I DIDN'T JUST PICK YOU UP IN A FERN BAR!
I KNOW! I KNOW! I'M SORRY! ;SOB! I'M ALL CONFUSED.
WILL YOU OPEN THE DOOR, PLEASE?
I'M TOO EMBARRASSED!
WHY? WE DIDN'T DO ANYTHING!
NO, BUT I WAS GOING TO! I WANTED TO!
AND THAT'S WHY YOU'VE LOCKED YOURSELF IN THE CLOSET!
FRANCINE, DO YOU SEE THE IRONY HERE?
WHAT?
...OH!
WAGH!!

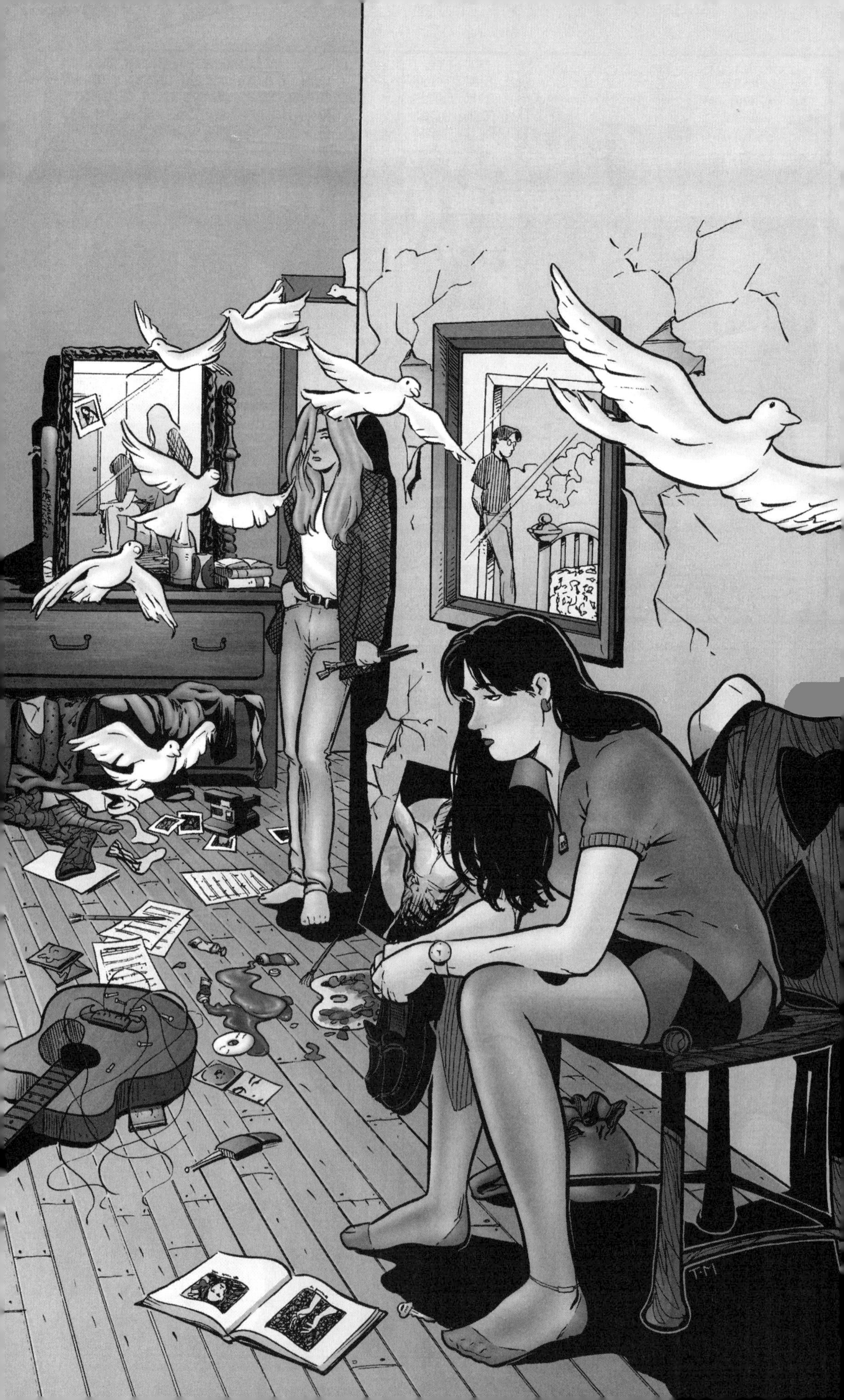
T·M

WHAT'S THE MOST **EMBARRASS-ING** THING THAT'S EVER HAPPENED TO YOU?

DID YOU SPEND YOUR FIRST DATE WITH FOOD ON YOUR TEETH?

DID YOU GET CAUGHT SHOP-LIFTING IN THE MALL WHEN YOU WERE 15?

DID YOUR ROBE COME OFF DURING THE SENIOR PLAY?

MAYBE YOU CALLED YOUR FIRST BOSS BILL FOR A WEEK BEFORE SOMEBODY TOLD YOU IT WAS BOB.

OR MAYBE YOU ALMOST HAD **SEX** WITH YOUR BEST FRIEND BUT COULDN'T GO THROUGH WITH IT AND LOCKED YOUR SELF IN THE CLOSET BE-CAUSE YOU WERE **SO EM-BARRASSED** AND YOU WOULDN'T COME OUT AND YOUR BEST FRIEND SAT OUTSIDE THE DOOR HALF THE NIGHT UNTIL SHE FELL ASLEEP AND YOU SPENT THE REST OF THE NIGHT ON THE COUCH AND TRIED TO **SNEAK OUT** TO WORK THE NEXT MORNING WITHOUT WAKING HER UP AND SHE CAUGHT YOU DOING IT AND TOOK A **POLOROID** OF YOU DOING IT TO SHOW YOU HOW **STUPID** YOU LOOKED DOING IT.

K-FLASH!

OKAY, SO MAYBE YOUR ROBE *DIDN'T* COME OFF DURING THE SENIOR PLAY. IT DOESN'T MATTER...

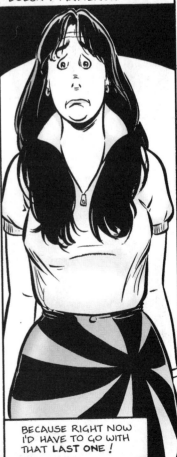

BECAUSE RIGHT NOW I'D HAVE TO GO WITH THAT **LAST ONE**!

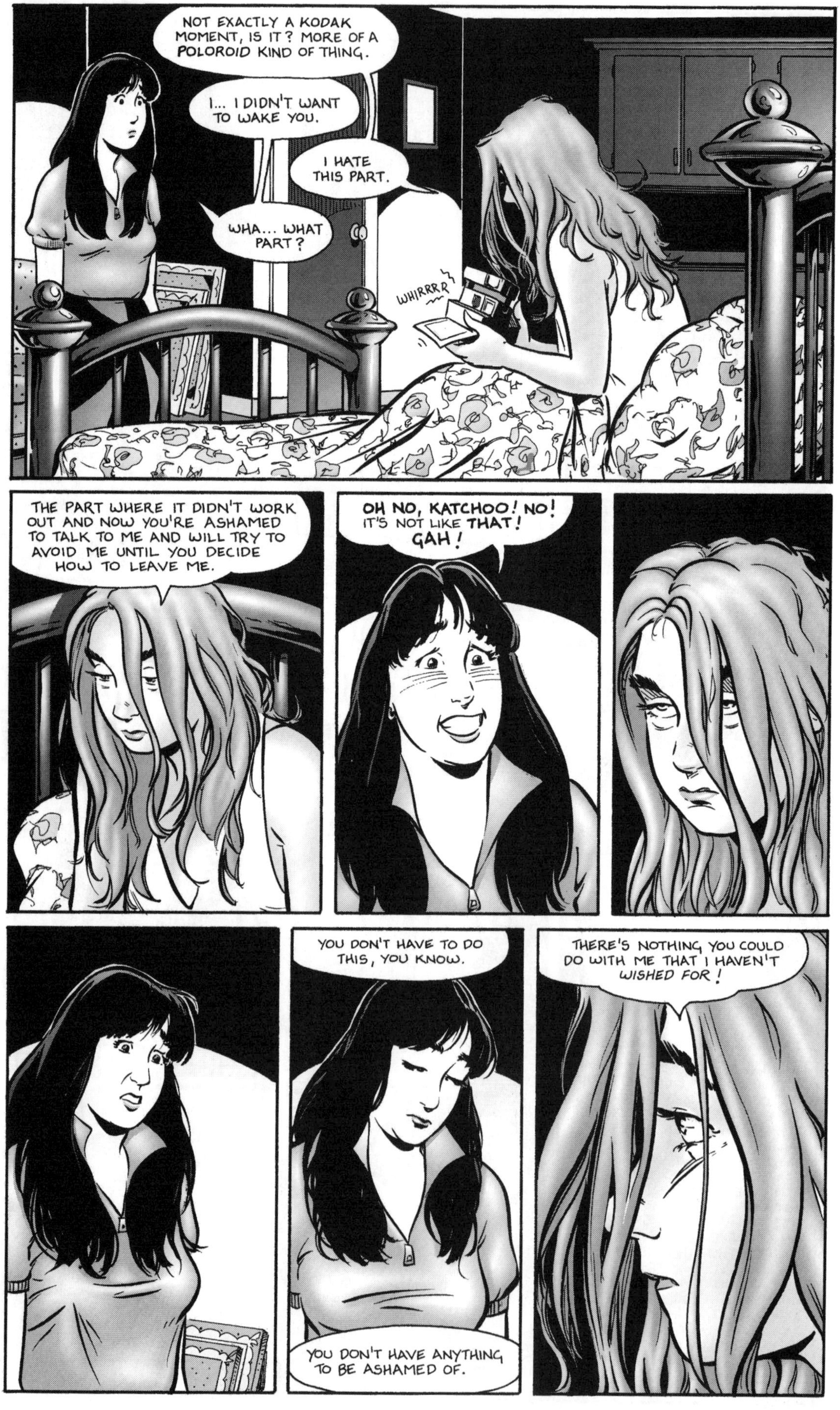
NOT EXACTLY A KODAK MOMENT, IS IT? MORE OF A POLOROID KIND OF THING.
I... I DIDN'T WANT TO WAKE YOU.
I HATE THIS PART.
WHA... WHAT PART?
WHIRRRR
THE PART WHERE IT DIDN'T WORK OUT AND NOW YOU'RE ASHAMED TO TALK TO ME AND WILL TRY TO AVOID ME UNTIL YOU DECIDE HOW TO LEAVE ME.
OH NO, KATCHOO! NO! IT'S NOT LIKE THAT! GAH!
YOU DON'T HAVE TO DO THIS, YOU KNOW.
YOU DON'T HAVE ANYTHING TO BE ASHAMED OF.
THERE'S NOTHING YOU COULD DO WITH ME THAT I HAVEN'T WISHED FOR!

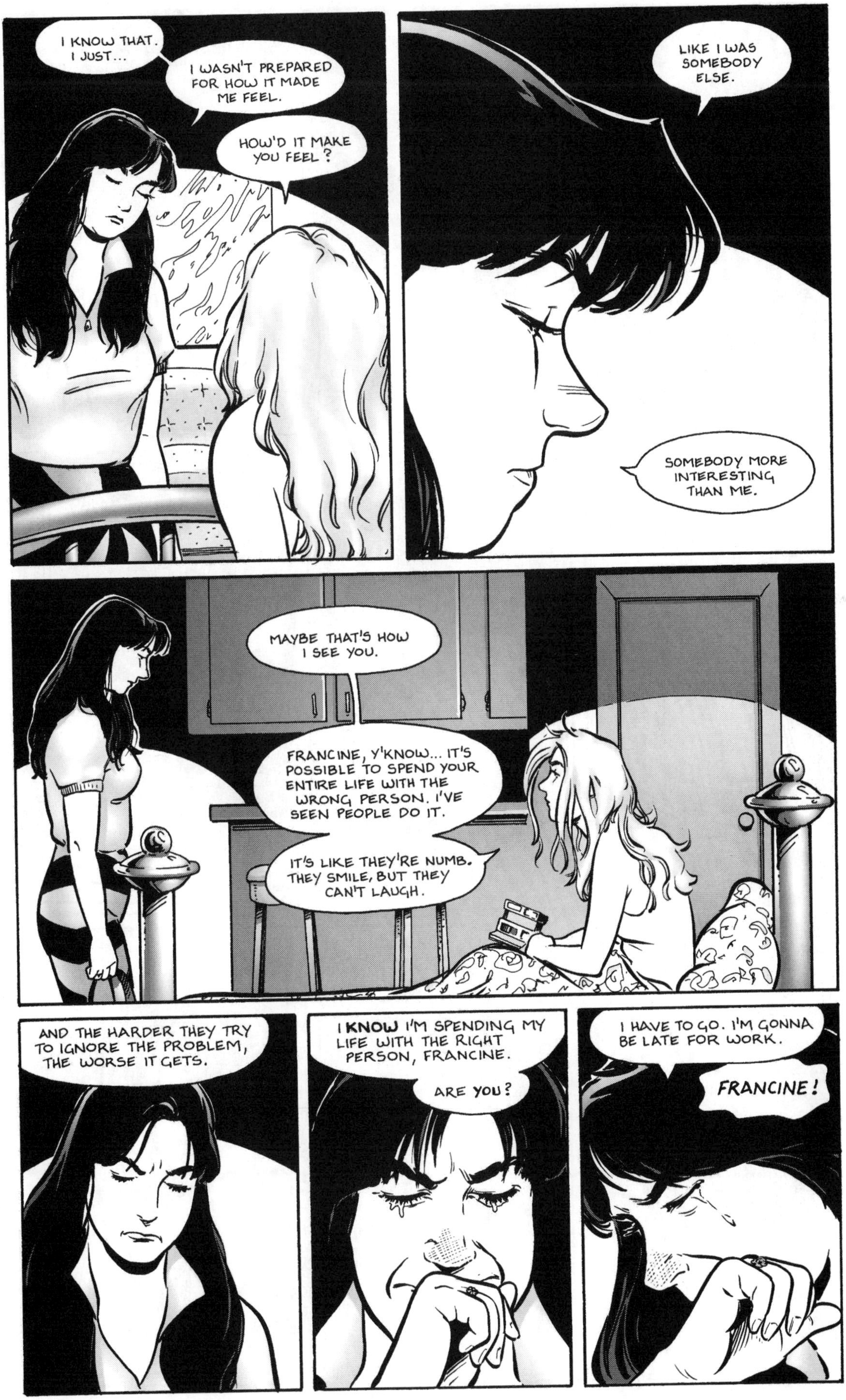
I KNOW THAT. I JUST...
I WASN'T PREPARED FOR HOW IT MADE ME FEEL.
HOW'D IT MAKE YOU FEEL?
LIKE I WAS SOMEBODY ELSE.
SOMEBODY MORE INTERESTING THAN ME.
MAYBE THAT'S HOW I SEE YOU.
FRANCINE, Y'KNOW... IT'S POSSIBLE TO SPEND YOUR ENTIRE LIFE WITH THE WRONG PERSON. I'VE SEEN PEOPLE DO IT.
IT'S LIKE THEY'RE NUMB. THEY SMILE, BUT THEY CAN'T LAUGH.
AND THE HARDER THEY TRY TO IGNORE THE PROBLEM, THE WORSE IT GETS.
I KNOW I'M SPENDING MY LIFE WITH THE RIGHT PERSON, FRANCINE.
ARE YOU?
I HAVE TO GO. I'M GONNA BE LATE FOR WORK.
FRANCINE!

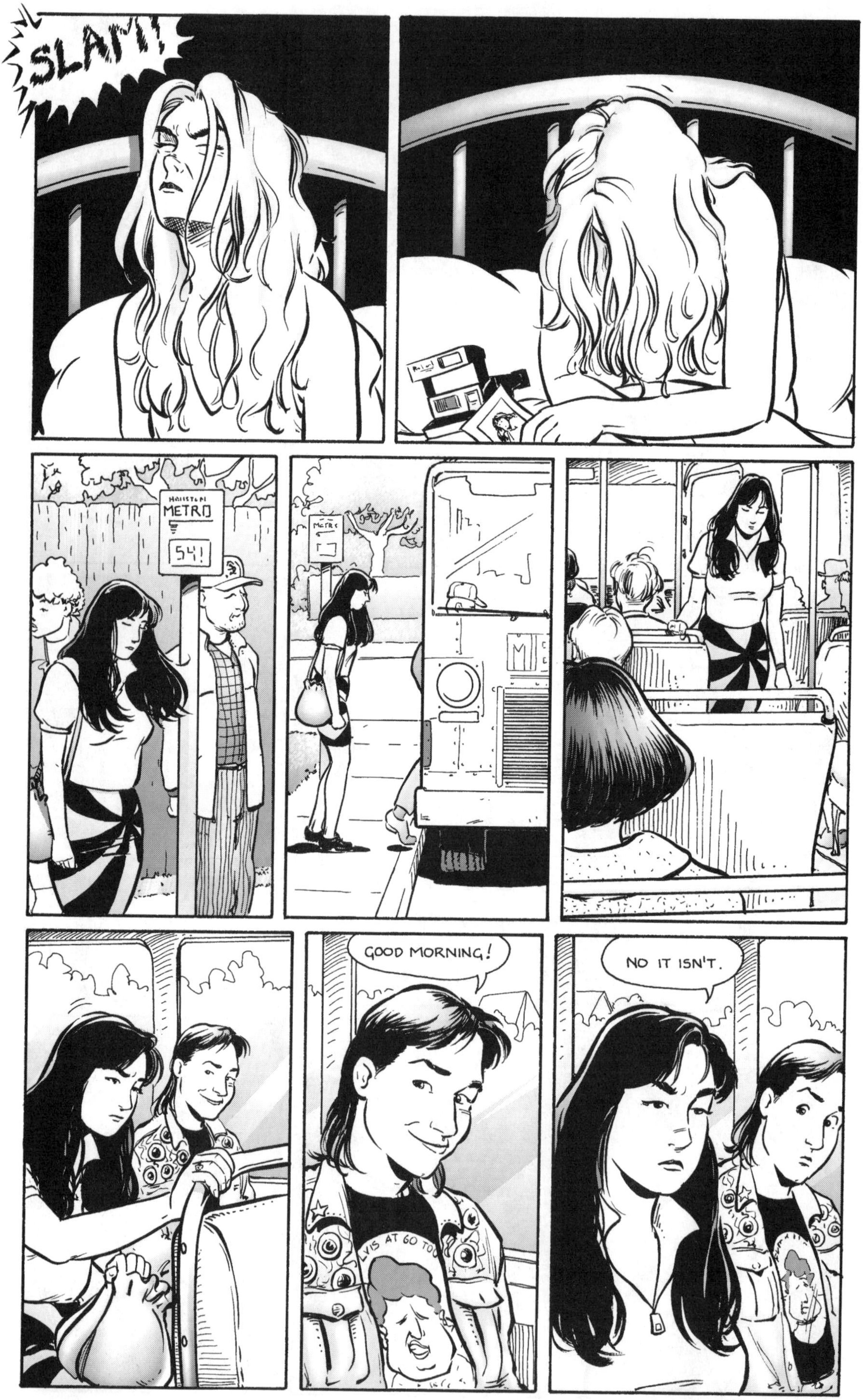
SLAM!
METRO
54!
METRO
GOOD MORNING!
NO IT ISN'T.

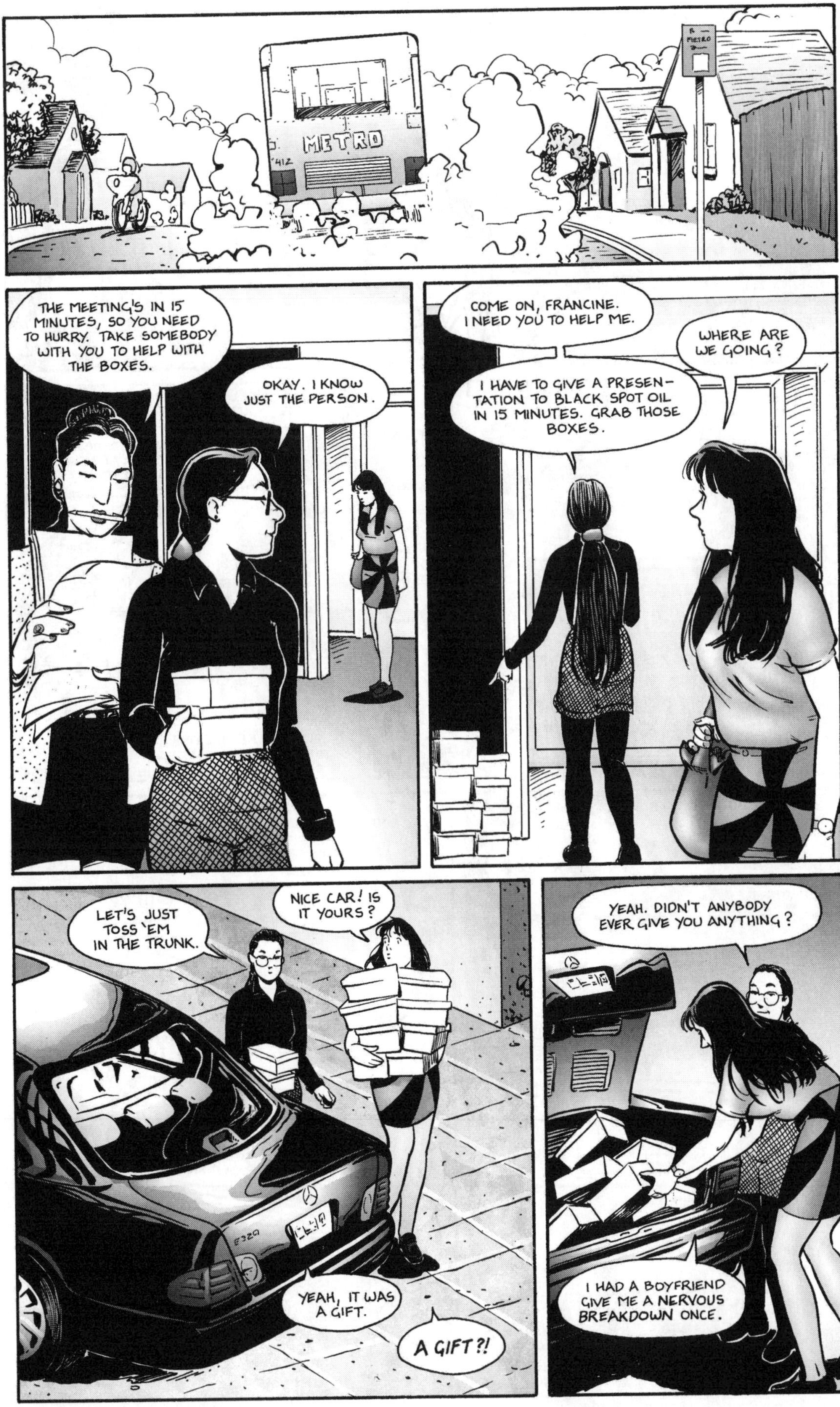
METRO
THE MEETING'S IN 15 MINUTES, SO YOU NEED TO HURRY. TAKE SOMEBODY WITH YOU TO HELP WITH THE BOXES.
OKAY. I KNOW JUST THE PERSON.
COME ON, FRANCINE. I NEED YOU TO HELP ME.
I HAVE TO GIVE A PRESENTATION TO BLACK SPOT OIL IN 15 MINUTES. GRAB THOSE BOXES.
WHERE ARE WE GOING?
LET'S JUST TOSS 'EM IN THE TRUNK.
NICE CAR! IS IT YOURS?
YEAH, IT WAS A GIFT.
A GIFT?!
YEAH. DIDN'T ANYBODY EVER GIVE YOU ANYTHING?
I HAD A BOYFRIEND GIVE ME A NERVOUS BREAKDOWN ONCE.

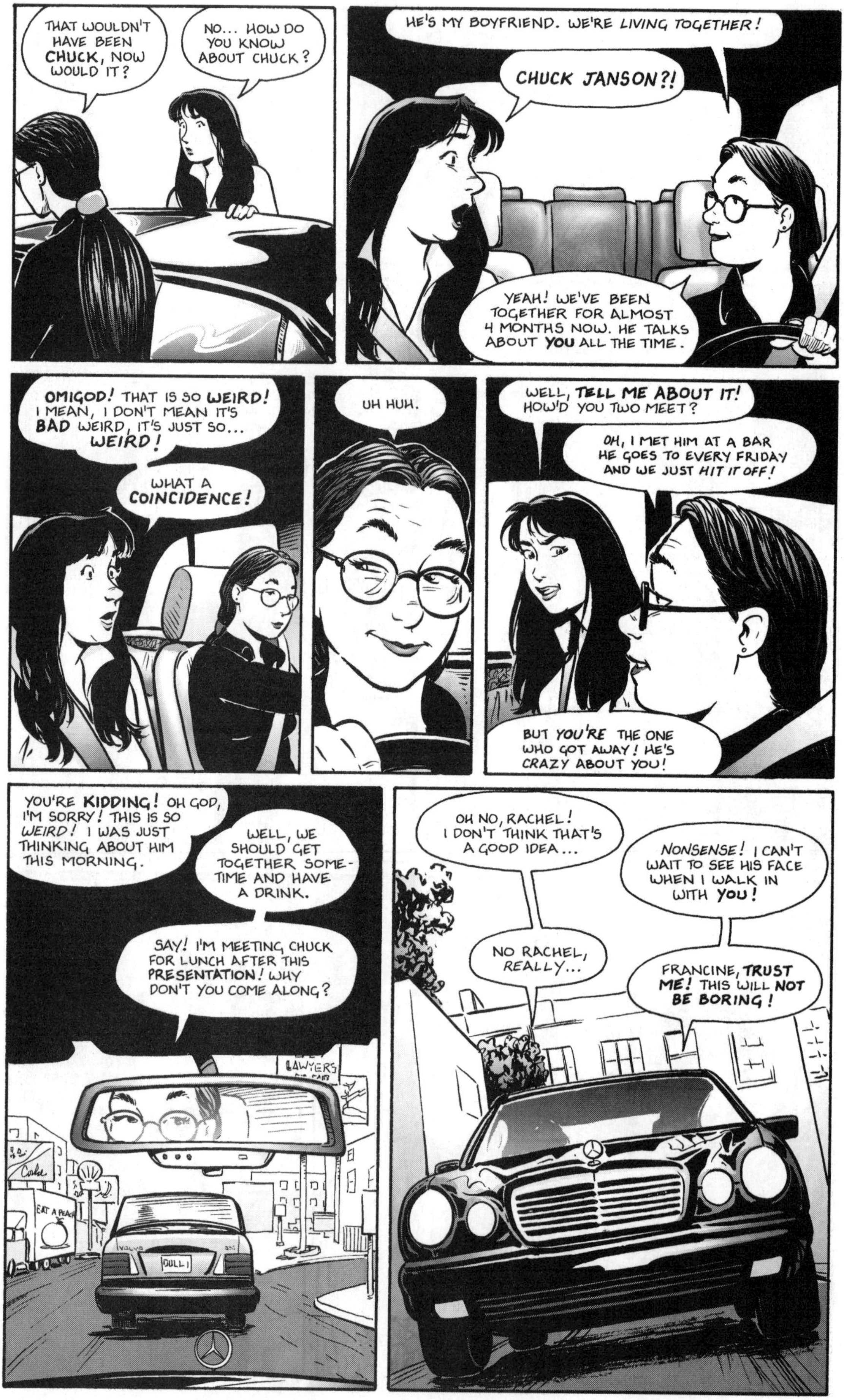
THAT WOULDN'T HAVE BEEN CHUCK, NOW WOULD IT?
NO... HOW DO YOU KNOW ABOUT CHUCK?
HE'S MY BOYFRIEND. WE'RE LIVING TOGETHER!
CHUCK JANSON?!
YEAH! WE'VE BEEN TOGETHER FOR ALMOST 4 MONTHS NOW. HE TALKS ABOUT YOU ALL THE TIME.
OMIGOD! THAT IS SO WEIRD! I MEAN, I DON'T MEAN IT'S BAD WEIRD, IT'S JUST SO... WEIRD!
WHAT A COINCIDENCE!
UH HUH.
WELL, TELL ME ABOUT IT! HOW'D YOU TWO MEET?
OH, I MET HIM AT A BAR HE GOES TO EVERY FRIDAY AND WE JUST HIT IT OFF!
BUT YOU'RE THE ONE WHO GOT AWAY! HE'S CRAZY ABOUT YOU!
YOU'RE KIDDING! OH GOD, I'M SORRY! THIS IS SO WEIRD! I WAS JUST THINKING ABOUT HIM THIS MORNING.
WELL, WE SHOULD GET TOGETHER SOME-TIME AND HAVE A DRINK.
SAY! I'M MEETING CHUCK FOR LUNCH AFTER THIS PRESENTATION! WHY DON'T YOU COME ALONG?
LAWYERS
EAT A PEACH
DULL
OH NO, RACHEL! I DON'T THINK THAT'S A GOOD IDEA...
NONSENSE! I CAN'T WAIT TO SEE HIS FACE WHEN I WALK IN WITH YOU!
NO RACHEL, REALLY...
FRANCINE, TRUST ME! THIS WILL NOT BE BORING!

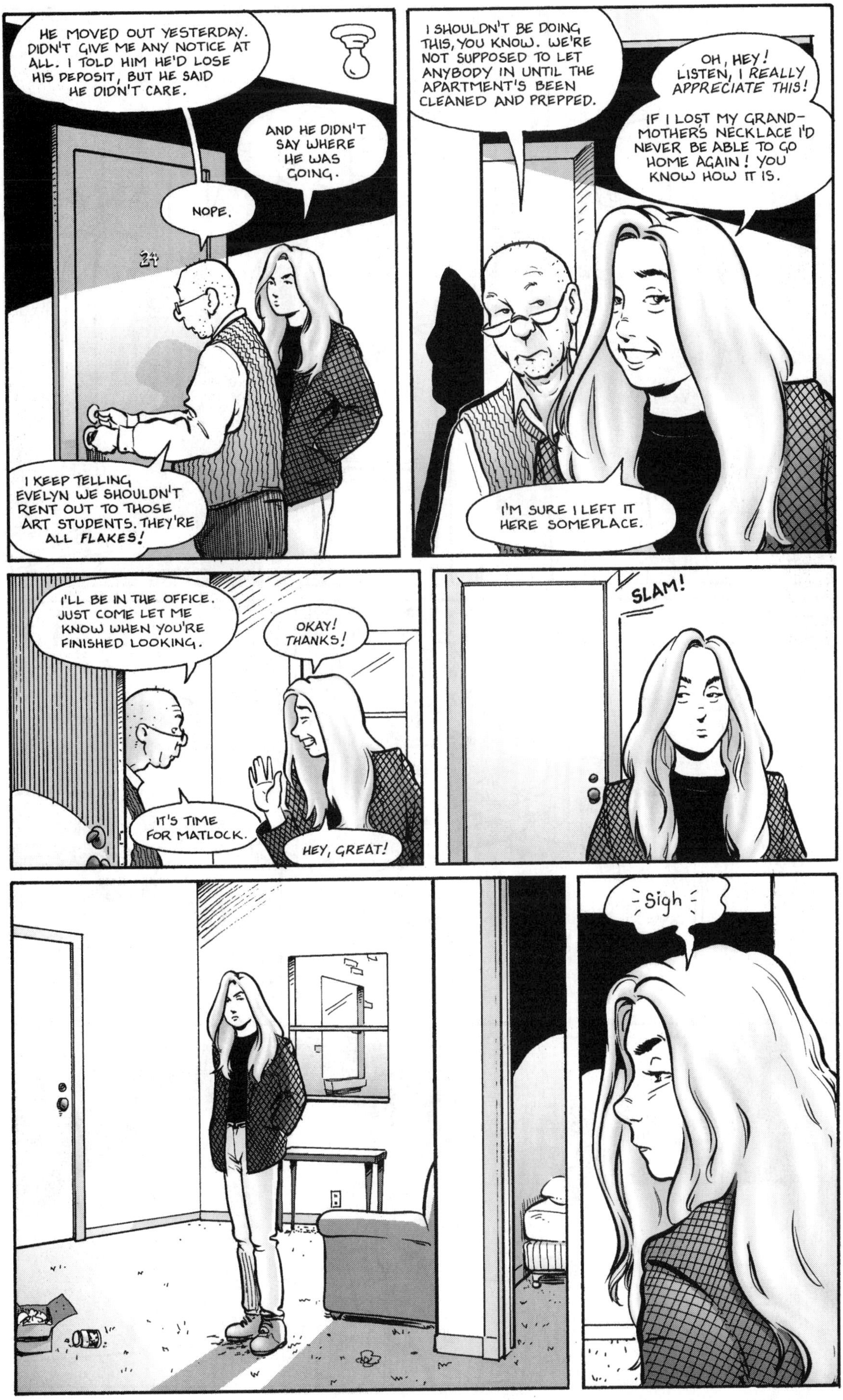
HE MOVED OUT YESTERDAY. DIDN'T GIVE ME ANY NOTICE AT ALL. I TOLD HIM HE'D LOSE HIS DEPOSIT, BUT HE SAID HE DIDN'T CARE.
AND HE DIDN'T SAY WHERE HE WAS GOING.
NOPE.
24
I KEEP TELLING EVELYN WE SHOULDN'T RENT OUT TO THOSE ART STUDENTS. THEY'RE ALL *FLAKES*!
I SHOULDN'T BE DOING THIS, YOU KNOW. WE'RE NOT SUPPOSED TO LET ANYBODY IN UNTIL THE APARTMENT'S BEEN CLEANED AND PREPPED.
OH, HEY! LISTEN, I *REALLY APPRECIATE THIS*!
IF I LOST MY GRAND-MOTHER'S NECKLACE I'D NEVER BE ABLE TO GO HOME AGAIN! YOU KNOW HOW IT IS.
I'M SURE I LEFT IT HERE SOMEPLACE.
I'LL BE IN THE OFFICE. JUST COME LET ME KNOW WHEN YOU'RE FINISHED LOOKING.
OKAY! THANKS!
IT'S TIME FOR MATLOCK.
HEY, GREAT!
SLAM!
Sigh

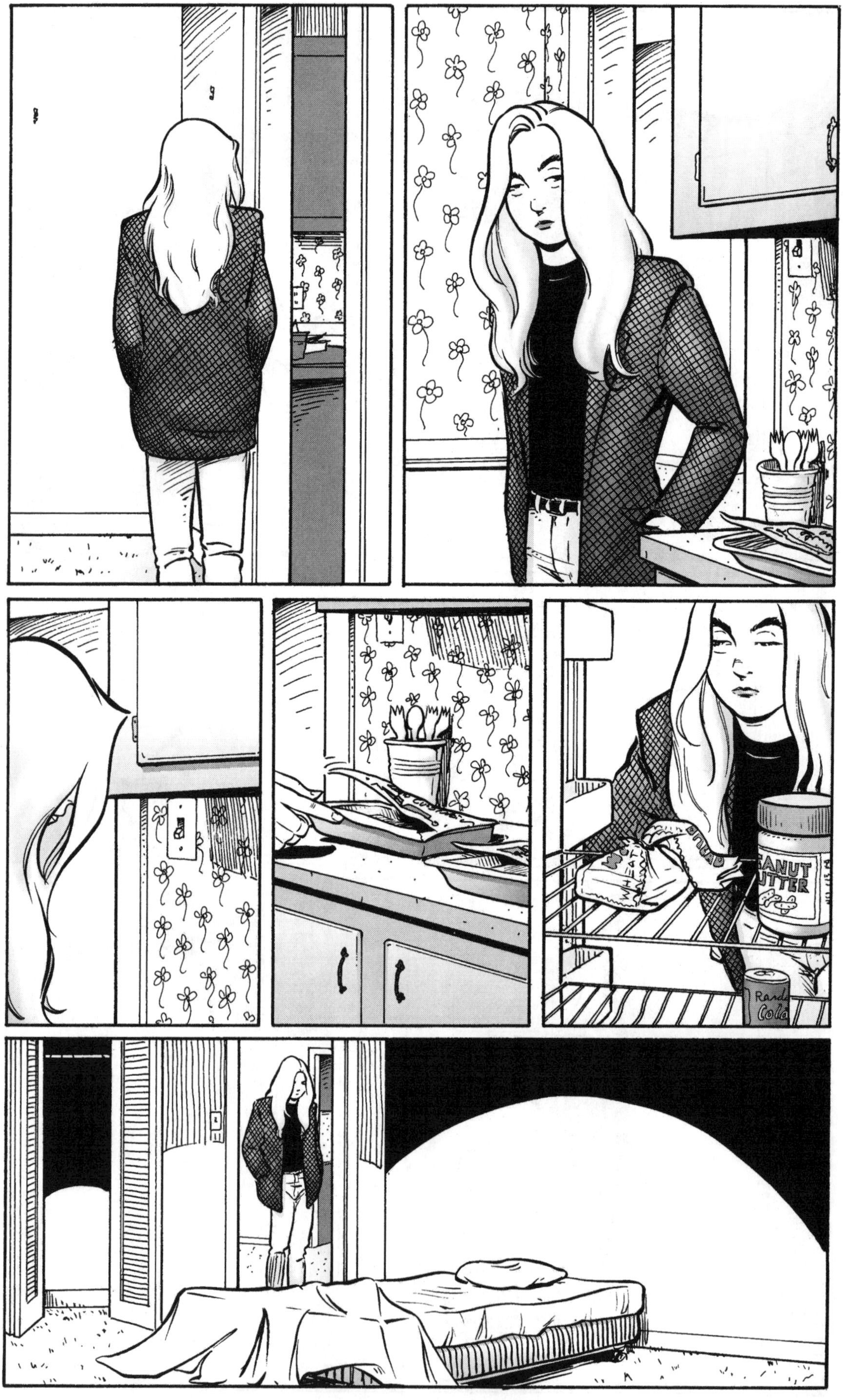
WHEAT
EANUT
UTTER
Rand
Cola

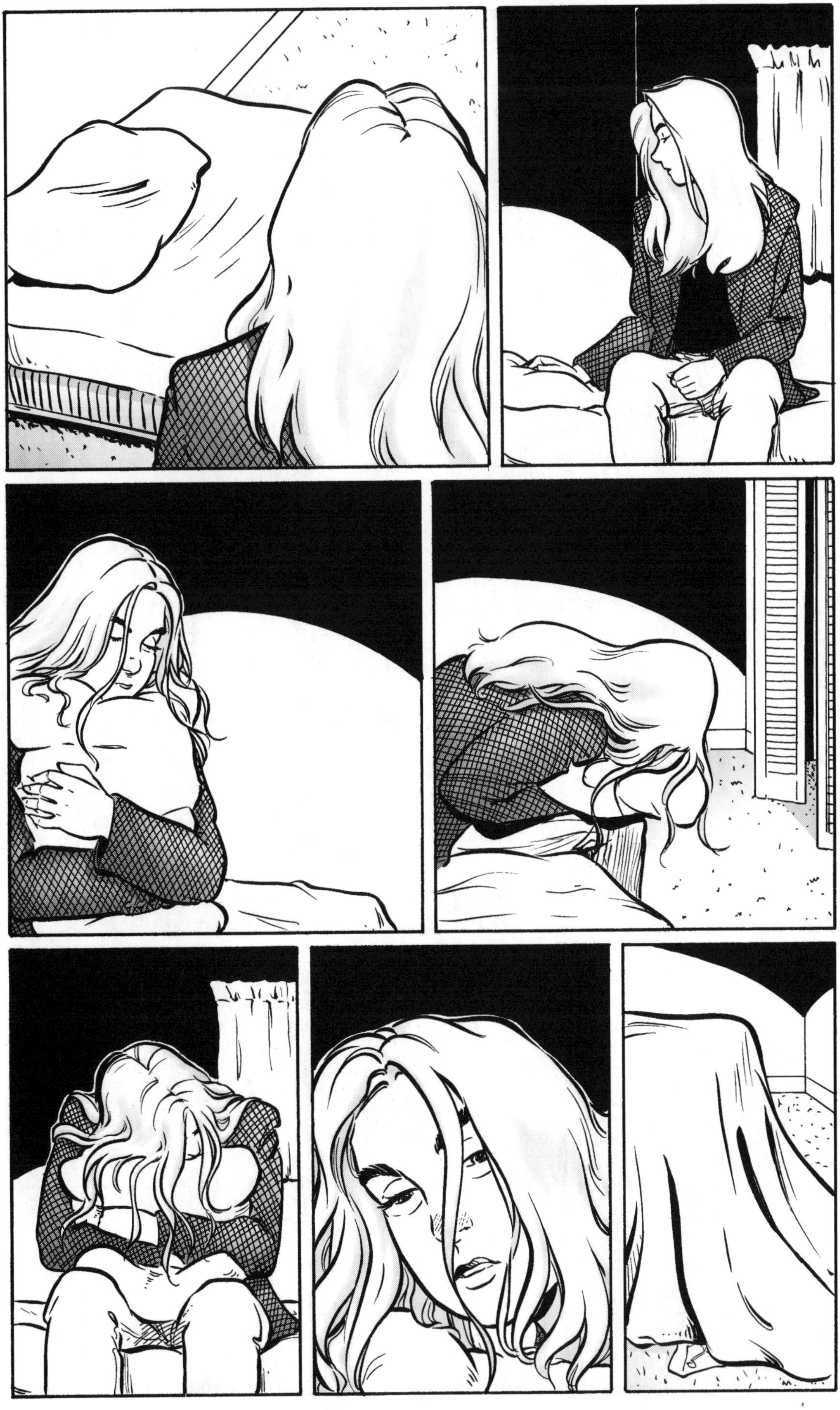

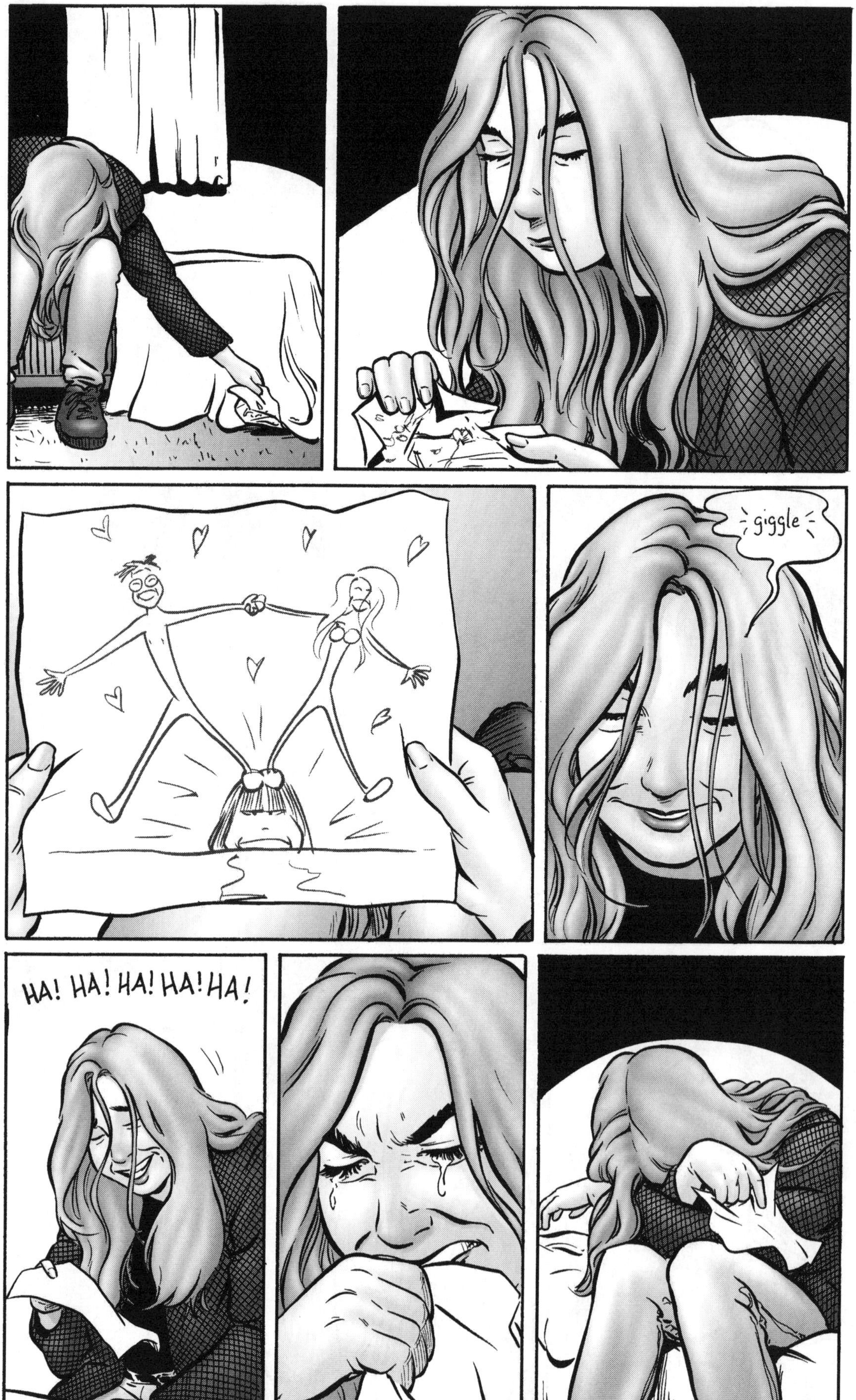

giggle
HA! HA! HA! HA! HA!

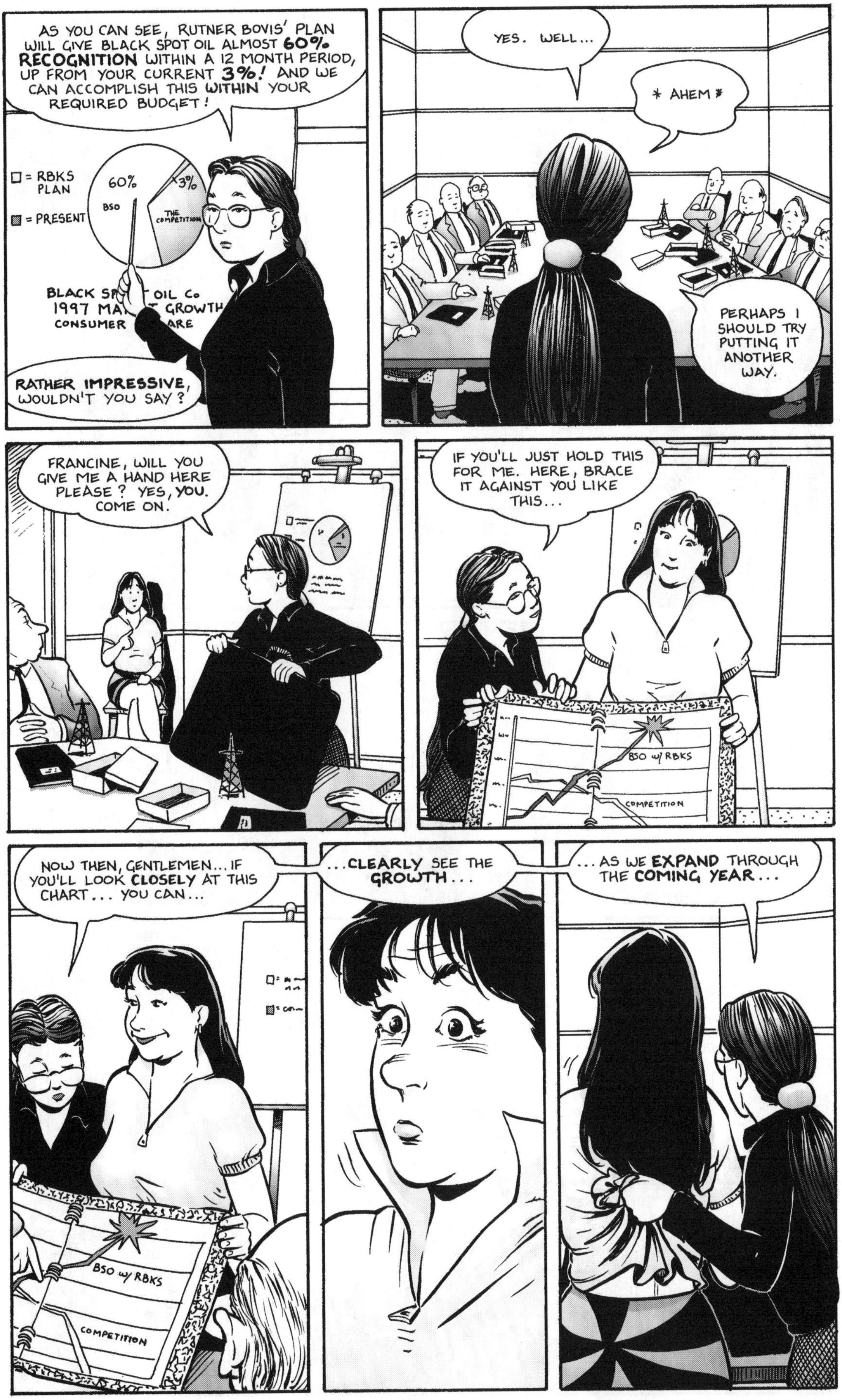
AS YOU CAN SEE, RUTNER BOVIS' PLAN WILL GIVE BLACK SPOT OIL ALMOST 60% RECOGNITION WITHIN A 12 MONTH PERIOD, UP FROM YOUR CURRENT 3%! AND WE CAN ACCOMPLISH THIS WITHIN YOUR REQUIRED BUDGET!
□ = RBKS PLAN
▨ = PRESENT
60%
BSO
3%
THE COMPETITION
BLACK SP OIL Co
1997 MA T GROWTH
CONSUMER ARE
RATHER IMPRESSIVE, WOULDN'T YOU SAY?
YES. WELL...
* AHEM *
PERHAPS I SHOULD TRY PUTTING IT ANOTHER WAY.
FRANCINE, WILL YOU GIVE ME A HAND HERE PLEASE? YES, YOU. COME ON.
IF YOU'LL JUST HOLD THIS FOR ME. HERE, BRACE IT AGAINST YOU LIKE THIS...
BSO w/ RBKS
COMPETITION
NOW THEN, GENTLEMEN... IF YOU'LL LOOK CLOSELY AT THIS CHART... YOU CAN...
BSO w/ RBKS
COMPETITION
...CLEARLY SEE THE GROWTH...
...AS WE EXPAND THROUGH THE COMING YEAR...

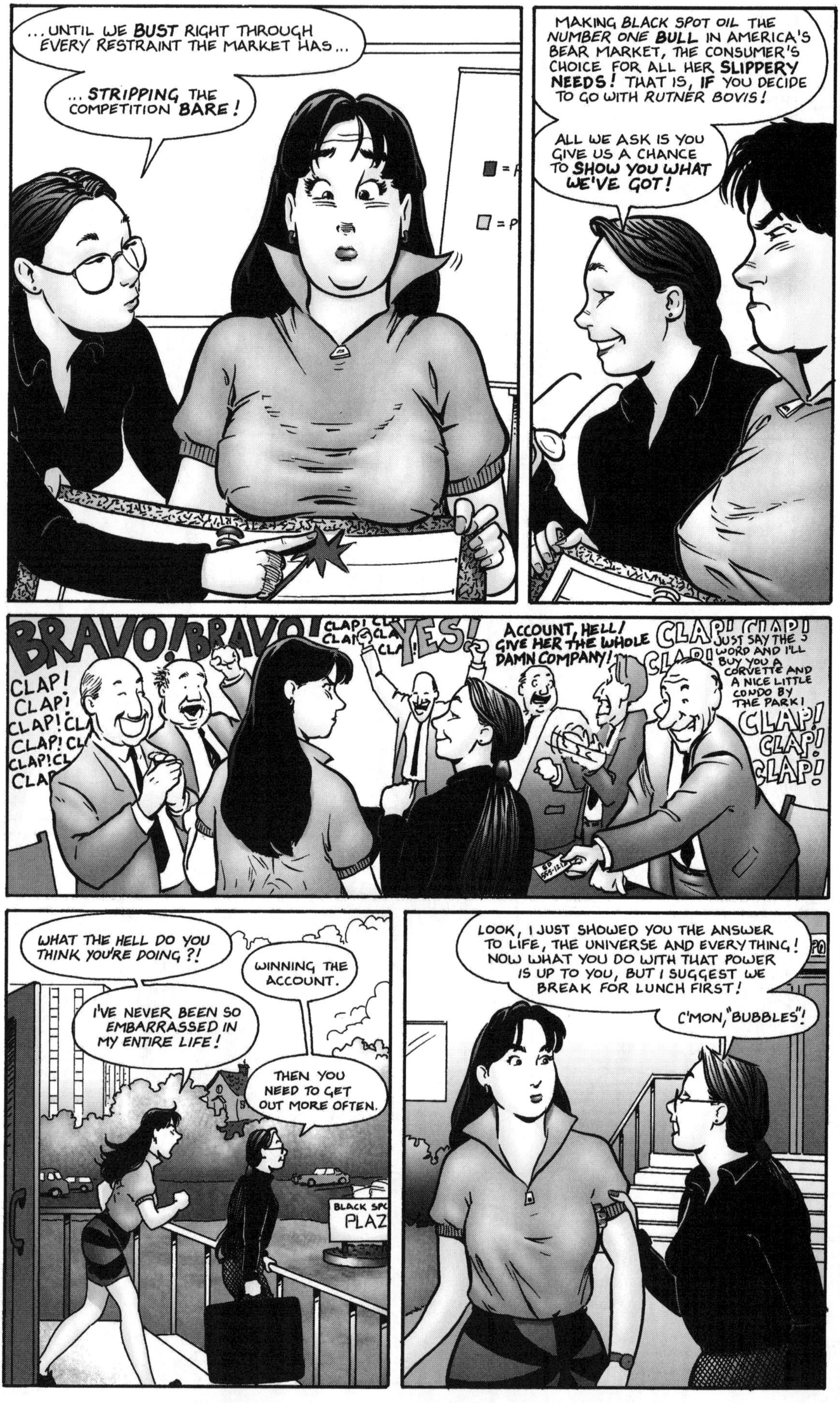
...UNTIL WE BUST RIGHT THROUGH EVERY RESTRAINT THE MARKET HAS...
...STRIPPING THE COMPETITION BARE!
MAKING BLACK SPOT OIL THE NUMBER ONE BULL IN AMERICA'S BEAR MARKET, THE CONSUMER'S CHOICE FOR ALL HER SLIPPERY NEEDS! THAT IS, IF YOU DECIDE TO GO WITH RUTNER BOVIS!
ALL WE ASK IS YOU GIVE US A CHANCE TO SHOW YOU WHAT WE'VE GOT!
BRAVO! BRAVO!
CLAP! CLAP! CLAP! CLAP! CLAP! CLAP!
YES!
ACCOUNT, HELL! GIVE HER THE WHOLE DAMN COMPANY!
CLAP! CLAP!
JUST SAY THE WORD AND I'LL BUY YOU A CORVETTE AND A NICE LITTLE CONDO BY THE PARK!
CLAP! CLAP! CLAP!
WHAT THE HELL DO YOU THINK YOU'RE DOING?!
WINNING THE ACCOUNT.
I'VE NEVER BEEN SO EMBARRASSED IN MY ENTIRE LIFE!
THEN YOU NEED TO GET OUT MORE OFTEN.
BLACK SPO
PLAZ
LOOK, I JUST SHOWED YOU THE ANSWER TO LIFE, THE UNIVERSE AND EVERYTHING! NOW WHAT YOU DO WITH THAT POWER IS UP TO YOU, BUT I SUGGEST WE BREAK FOR LUNCH FIRST!
C'MON, "BUBBLES"!

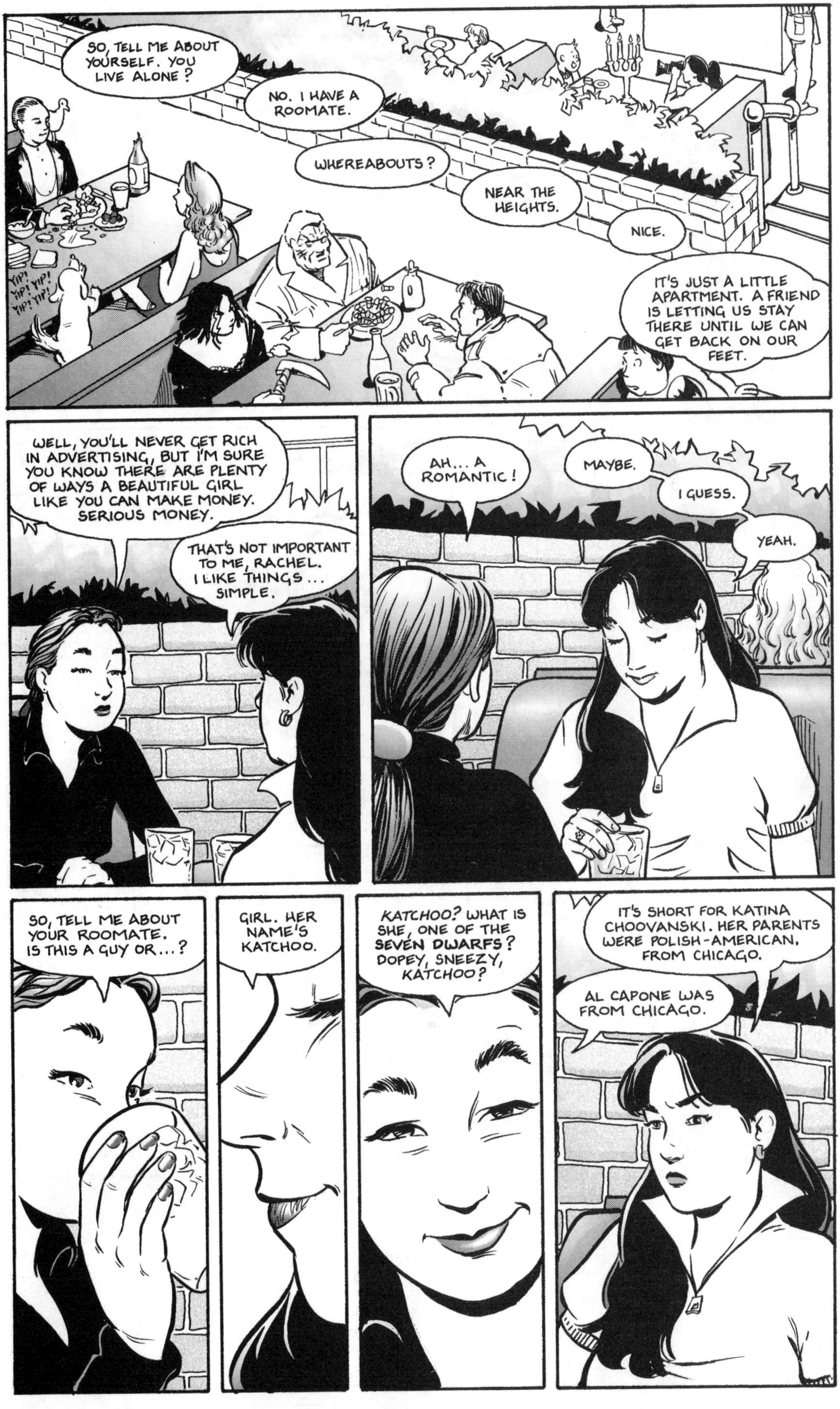

SO, TELL ME ABOUT YOURSELF. YOU LIVE ALONE?
NO. I HAVE A ROOMATE.
WHEREABOUTS?
NEAR THE HEIGHTS.
NICE.
IT'S JUST A LITTLE APARTMENT. A FRIEND IS LETTING US STAY THERE UNTIL WE CAN GET BACK ON OUR FEET.
YIP! YIP! YIP! YIP! YIP!
WELL, YOU'LL NEVER GET RICH IN ADVERTISING, BUT I'M SURE YOU KNOW THERE ARE PLENTY OF WAYS A BEAUTIFUL GIRL LIKE YOU CAN MAKE MONEY. SERIOUS MONEY.
THAT'S NOT IMPORTANT TO ME, RACHEL. I LIKE THINGS... SIMPLE.
AH... A ROMANTIC!
MAYBE.
I GUESS.
YEAH.
SO, TELL ME ABOUT YOUR ROOMATE. IS THIS A GUY OR...?
GIRL. HER NAME'S KATCHOO.
KATCHOO? WHAT IS SHE, ONE OF THE SEVEN DWARFS? DOPEY, SNEEZY, KATCHOO?
IT'S SHORT FOR KATINA CHOOVANSKI. HER PARENTS WERE POLISH-AMERICAN, FROM CHICAGO.
AL CAPONE WAS FROM CHICAGO.

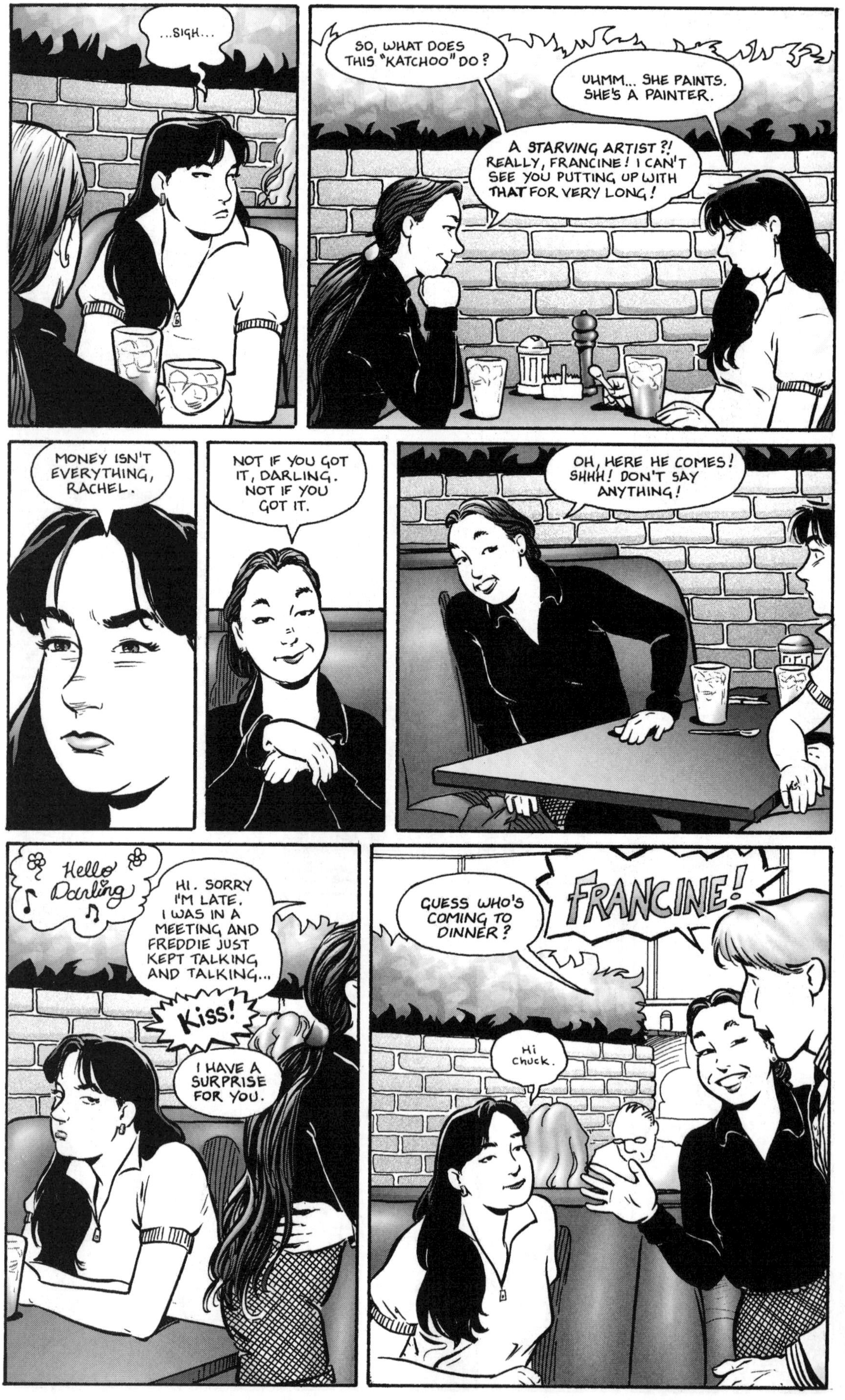
...SIGH...
SO, WHAT DOES THIS "KATCHOO" DO?
UHMM... SHE PAINTS. SHE'S A PAINTER.
A STARVING ARTIST?! REALLY, FRANCINE! I CAN'T SEE YOU PUTTING UP WITH THAT FOR VERY LONG!
MONEY ISN'T EVERYTHING, RACHEL.
NOT IF YOU GOT IT, DARLING. NOT IF YOU GOT IT.
OH, HERE HE COMES! SHHH! DON'T SAY ANYTHING!
Hello Darling
HI. SORRY I'M LATE. I WAS IN A MEETING AND FREDDIE JUST KEPT TALKING AND TALKING...
Kiss!
I HAVE A SURPRISE FOR YOU.
GUESS WHO'S COMING TO DINNER?
FRANCINE!
Hi Chuck.

Y'KNOW, FRANCINE, YOU'RE ALL CHUCK HERE EVER TALKS ABOUT! SOM...

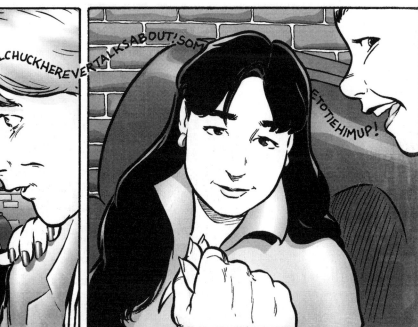

...E TO TIE HIM UP!

COURSE I TOLD HIM I DIDN'T MIND, JUS...

...BUT...

WELL! DON'T JUST STAND THERE LIKE AN IDIOT, CHUCKLES! KISS HER! YOU HAVE MY PERMISSION!

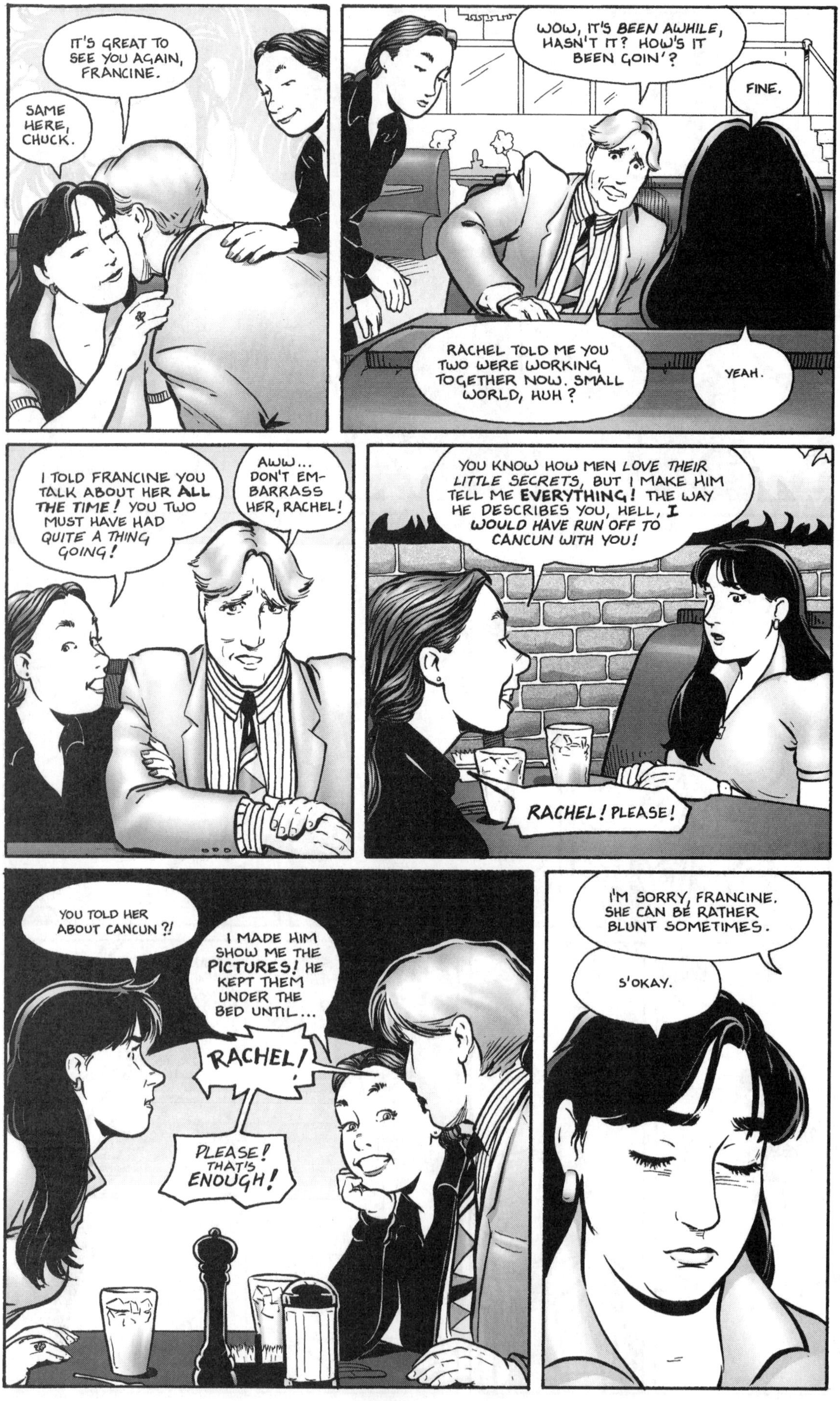
IT'S GREAT TO SEE YOU AGAIN, FRANCINE.
SAME HERE, CHUCK.
WOW, IT'S BEEN AWHILE, HASN'T IT? HOW'S IT BEEN GOIN'?
FINE.
RACHEL TOLD ME YOU TWO WERE WORKING TOGETHER NOW. SMALL WORLD, HUH?
YEAH.
I TOLD FRANCINE YOU TALK ABOUT HER ALL THE TIME! YOU TWO MUST HAVE HAD QUITE A THING GOING!
AWW... DON'T EM-BARRASS HER, RACHEL!
YOU KNOW HOW MEN LOVE THEIR LITTLE SECRETS, BUT I MAKE HIM TELL ME EVERYTHING! THE WAY HE DESCRIBES YOU, HELL, I WOULD HAVE RUN OFF TO CANCUN WITH YOU!
RACHEL! PLEASE!
YOU TOLD HER ABOUT CANCUN ?!
I MADE HIM SHOW ME THE PICTURES! HE KEPT THEM UNDER THE BED UNTIL...
RACHEL!
PLEASE! THAT'S ENOUGH!
I'M SORRY, FRANCINE. SHE CAN BE RATHER BLUNT SOMETIMES.
S'OKAY.

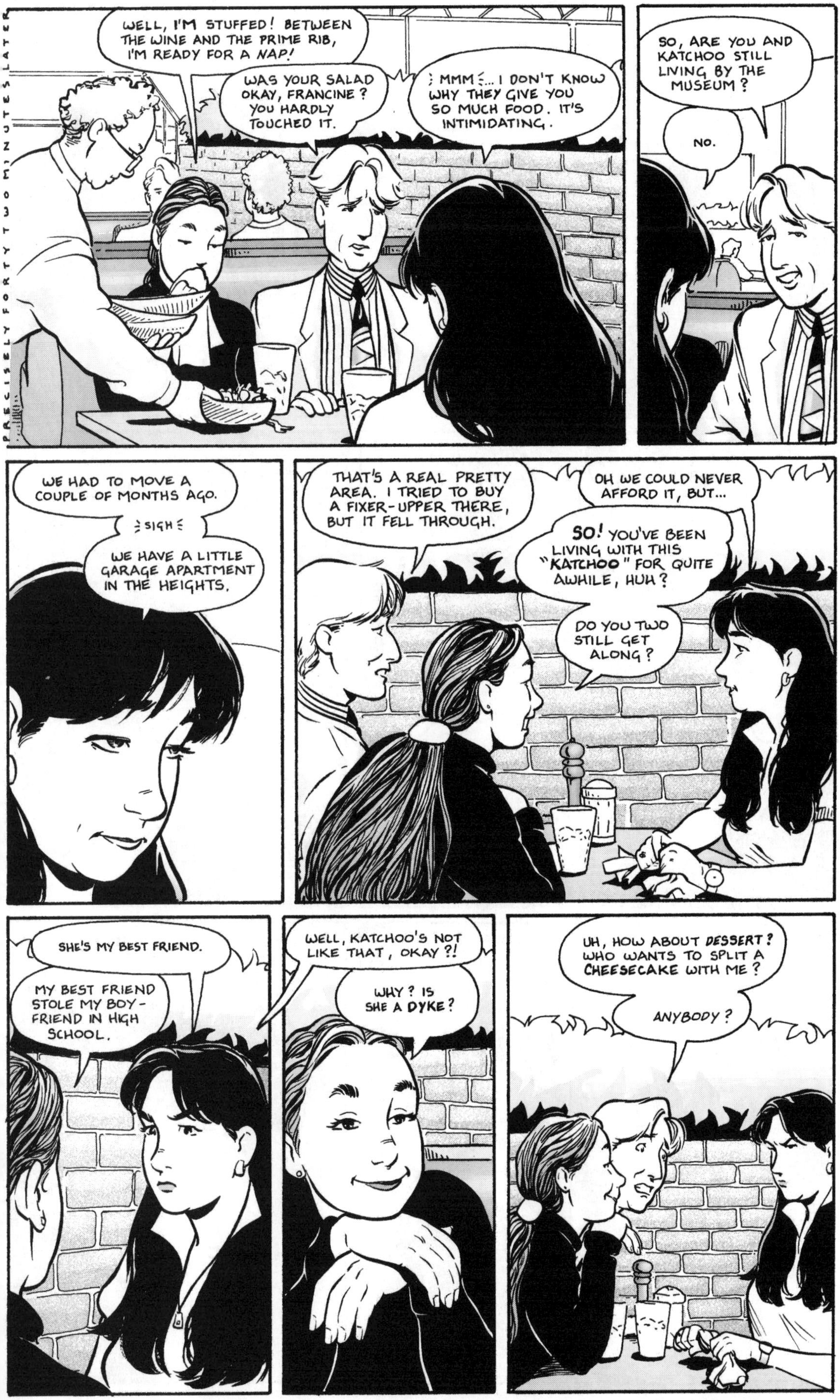
PRECISELY FORTY TWO MINUTES LATER
WELL, I'M STUFFED! BETWEEN THE WINE AND THE PRIME RIB, I'M READY FOR A *NAP!*
WAS YOUR SALAD OKAY, FRANCINE? YOU HARDLY TOUCHED IT.
MMM... I DON'T KNOW WHY *THEY* GIVE YOU SO MUCH FOOD. IT'S INTIMIDATING.
SO, ARE YOU AND KATCHOO STILL LIVING BY THE MUSEUM?
NO.
WE HAD TO MOVE A COUPLE OF MONTHS AGO.
SIGH
WE HAVE A LITTLE GARAGE APARTMENT IN THE HEIGHTS.
THAT'S A REAL PRETTY AREA. I TRIED TO BUY A FIXER-UPPER THERE, BUT IT FELL THROUGH.
OH WE COULD NEVER AFFORD IT, BUT...
SO! YOU'VE BEEN LIVING WITH THIS "**KATCHOO**" FOR QUITE AWHILE, HUH?
DO YOU TWO STILL GET ALONG?
SHE'S MY BEST FRIEND.
MY BEST FRIEND STOLE MY BOY-FRIEND IN HIGH SCHOOL.
WELL, KATCHOO'S NOT LIKE THAT, OKAY?!
WHY? IS SHE A **DYKE**?
UH, HOW ABOUT **DESSERT**? WHO WANTS TO SPLIT A **CHEESECAKE** WITH ME?
ANYBODY?

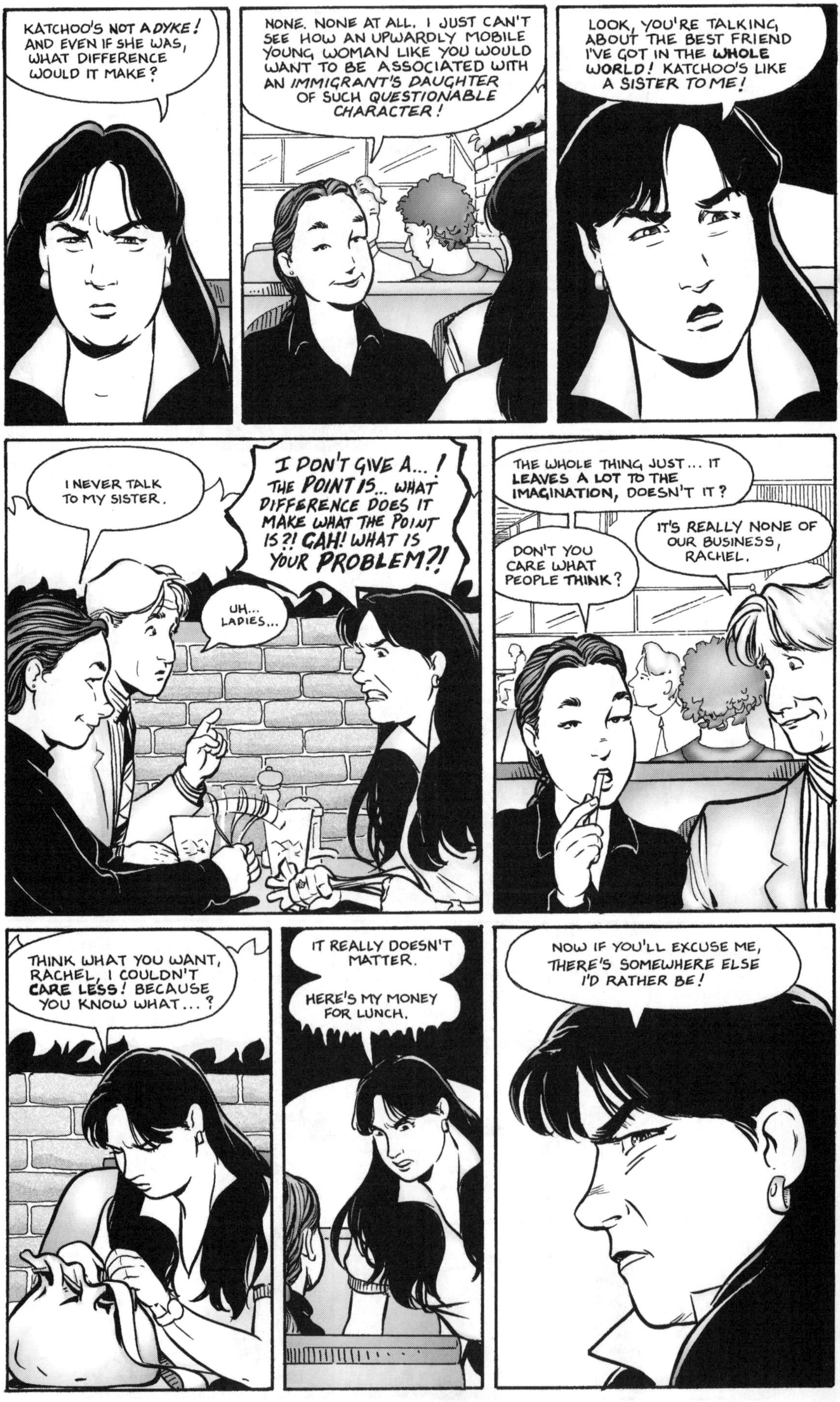
KATCHOO'S NOT A DYKE! AND EVEN IF SHE WAS, WHAT DIFFERENCE WOULD IT MAKE?
NONE. NONE AT ALL. I JUST CAN'T SEE HOW AN UPWARDLY MOBILE YOUNG WOMAN LIKE YOU WOULD WANT TO BE ASSOCIATED WITH AN IMMIGRANT'S DAUGHTER OF SUCH QUESTIONABLE CHARACTER!
LOOK, YOU'RE TALKING ABOUT THE BEST FRIEND I'VE GOT IN THE WHOLE WORLD! KATCHOO'S LIKE A SISTER TO ME!
I NEVER TALK TO MY SISTER.
I DON'T GIVE A...! THE POINT IS... WHAT DIFFERENCE DOES IT MAKE WHAT THE POINT IS?! GAH! WHAT IS YOUR PROBLEM?!
UH... LADIES...
THE WHOLE THING JUST... IT LEAVES A LOT TO THE IMAGINATION, DOESN'T IT?
IT'S REALLY NONE OF OUR BUSINESS, RACHEL.
DON'T YOU CARE WHAT PEOPLE THINK?
THINK WHAT YOU WANT, RACHEL, I COULDN'T CARE LESS! BECAUSE YOU KNOW WHAT...?
IT REALLY DOESN'T MATTER.
HERE'S MY MONEY FOR LUNCH.
NOW IF YOU'LL EXCUSE ME, THERE'S SOMEWHERE ELSE I'D RATHER BE!

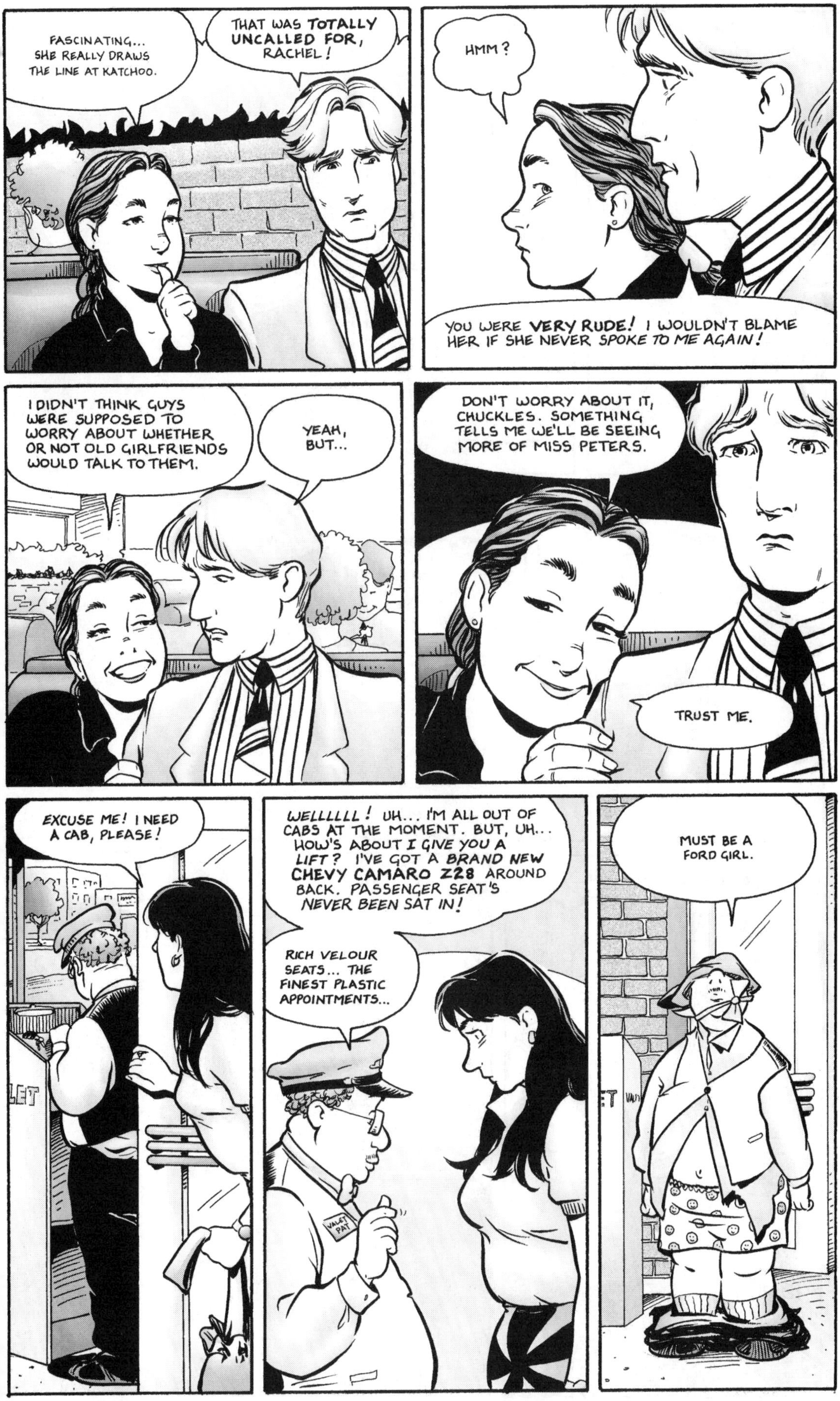
FASCINATING... SHE REALLY DRAWS THE LINE AT KATCHOO.
THAT WAS TOTALLY UNCALLED FOR, RACHEL!
HMM?
YOU WERE VERY RUDE! I WOULDN'T BLAME HER IF SHE NEVER SPOKE TO ME AGAIN!
I DIDN'T THINK GUYS WERE SUPPOSED TO WORRY ABOUT WHETHER OR NOT OLD GIRLFRIENDS WOULD TALK TO THEM.
YEAH, BUT...
DON'T WORRY ABOUT IT, CHUCKLES. SOMETHING TELLS ME WE'LL BE SEEING MORE OF MISS PETERS.
TRUST ME.
EXCUSE ME! I NEED A CAB, PLEASE!
WELLLLLLL! UH... I'M ALL OUT OF CABS AT THE MOMENT. BUT, UH... HOW'S ABOUT I GIVE YOU A LIFT? I'VE GOT A BRAND NEW CHEVY CAMARO Z28 AROUND BACK. PASSENGER SEAT'S NEVER BEEN SAT IN!
RICH VELOUR SEATS... THE FINEST PLASTIC APPOINTMENTS...
VALET PAT
MUST BE A FORD GIRL.

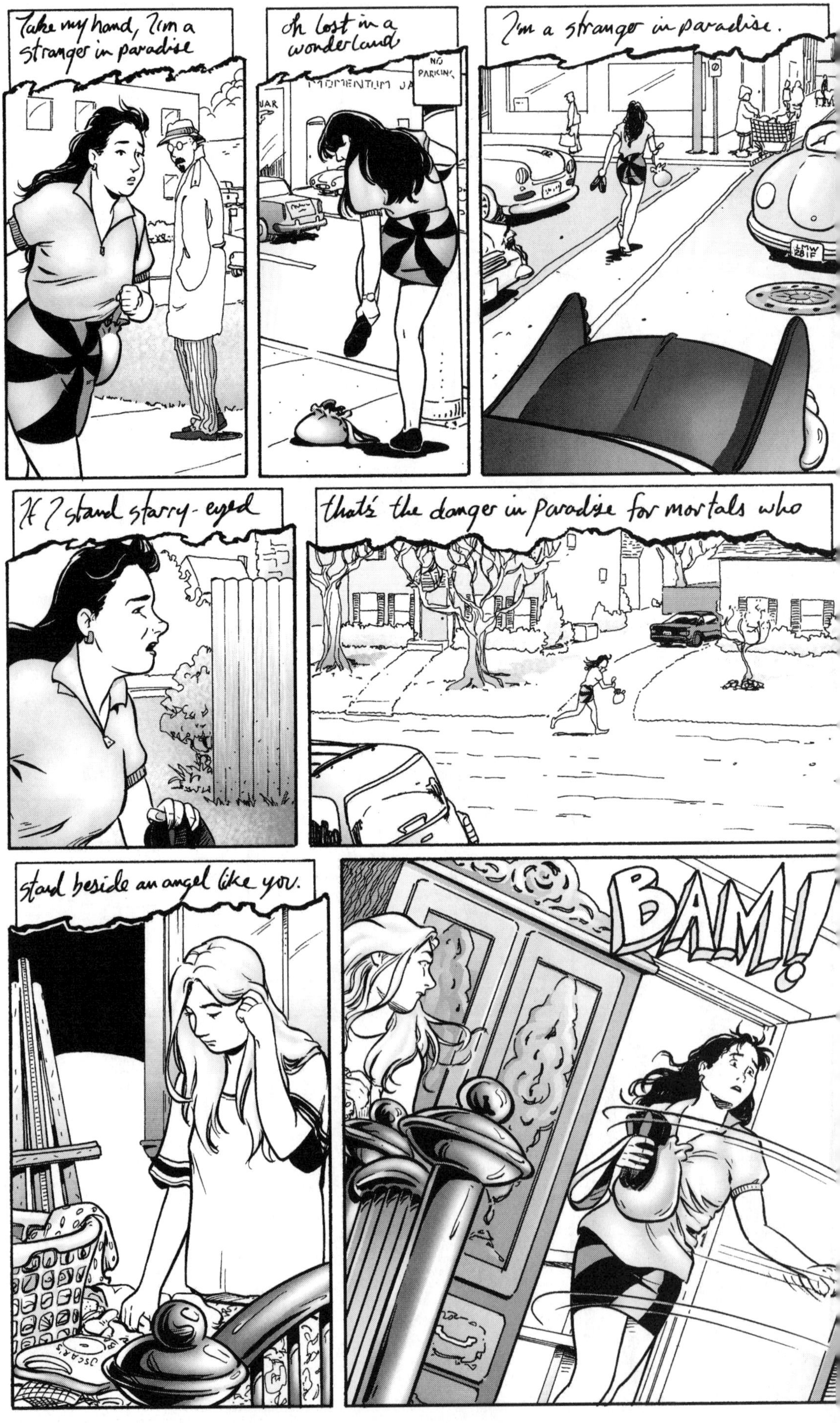
Take my hand, I'm a stranger in paradise
Oh lost in a wonderland
NO PARKING
I'm a stranger in paradise.
If I stand starry-eyed
that's the danger in paradise for mortals who
stand beside an angel like you.
BAM!

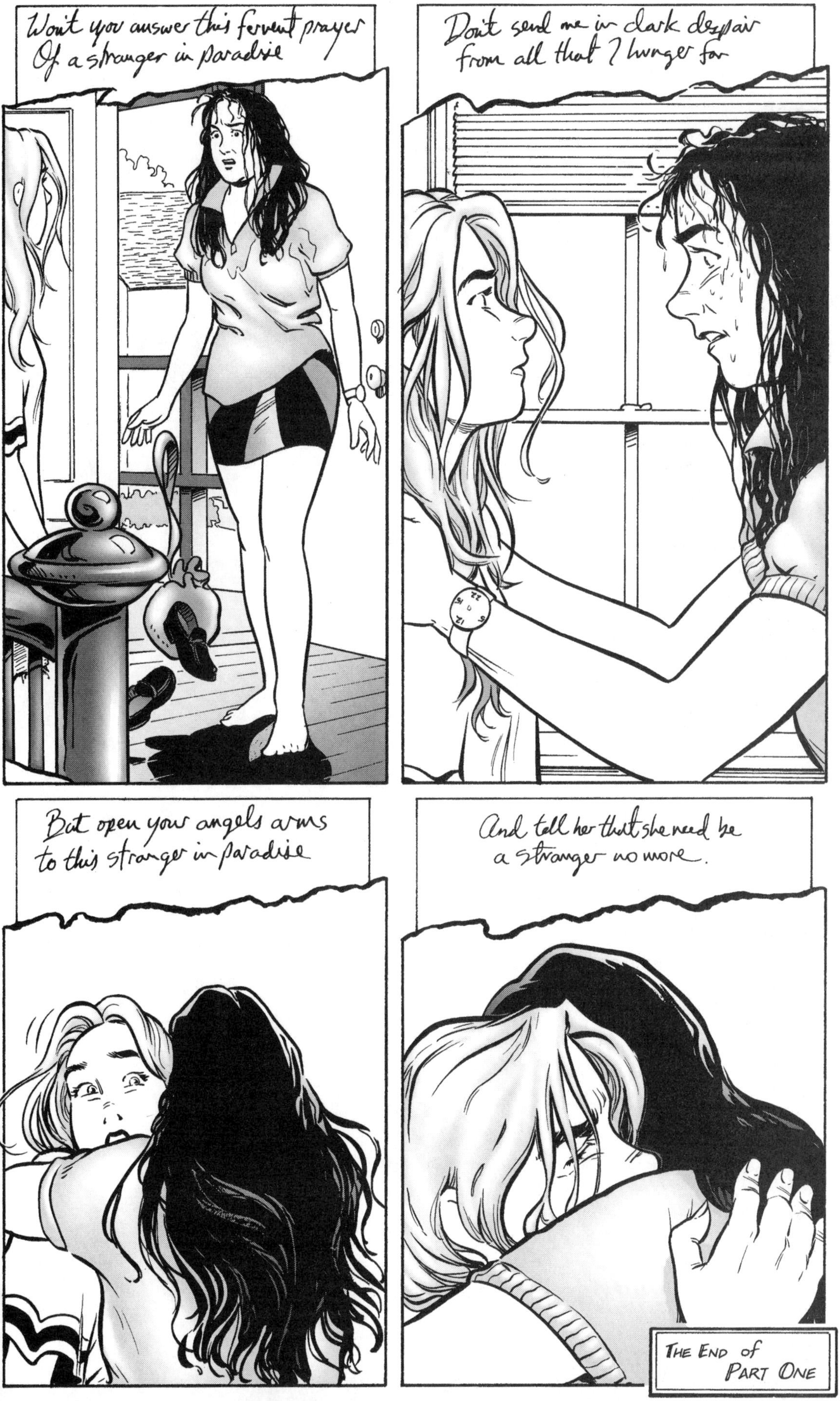
Won't you answer this fervent prayer
Of a stranger in paradise
Don't send me in dark despair
from all that I hunger for
But open your angels arms
to this stranger in paradise
And tell her that she need be
a stranger no more.
THE END of
PART ONE

Grateful acknowledgement to the
following artists for the use of their material:

"Is This Anyway To Fall In Love"
sung by
Linda Eder
Lyrics by Jack Murphy
Music by Frank Wildhorn
©1992 Bronx Flash Music, Inc.

"Stranger In Paradise"
sung by
Tony Bennett
Lyrics and Music by Wright/Forrest
©1986 CBS, Inc.